DIPLOMACY, ROGER MAKINS AND THE ANGLO-AMERICAN RELATIONSHIP

For Lin, Emma, Carla, Amy, Freddie and Alfie

Diplomacy, Roger Makins and the Anglo-American Relationship

RICHARD WEVILL

ASHGATE

Published by
Ashgate Publishing Limited
Wey Court East
Union Road
Farnham
Surrey, GU9 7PT
England

Ashgate Publishing Company
110 Cherry Street
Suite 3-1
Burlington
VT 05401-3818
USA

www.ashgate.com

British Library Cataloguing in Publication Data
A catalogue record for this book is available from the British Library.

The Library of Congress has cataloged the printed edition as follows:
Wevill, Richard.
Diplomacy, Roger Makins and the Anglo-American relationship / by Richard Wevill.
pages cm
Includes bibliographical references and index.
ISBN 978-1-4724-4649-7 (hardcover) -- ISBN 978-1-4724-4650-3 (ebook) -- ISBN 978-1-4724-4651-0 (epub) 1. Sherfield, Roger Mellor Makins, Baron, 1904-1996. 2. Ambassadors--Great Britain--Biography. 3. Great Britain--Foreign relations--1945- 4. Great Britain--Foreign relations--United States. 5. United States--Foreign relations--Great Britain. I. Title.
DA585.M36W38 2014
327.41073092--dc23
[B]

2014026567

ISBN 9781472446497 (hbk)
ISBN 9781472446503 (ebk – PDF)
ISBN 9781472446510 (ebk – ePUB)

MIX
Paper from responsible sources
FSC® C004959

Printed and bound in Great Britain
by Printondemand-worldwide.com

Contents

About the Author

Richard Wevill turned to the study of history after a successful career in investment banking. Richard gained his PhD from the University of Exeter where he is currently a Research Fellow. Richard is also a Fellow of the Royal Historical Society. He is the author of *Britain and America after World War II: Bilateral Relations and the Beginnings of the Cold War* (2012). He is currently working on his next book which is concerned with the role of the Treasury and Treasury officials in Anglo-American relations 1945–1960.

Acknowledgements

In undertaking to write *Diplomacy, Roger Makins and the Anglo-American Relationship* I have acquired debts to many people and certain institutions. Their mention here is only a small part of my gratitude.

I would like to express my thanks to Ashgate Publishing for agreeing to publish this book and I am particularly grateful to Emily Yates, the Commissioning Editor, for the efficient and impressive way she dealt with my book proposal. I would also like to thank the University of Exeter, and my colleagues in the History Department for their help and support, in particular, Professor Jeremy Black who undertook the burdensome task of reading an entire draft. Professor Black made many helpful and constructive comments and afforded me introductions to others who have also been helpful. I am also grateful to Dr Saul Kelly, Reader in International History at Kings College London, who gave me papers relating to his earlier work on Makins and for giving me helpful background information on him. I also benefitted from meeting with Professor Simon Green Reader in Modern British History at the University of Leeds and an Extraordinary Fellow of All Souls College and D.R.Thorpe, a senior member of Brasenose College. Professor Green offered many insights into Makins' character and gave practical help in verifying points relating to Makins' time at All Souls College. D.R.Thorpe, who had interviewed Makins several times, offered a very interesting assessment of the man and his career.

Almost without exception the staff at the various archives I have visited have proved to be both professional and helpful. I am especially grateful to both Patrick Maclure and Suzanne Foster at Winchester College, and to Judith Curthoys at Christ Church College for the time they spent with me and the trouble they went to in order to provide assistance. I have also benefitted considerably from meeting with many people who knew and worked with Makins. These include Sir John Herbecq, Sir Peter Marshall and Sir David Butler, Virginia Makins and David Shapiro.

I would also like to thank Lin who kindly proofread several drafts; a tedious job and I am grateful to her for undertaking the task. Finally, I would like to thank Freddie and Alfie, who between them have managed to impart a sense of reality during the more frustrating moments experienced while writing this book.

Introduction

Diplomacy, Roger Makins and the Anglo-American Relationship explores the Anglo-American relationship through the prism of the life and career of Roger Makins. In doing so, it will not only provide an account of the life of one of the most influential civil servants in the twentieth century, but also emphasise the importance of the contribution made to British post-war history by diplomacy at the official, rather than the political level. Makins served as the British Ambassador in Washington from 1953 until 1956; he was Joint Permanent Secretary to the Treasury from 1956 until 1959 and he was the Chairman of the UK Atomic Energy Authority from 1960 until 1964. His influence extended into both the Labour and the Conservative post-war administrations and across several policy areas, including atomic energy and economic policy. The common thread, however, which underlies all of his work, is the furtherance of the relationship between Britain and America.

The history of Britain in the twentieth century is a story with many[1] variations, but the essential theme is the portrayal of Britain's decline. By decline what is really meant is Britain's loss of great power status and her relegation to that of a middle ranking major power. There are, of course, many sources of a country's power and there is a tendency when discussing Britain's relative decline to focus on those sources of power which are tangible, and are therefore capable of measurement. These might include the size of a country's armed forces, her Gross Domestic Product or her energy reserves. There are, however, other sources of power which are not so easily measured but are real nevertheless. The morale of a nation, the quality, integrity and stability of a country's political system and a nation's sense of unity are all examples of intangible sources of power. Yet another is diplomatic skill.[2] Power might be discussed in terms of a nation's ability to produce intended results and, on this level, power comes close to the notion of influence.[3] Diplomatic skill, whether it be exercised at the official level or at the political level, is central to the ability of one country to

---

1 See for example: Reynolds, David, *Britannia Overruled British Policy and World Power in the Twentieth Century*, New York: Longman, 1991; Young, John, *Britain and the World in the Twentieth Century*, London: Arnold, 1997; Bartlett, C. J., *A History of Post War Britain 1945–1974*, London: Longman, 1976.

2 For more on this see Frankel Joseph, *British Foreign Policy 1945–1973*, Oxford: Oxford University Press, 1975 and Reynolds, *Britannia Overruled.*

3 Frankel, *British Foreign Policy*, p. 71.

influence another. Diplomatic skill then, or indeed the lack of it, is an important consideration when discussing the events which mould a country's history.

Allied to the study of a country's decline is a consideration of the strategies which a country might adopt in order to arrest that decline or to extend her influence beyond that which may be implied by her natural resources. There were a number of strategies which Britain might have adopted in order to enable her to better cope with the post-war world including, for example, closer connections with the Commonwealth and/or responding to both Continental European and American overtures for a more integrated Europe. One such strategy, however, which came to dominate, was the attempt by Britain to harness America's power for her own ends. The considerable drain on Britain's resources during the war and the rapid decline in her relative position in the post-war period made the pursuit of effective Anglo-American relations an attractive strategy. An essential component of that strategy was diplomatic skill. This book is a case study in the application of power in the form of diplomatic skill in the pursuit of the Anglo-American strategy.

The case study approach takes the form of assessing the contribution one man, Roger Makins, made to the process described above and why he is considered an important figure in twentieth-century British history. It is, therefore, a study focused on the official rather than the political level. In the two decades following the Second World War he held positions of crucial importance within the British establishment. He was the civil servant at the centre of the post-war atomic energy debate in both London and Washington and, unusually for a Foreign Office official, reported on such matters directly to Clement Attlee, the Prime Minister. He was a close confidant of Ernest Bevin, the Foreign Secretary at the time when Britain was attempting to cement the post-war Anglo-American relationship. Makins, who had worked with Anthony Eden in the 1930s, was appointed by him to become the British Ambassador to America at a time when the Eisenhower administration was taking over in Washington. Subsequently Makins was seconded from the Foreign Office to run the Treasury for three years, where his contribution in the immediate aftermath of the Suez Crisis was crucial. He ended his official career as the Chairman of the UK Atomic Energy Authority, a position to which his old friend Harold Macmillan appointed him shortly after the Windscale accident. In all of these positions, the unifying theme is Makins' determination to strengthen the Anglo-American relationship.

There have, of course, been many studies of the Anglo-American relationship; what this book is concerned with is the detail of that relationship.[4] Historians often use phrases such as 'America used her power wisely' or 'Britain responded

---

4 See for example: W.M.Roger Louis and Hedley Bull (eds), *The Special Relationship: Anglo-American Relations Since 1945,* Oxford: Clarendon Press, 1986; Bartlett C.J., *The Special Relationship: A Political History of Anglo-American Relations Since 1945*, London:

to her decline'. Personalities are often used as shorthand for policy: 'Eden secured an agreement in Indo-China' or 'Bevin was responsible for NATO.' It is a tempting and often useful habit, but it carries with it the risk of over simplification. For a fuller understanding we need to consider what all the key players were doing, not just the politicians, but also the diplomats and the civil servants. What advice were they giving, what was the nature of their relationship with each other, the politicians and their counterparts in other countries?

We know, for example, that Harold Macmillan was a great success in North Africa during the Second World War and that his success was, in part, based upon his relationship with Eisenhower, the Allied Forces Commander at the time, but what was underneath that? What was it that secured that relationship – there was more to it than Macmillan's charm. We know that Attlee sought and failed to achieve continued cooperation over atomic energy with the Americans in 1946. But was it Attlee who failed to achieve it or was he let down by his advisers or diplomats at the time? It has been noted many times that Eden walked into the Suez Crisis without much discussion with his diplomats or advisers, but why? In order to understand this or at least get nearer to a better understanding of it we need to know, amongst other things, what his ambassador in Washington had been saying to him in the three years preceding Suez. Britain, desperate for liquidity in the post-Suez period, needed funds from America. Was it the British Chancellor at the time telephoning the American Treasury Department which secured the finance or was it his Permanent Secretary who had close personal contacts with the Secretary of the Treasury and his officials? In short, if we want to get a fuller picture then we need to consider what the key players, including diplomats and civil servants, were doing or saying at the time.

Context is also important. It is not surprising that Britain, in the post-war period, sought to harness American power for her own ends: and America had a great deal of power, having emerged from the Second World War richer and stronger than ever before. With more than two thirds of the world's gold reserves and three fourths of its invested capital. More than half of the entire world's manufacturing capacity was located in the United States, and the nation was turning out more than a third of all goods produced around the world. It owned half of the world's supply of shipping and was the world's largest exporter of goods and services. The Gross National Product of the United States was three times Soviet Russia's and more than five times Great Britain's.'[5] By contrast, Britain, the only country to have fought the war from beginning to end, emerged in a severely weakened condition. She had lost a quarter of her wealth, had external

Longman, 1992; Cameron Watt, *Succeeding John Bull: America in Britain's Place 1900–1975*. Cambridge: Cambridge University Press, 1984.

5 Leffler, Melvyn, *A Preponderance of Power*, Stanford: Stanford University Press, 1992.

debts of $14 billion and the volume of her exports had declined by over two thirds. As the war ended Britain had the largest external debt in history.

However, as has already been pointed out, material resources are not the only source of power and Britain's experience in the conduct of Foreign affairs was highly valued. Leaving aside the absurd notion that Britain could play Greece to America's Rome[6] there was a feeling in Washington that despite America's preponderance of power, she was in need of allies and there was something to be learnt from the British experience of international affairs. The door was therefore, open to British diplomats to seek advantage where they could, and Roger Makins was one of the key players at the time who ensured that they did.

In assessing the work of officials, it is often difficult to discern where administration ends and policy making begins. The problem is compounded when more than one government department is involved, and where civil servants coordinate advice to more than one minister. This was true in the immediate post-war period where certain aspects of economic policy were seen as a matter for the Foreign Office as well as the Treasury. It is even more difficult to disentangle policy and administration in new fields where there is no set structure for policy development. Atomic energy was one such: several bodies were involved, and, because of the sensitivity of the subject, much of the discussion was kept secret. More often than not it is inappropriate to claim that any one person, whether a politician or a civil servant, was responsible for a particular decision: policy making is a collaborative process.

This book, however, examines areas where officials seemed to have a particular influence. It is important to remember that civil servants have a permanence that politicians do not. This is not merely to say that civil servants stay working on an issue as politicians come and go: there was basically broad agreement on post-war foreign policy between the Labour and Conservative governments. But unlike politicians, officials see events at first hand on a day-to-day basis. Officials were regularly visiting Washington to explain the latest sterling crisis, or to inform the State Department that Britain could no longer afford to maintain her overseas commitments in places such as Greece and Turkey, or to plead for a special place in the allocation of Marshall Aid. Unlike politicians, they faced the practicalities of dealing with the American administration. With differing perceptions of the realities, a tension could develop between the officials and the politicians, a tension which was exacerbated by Britain's decline. An example which this book considers is the extent to which Eden was out of touch when he returned to office in 1951, and the problems this caused.

6 This is a reference to Macmillan's notion that Britain could tutor America in international affairs after the war ended. See Macmillan, Harold, *The Blast of War*, London: Macmillan, 1967.

The aim here is to provide a clear demonstration that diplomatic skill, as found at the official level, is an important asset for a nation and, indeed, that there can be adverse consequences when that skill is lacking. One of the facts which is highlighted is that the Anglo-American relationship is not some abstract notion, but rests upon individual relationships between people. There have, of course, been many studies on the subject of the Anglo-American relationship and it can be analysed on a number of levels, these might include the political level, the cultural level and the official level. This study focusses on the official level.[7]

It's important to begin with a consideration of Makins' background, education and early experiences of diplomacy. He was typical of a group of men who became influential in the development of foreign policy in the period immediately after the Second World War, men such as Gladwyn Jebb, Harold Caccia and Frank Roberts, all of whom were from wealthy and well-connected backgrounds, all clever and well educated. Makins was perhaps different, however, in that his early foreign office work focused on the Americas rather than Europe or countries in the Far and Middle East. It was perhaps during this early period, after Makins was posted to the Washington embassy in the 1930s, that his lifelong pursuit of the Anglo-American relationship began to take hold. Chapter 2 considers the part which diplomats, Makins in particular, played during the Second World War. It might be said that the Anglo-American relationship was forged during the war and diplomats such as Makins played key roles in cementing that relationship throughout the theatre of war.

Makins' second posting to the Washington embassy is considered in Chapter 3, where the role he played in the discussions relating to Anglo-American cooperation in the field of atomic energy is discussed. Britain failed to obtain any meaningful assistance from the Americans and Makins' misplaced faith in American benevolence may have contributed to this result. After Washington, Makins returned to the Foreign Office in London and served under Bevin. In this chapter we discuss the part Makins played in facilitating closer relations with the Americans while, at the same time, attempting to distance Britain from the notion of an integrated Europe.

Chapter 5 discusses Makins' third posting to the Washington embassy, this time as Ambassador. In some ways it might be seen as the zenith of Makins' career, in others it might be seen as something of a failure. Makins' ambassadorship was probably doomed from the start. Eden, in a paper to the cabinet in 1952, insisted that American power and in particular her foreign policy objectives could be moulded to suit British ends. Makins regularly reported that the Americans would not always be as obliging as Eden desired.

---

7 For an interesting study on the cultural level see Leventhal, Fred and Quinault, Roland, *Anglo-American Attitudes: From Revolution to Partnership*, Aldershot: Ashgate, 2000.

The tone of Makins' reports grated within the Foreign Office and with Eden. This friction ultimately led to Makins' recall from Washington. Makins returned to London at a critical moment in the unfolding Suez Crisis.

Upon his return to London, Makins in a dramatic breach of convention, was appointed Permanent Secretary to the Treasury. Chapter 6 discusses this appointment and concludes that it was something of a disaster. One irony, however, given his recall from Washington, was that he was able, through his very close contacts with George Hunphrey, the Secretary of the American Treasury Department, to secure financial support for Britain at a critical moment in the Suez Crisis. It is interesting to note that close connections with the American establishment can have both advantages and disadvantages. The final chapter considers Makins' appointment as head of the UK Atomic Energy Authority, and his subsequent appointment to the House of Lords. In both of these roles Makins never failed to press home the advantages of closer ties to America.

As was indicated above the Anglo-American relationship in the immediate post-war period is one which has been described many times. This book demonstrates that, at least in part, the relationship has been influenced at the official level as well as the political level. As importantly it also demonstrates that whilst relationships between diplomats and politicians of different countries are important, the relationship between diplomats and politicians of the same country can have a significant impact on outcomes. The important point to be made is that if one wants a complete picture of events in the post war world then one needs to talk about the diplomats and civil servants, as well as the politicians.

Chapter 1

Formative Years

The driving force for policy formation within the Foreign Office during the post-war period came not so much from the Permanent Under Secretaries, men such as Orme Sargent, William Strang and Ivone Kirkpatrick, but rather from the men who occupied positions at the next level down, the Deputy and Assistant Under Secretaries.[1] These men, and they invariably were men, included people such as Harold Caccia, Piers Dixon, Gladwyn Jebb, Frank Roberts and Evelyn Shuckburgh. They shared a common background. They were too young to fight in the First World War, but had been educated in its aftermath. They attended private schools and university, which in practice meant Oxford or Cambridge, and they usually achieved Firsts, often winning academic prizes. Equally, they excelled in the Foreign Office entrance exams, often coming top. Makins was a part of this elite group, and his background and education, which is discussed below, would not have been untypical of those diplomats who were so influential in foreign policy in the period after the Second World War.

In addition to a consideration of Makins' education, this chapter also sets out his early career, including his first posting to the British Embassy in Washington. It is not difficult to see why Makins, at an early stage, developed an attraction to and indeed understanding of the American approach. It was fortuitous for Makins, in terms of his career and prospects, that he made these early connections with the American establishment. Connections which were to become so much more valuable as America emerged from her isolationist shell and became the most powerful nation the world had ever seen.

On the morning of 27 January 1904, his father, Ernest Makins then a major in The Royal Dragoons, boarded a troop ship bound for Bombay. As he sailed down the English Channel, his thoughts would have been with Florence, the woman he had married almost exactly a year earlier. It took several days to cross the Bay of Biscay, progress being slowed by south-westerly gales. On 3 February, having rounded the Straits of Gibraltar, the ship was off the coast of Algeria.

---

1 For more background on this see two articles by Adamthwaite, Anthony. 'Britain and the World 1945–1949: The View from the Foreign Office' *International Affairs*, 61 (Spring 1985), pp. 223–35 and 'Overstretched and Overstrung: Eden, the Foreign Office and the Making of Policy, 1951–5' *International Affairs,* Vol. 64 No.2 (Spring 1988), pp. 241–9.

Ernest noted in his diary, 'a mountainous coast much greener than expected'.[2] What he did not know at the time was that his first child, Roger, had been born on that day. It is a curiosity of both time and place that Ernest Makins was, at the time of his son's birth, gazing at a country which would, albeit indirectly, play such a big part in the shaping of that child's career.

Roger Makins was born into privilege. His family was neither noble nor gentry, but they were wealthy and well connected. The family originally came from Yorkshire, where they were bankers. Makins' paternal grandfather, Henry, moved to London in the 1860s. 'Mr H F Makins ... was one of those, intelligent, cultivated, but rather retiring Englishmen, who, though they lived in the nineteenth century, were not in the least Victorian.'[3] Henry had an eye for promising artists and built an art collection which included paintings by Millais and other pre-Raphaelites, and he commissioned family portraits by Romako. He was a shrewd businessman and he made a substantial fortune through judicious investments. In 1866 he married Keziah Hunt, 'a small, very pretty, rather shy woman noted for her unpunctuality',[4] and together they had seven children including Roger Makins' father Ernest. The family settled at 180 Queens Gate, a 'remarkable house' designed by Norman Shaw and built for Henry in the 1880s, with William Morris wallpapers, curtains and furniture. Queens Gate remained the family residence, until Roger Makins sold it in 1960, not long after his father's death, to Imperial College, which owned all the surrounding property.

Ernest Makins was born in 1869. He was educated at Winchester and Christ Church, Oxford, although he left after only one year to join the Army. Serving in the Royal Dragoons, he fought with distinction during the Boer War and was awarded the Distinguished Service Order in 1902. He fought again in the First World War, where both of his brothers were killed, and was again mentioned in despatches. He fell ill, however, and needed to be invalided home in 1915 for a period of convalescence. He returned to France in 1917 and ended the war in command of the 6th Cavalry Brigade. In 1922 he successfully stood for Parliament as the Conservative candidate in Knutsford, Cheshire, holding the seat until he retired from politics in

---

2 Bodleian Library, University of Oxford, Sherfield Papers, B Papers of Brigadier General Sir Ernest Makins and his wife Florence (Henceforth Ernest Makins Papers) MS Sherfield 91, Diary entry Tuesday 3 February 1904.

3 Bodleian Library, University of Oxford, Papers of Roger Mellor Makins, 1st Baron Sherfield and his wife, Alice, 1820–1996 (Henceforth Makins Papers) MS Sherfield 822, Extract from *Country Life* 30 August 1956.

4 Lord Sherfield's Memoirs, section entitled *A Biographical Sketch, Early Years and Family* (Henceforth *Early Years and Family*), p. 4. The version of Lord Sherfield's Memoirs used throughout this book are those in the possession of Virginia Makins, they do not necessarily correspond with those deposited at the Bodleian Library.

1945. Florence Mellor, Makins' mother, was born in 1877. She came from a family of lawyers; her father, James R. Mellor, was the Master of the Crown Office and King's Remembrancer and was knighted for his services, as was her brother, Gilbert Mellor, who became Deputy Judge Advocate General during the First World War. The Mellor family came from Liverpool, but was of Scottish origin. Florence was the third daughter and one of six children. She was an accomplished violinist who, according to Makins, could have become professional.[5] She married Ernest Makins on 31 January 1903 at Christ Church, Lancaster Gate. It was a successful marriage which survived until Ernest's death some 60 years later.

Makins was born into a family in which the ideal of service played an important part – service, that is, to the British Empire. He was born only three years after the death of Queen Victoria, at a time when the Empire was near its zenith; it covered a quarter of the globe and contained 400 million people. The Empire needed soldiers and bureaucrats to run it and the Makins and Mellor families helped to provide them. Roger Makins was destined to follow the tradition of public service, although he would spend his time wrestling with the decline of the Empire rather than running it.

His early years were spent in the care of a series of nurses and governesses while his parents were stationed in India. He was not, however, forgotten. Both his mother and father wrote to him on a regular basis. His father took considerable trouble over his letters to Roger, including drawing pictures of animals, such as the elephant he rode on a tiger shoot, and describing events in India. In 1912 the Royals were transferred from India to South Africa, and Makins was able to be with his parents. His memories of his two years in South Africa were sketchy: he recalls the thunderstorms rolling across the Veldt, catching crayfish in the muddy waters of Potchefstoom in the Orange Free State and being taught to ride by the Regimental Sergeant Major. After two years, however, as was normal at that time, he was sent off to school in England. By the time he went he could read, write and recite the names and dates of the Kings and Queens of England.

Makins attended West Downs Preparatory School from March 1914 until July 1917. The school, situated on a hill outside Winchester, had been founded by Lionel Helbert 'if not ... a genius, then at any rate ... a man with a genius for teaching small boys and for managing them and their parents'.[6] Alumni included Sir Oswald Mosley, Duncan-Sandys and David Astor. Perhaps unusually for the time, the school was a caring place, interested as much in the boys' happiness as in their academic achievements. Makins, however, must have felt the pain all boys

---

5 *Early Years and Family*, p. 2.

6 Makins Papers, MS Sherfield 941, A Foreword written by Makins in the book *A History of West Downs* by Mark Hitchens.

do at being sent away from a loving home. In one letter to his mother he wrote 'my nick name is either fatty, the fat one or fatty miss Makins.'[7] Nevertheless, as he recorded some sixty years later: 'It was a very well managed school, the boys were happy, there was no bullying and the teaching remained good even during the war.'[8] There was drama in the form of Shakespeare plays, something at which Makins did not excel, and although he had piano lessons he, unlike his mother, had no talent for music. In common with other preparatory schools the curriculum was driven by the common entrance requirements, consequently the school taught no science and concentrated on the classics. Makins thrived at the school; he had good reports, was Head of School and, perhaps more importantly for him at the time, captain of the cricket team.

In September 1917, at the age of 13, the time came to 'move down the hill' to Winchester College, where he stayed until July 1922. He was fortunate in that he followed his father into D House (Kennys) which was a friendly, well run house, in contrast to other houses at that time, which could be brutal. Makins tried for, but did not get a scholarship to Winchester. This was curious, since, being the top of school at West Down, a scholarship might have been expected. Makins suggests that his papers were mixed up with someone else's.[9] This assertion is consistent with his Winchester record card. It shows that he was put in the lowest class on arrival at Winchester, but there is a note 'hot up after 1 month', so he was evidently moved to a higher division after one month, rather than waiting until the end of term.[10] Makins wrote to his mother proclaiming his achievements, something which he was apt to do and indeed never stopped doing, 'Rejoice! Rejoice!! Rejoice!!! I have been raised a remove into Middle Part III'.[11] The record card shows continued rapid progress through the various divisions within the school.[12]

Makins passed the School Certificate at the end of his second year, at which point, having scraped through the mathematics paper, he dropped the subject altogether. He thus ended his 'school career finding difficulty in adding and subtracting and unable to understand even the logarithmic scale, let alone differential calculus'.[13] After the School Certificate he chose to study the classics. However, as the time to consider university entrance approached, Makins who could just about write 'passable Greek and Latin verse', was told that he would not 'be up to scholarship standard in classics' and that his best chance of a scholarship

7 Makins Papers, MS Sherfield 204, Letter to mother, 1 June 1913.

8 *Early Years and Family*, p. 7.

9 *Early Years and Family*, p. 8.

10 Winchester College Archives, Makins record card.

11 Makins Papers, MS Sherfield 204, letter to mother, 2 November 1917.

12 Winchester College Archives, Makins record card.

13 *Early Years and Family*, p. 10.

to Oxford was to go for a history one.[14] He told his father that he was more likely to make progress in a subject he enjoyed than in one which he did not. Makins was fortunate: History at that time was taught by Winchester's Second Master, Alwyn Williams. Williams was a brilliant scholar; he had taken a Triple First at Oxford in Classic Moderations (1908), Greats (1910) and Modern History (1911); he was also an outstanding teacher. Makins recalled that 'my essays for him were a source of fruitful discussion and criticism ... he was highly discriminating in his selection of reading matter for me and he introduced me to American History as well as British and European'.[15]

Rather than join the conveyor belt from Winchester to New College, Makins tried for a place at Christ Church (sometimes called 'the House'), his father's old college. Whether this was his decision or his father's is not clear. In 1920, when Makins was just sixteen, Ernest Makins wrote to the Dean of Christ Church. 'I am very anxious that my son Roger Mellor Makins should go to my old college "the House" ... I am advised that it is time to take steps about his entering the University and should be much obliged to you if you could arrange for his arrival.'[16] Two years after this letter was written, Makins travelled up to Oxford in the company of his fellow Wykeamist Kenneth Clark (later Lord Clark, the art historian) to sit their respective scholarship examinations. Clark was successful, Makins was not. However, he did well enough to be offered a place without having to sit the college examination. He reflected in his memoirs, that while Clark may have got a scholarship to Magdalen, he only managed a fourth class degree.

Makins went up to Oxford in August 1922. By then 'the survivors of the war who had gone up or back to Oxford had gone down again, and there was a gulf in experience and outlook – between them and my generation who had just missed military service'.[17] A.L. Rowse, who went up to Christ Church at the same time as Makins, recalled the post-war atmosphere. 'The grim experience of the first war had reinforced the strength of idealism. There was a real belief ... in bettering the world. "It must not happen again" was our attitude to the war; the sacrifice of the generations before us must not be in vain.'[18] Makins records 'we were ... both naïve and immature'.

Christ Church was dominated by boys from Eton and Westminster. The Christ Church of 1922 was the college depicted in *Brideshead Revisted* and

---

14 Ernest Makins Papers, MS Sherfield 193, letter Makins to father, undated.

15 *Early Years and Family*, p. 11.

16 Christ Church College Archives, Roger Makins file, letter Ernest Makins to Dean of Christ Church, 20 February 1920.

17 Lord Sherfield's Memoirs, *A Biographical Sketch, Oxford and Beyond* (henceforth *Oxford and Beyond*), p. 25.

18 A.L. Rowse, *A Cornishman at Oxford*, London: Jonathan Cape, 1965, p. 26.

'Makins ... must have known all the characters'.[19] He was not one of the rich undergraduates of whom there were many in the House. He did, however, have an adequate allowance, and was sufficiently well off to run a two-seater Talbot convertible, and keep two horses for hunting, joining both the South Oxfordshire and the Bicester Hunts. In the vacations, when he returned home to the family house at 180 Queens Gate, he had the services of the family's butler, chauffeur and housemaids to look after him. It was a comfortable existence, but by no means special in the context of Christ Church.

On arrival at Christ Church Makins had rooms which were on the corner of Peckwater and Canterbury Quads, moving from the ground floor to more spacious and expensive rooms on the second floor after his first year. At first he knew few people in Oxford, but he soon acquired a circle of friends. Makins wrote to his father 'I am settling down very gradually; it is somewhat nervous work at first, but I am getting to know one or two people by degrees'.[20] He shared a staircase with Dick Heathcoat Amory (who became a stockbroker and was Makins' best man), Alan Lennox Boyd (later an MP and Colonial Secretary) and Bill Anstruther Gray (later an MP having defeated Jenny Lee in the 1931 General Election, and later became Deputy Speaker of the House of Commons). Beyond Christ Church, Makins made friends with Jim Wedderburn (later an MP and Parliamentary Under Secretary of State for Scotland) Kit Steel (who joined the Foreign Office and became the Ambassador in Bonn) and Evelyn Baring (later Lord Howick and Governor of Kenya). All these men became lifetime friends.

The group was all Conservatives. Makins belonged to two University Conservative clubs; the Canning, for which he was Secretary for a time, and the Chatham. Although he was a member of the Oxford Union, he did not take part in its debates, 'being far too diffident'. His diffidence was longstanding: several years earlier, while at Winchester he wrote 'I went to my first debate last Thursday, it was most amusing, needless to say I did not make a remark'.[21] His political activities outside of university were restricted to helping his father in the November 1922 general election, and the occasional dalliance with the Young Conservative Union, for example he helped out in London's North Camberwell division during general elections.[22]

Aside from the political societies at Oxford, Makins was a member of two social clubs, the Carlton and the Gridiron. His group 'were not in the main heavy drinkers,' they 'smoked but only the choicest brands of Macedonia or

---

[19] Cairncross, Alec (ed.), *The Robert Hall Diaries 1947–1953*, London: Unwin Hayman, 1989, p. 68.

[20] Ernest Makins Papers, MS Sherfield 195, Letter to father, 15 August 1922.

[21] Ernest Makins Papers, MS Sherfield 204, Letter to mother, 12 October 1919.

[22] Makins Papers, MS Sherfield 777, letter Dame Helen Gwynne-Vaughan to Makins, undated but probably written in 1924.

Turkish tobacco and ... played a good deal of bridge, poker and vingt-et-un, but never for high stakes'.[23] Makins played soccer for the House in winter, and cricket in the summer. Together with Alec Douglas Home (later Lord Home and the Prime Minister), who was also at Christ Church, and Dick Heathcoat Amory, he formed a cricket club called the 'Coconuts', so called because they bowled a coconut as the first ball instead of a cricket ball. This got them into trouble, but it seems to be the most 'riotous' activity that Makins became involved in at Oxford. The historian A.L. Rowse, who shared tutorials with Makins in his second and third years, described him as 'immensely distinguished to look at even then, very lofty with prominent bony nose and slightly mongoloid cast of features; very alert and intelligent, with a quick, engaging sense of humour'.[24]

Makins was fortunate to be at Christ Church at a time when both John Masterman and Keith Feiling were teaching there. Masterman who taught at Christ Church from 1921–6, was also a Censor, responsible for welfare and discipline when Makins was an undergraduate. Feiling was elected a student (that is a Fellow) of Christ Church in 1911. He remained there for over 30 years and was largely responsible for Christ Church's prowess in history. Rowse noted that Masterman, perhaps the less serious historian, 'saw that we worked' while Feiling who eventually held the Chichele Chair of Modern History at Oxford 'undoubtedly had a living interest in history'.[25] 'Their complementary talents and sympathetic cooperation explain their outstanding success. Between 1921 and 1936 ... Christ Church won thirty one First Classes.'[26] Makins was one of them. He regarded Masterman as a 'first class history tutor' and spoke of Feiling as a 'sensitive and charming man ... a stimulating and imaginative tutor to whom I owed a good deal of my success in the schools [final exams]'.[27]

Good teaching was one ingredient; hard work was another. Rowse noted 'Everyone who knows Oxford knows that taking the Honour School of Modern History seriously is a great strain – more than probably any other school'.[28] Makins' response was to cram in the vacations. Every year during the summer vacation he would disappear to stay with the Septenville family at Chateau Bois du Robin in Northern France, armed with a box of history books. He had first stayed there immediately after leaving Winchester in order to learn French from Madame Septenville. Makins worked on his history books every day, for ten hours a day. It paid off. Out of the 270 candidates who sat history finals in the

---

23 *Oxford and Beyond*, p. 32.

24 Rowse, *A Cornishman at Oxford*, p. 192.

25 Rowse, *A Cornishman at Oxford*, p. 192.

26 Charles Stuart, 'Feiling, Sir Keith Grahame (1884–1977)', *Oxford Dictionary of National Biography*, Oxford University Press, 2004 Online edition.

27 *Oxford and Beyond*, p. 26.

28 Rowse, *A Cornishman at Oxford*, p. 191.

summer of 1925, there were 15 Firsts; Makins' was one of the best.[29] He wrote to his father 'all my plans have been altered by a most miraculous occurrence, not only have I got a first, but one of the best firsts of the year'.[30] At his Viva (oral examination) the Board of Examiners congratulated Makins on his papers 'a blessing which is pronounced over two or three people every year'.[31] He had intended immediately to apply for the Foreign Office, but given his academic success he decided to try for an All Souls Prize Fellowship instead – 'one of the hardest examinations there is'.[32]

In September 1925 he motored down to Oxford to sit the All Souls College examinations along with 15 others. In the first paper, the essay paper, he was confronted with one word 'Possessions'. After an hour he had written two lines. There was some relief in the afternoon with the first history paper. The next morning came a general paper of 'appalling difficulty', mostly aesthetics and philosophy, and that was followed by another history paper. The rest of the week saw English History, Spanish, French and Latin translations and the Viva. Makins did not leave the examinations with any great hope of success, but neither perhaps, did any other candidate. Nevertheless, on 3 November, Makins was informed that he had been elected to a Prize Fellowship.[33]

Makins noted in his diary 'I suppose I always had a vague premonition, against every rational supposition, that I had a good chance of success ... I have never known such perfect satisfaction or had my hopes set for two months uniquely on one object, and had that object not been attained, my whole outlook might have been altered'.[34] His success in the All Souls examinations was, perhaps, the most significant event in his life thus far. Shortly after election Makins wrote to this father 'I have no doubt that it is the best thing there is to be a Fellow here, it must be an institution quite unlike any other in the world, through which pass either as Fellows or as guests most of the worlds distinguished and clever men.' Makins continued, perhaps with his feet nearer the ground 'and reducing it to its lowest and most material terms £300 per year'.[35]

The next day Makins moved into All Souls College amid a shower of congratulatory messages, together with a notice of his achievements on the front page of *The Times*. He was one of two Prize Fellows elected that year. The other was A.L. Rowse, who was elected ahead of Makins, which meant that Rowse was

---

29 Ibid., p. 232.

30 Ernest Makins Papers, MS Sherfield 195, letter Makins to father, 29 July 1925.

31 Ibid.

32 Ibid.

33 The Sherfield Diary 1925/1926, dated 3 October but he must mean 3 November.

34 Ibid.

35 Ernest Makins Papers, MS Sherfield 1925, letter Makins to father, 5 November 1925.

given the choice of rooms 'which he exercised for the best'.[36] There are perhaps two kinds of Prize Fellows, those who intend to pursue an academic career and those who do not. Makins was in the latter category. He had little interest in becoming an academic historian. Nominally he was at All Souls to research 'The Grenville Connection in English Politics from 1760 to 1834', a subject which he had chosen and which the College had approved.[37] This requirement, however, was not strictly enforced and the Grenville Connection was one which continued to be ignored. Makins instead decided to read law and pursue a career at the Bar.

Anyone elected to a Prize Fellowship had to live at All Souls for two years, so Makins' plan to go abroad and study for the Foreign Office examination was not possible. In 1925 he joined the Inner Temple and began reading for the Bar. At least at the beginning he does not seem to have taken the work too seriously; he managed to fail two out of four of his preliminary examinations. His diary entry for 26 April 1926 noted 'Bar exams not a success. Bit off more than I could chew'.[38] A more plausible reason might be his lifestyle at the time. As Simon Green has pointed out, to read the Makins' diary for his first six months at All Souls is seemingly to enter a world otherwise better described by P.G. Wodehouse:

> Friday 6 November "Great dinner in Christ Church ... Many golfing hearties there ... Had a smash in the Studebaker ... Shot with old Arthur Johnson in Bagley Wood ... three pheasants ... then a rabbit"
> Saturday 7 November "horrible rich dinner ... at Claridges ... Heaps of people there"
> Sunday 8 November "First Sunday dinner at All Souls ... made a terrific hash of the screwing and had to be helped out"
> Wednesday 19 December "I have got into the terrible habit of not being able to wake up in the morning"[39,40]

After his failure in the spring of 1926, no doubt recognising his hubris, he applied himself and retook the two preliminary examinations in the autumn of 1926. This time he passed. Towards the end of 1926, Makins whose confidence must have been dented by his failure in the preliminary examinations, wrote

---

[36] All Souls College, Codrington Library LR 5.a.10., Ms cccc 1(k), All Souls Minute Book, 1915–1925.

[37] All Souls College, Codrington Library, LR.5.a.11; Ms ccccl(l) All Souls Minute Book, 1926–1946.

[38] The Sherfield Diary 1925/26, 20 April 1926.

[39] Extracted from the transcript of a lecture given by Professor Simon Green 'Wykehamists and Public Servants: The Recasting of the Ansonian Deal'.

[40] Note the Makins diary records these dates as being in October/November in fact they were in November/December.

to his father asking for advice. 'The question is what I should do best and what would be best for me to do in the near future', adding 'I am quite sure that ultimately I shall want to go into politics'.[41] He then outlined his immediate options, diplomacy or the Bar. He feared keeping both options open lest he fell between two stools; the Bar required a good showing in the final bar examinations if there was to be any hope of entering good chambers, and the Foreign Office required a long period of study in order to achieve satisfactory marks in its language papers. Ernest Makins' advice was clear and decisive. Concentrate on the Bar examinations when sitting them in May 1927, try the law first, the training will not be wasted, and if it transpired that the law did not suit, then wait a year and sit the Foreign Office exams in the summer of 1928.[42] This strategy also maximised the chances of Makins retaining a Fellowship of All Souls, which was up for renewal in November 1927.

Makins followed his fathers' advice. He passed his law finals 'by an adequate margin' and, courtesy of Donald Somervell, a Fellow of All Souls, then Solicitor General, entered a prestigious set of chambers in Inner Temple, of which Colin Pearson, later a Law Lord, and Cis Asquith, later a Lord of Appeal, were members. Makins, however, did not find the work very interesting, consisting as it did of several large long-running commercial cases and a miscellany of small, mainly divorce cases. It did not take him very long to realise that the law was not for him. In October 1927 he left Chambers: he had not had a brief of his own, and rarely ventured into court. His dislike of the work was one factor which influenced his decision to leave; another was his diffidence about public speaking.

That left him nine months to prepare for the Foreign Office examinations. He had a good knowledge of French but spoke it poorly, and had no German. The rest of the examination was according to Makins 'exactly the same as the History Finals at Oxford with a wide range and choice of subject'.[43] He felt confident that he could tackle these papers with the minimum of revision and so he decided to travel abroad to study languages. He knew that his Fellowship of All Souls would continue: on 3 November 1927 the college unanimously agreed that it would be extended for a further period of five years.[44] The extension recognised his lack of interest in academic matters and Makins became a 'fifty pound' fellow, a type of Fellowship reserved for those who did not intend to work exclusively at Oxford.

Makins joined the familiar tour undertaken by Foreign Office hopefuls. There were a number of families who regularly took in the aspirants. Makins

41 Ernest Makins Papers, MS Sherfield 195, letter Makins to father, 4 December 1926.

42 Makins Papers, MS Sherfield 427, letter father to Makins, 10 December 1926.

43 *Oxford and Beyond*, p. 45.

44 All Souls College, Codrington Library, LR.5.a.11; Ms ccccl(1) All Souls Minute Book, 1926–1946. Statutory General Meeting 3 November 1927, p. 34.

travelled first to the Hepners in Potsdam, then the Mirbuchs in Munich and then the Menzen family in Bonn. It was a dull existence and something of a contrast to Makins' Bertie Wooster-like existence in England. But the lack of any significant distractions in Germany paid off and by the Easter of 1928 Makins, who found German 'interesting and easy to learn', was fluent.[45] Easter was followed by a spell in Paris to brush up his French and then back to London in July to sit the Foreign Office examinations. He was staying with Evelyn Baring at Howick when news came that he had not only passed the Foreign Office Examinations, but that he had come top of the list.

The Foreign Office which Makins joined was very small indeed compared with the service today. Reforms in 1906 had expanded its staff beyond a Permanent Under Secretary and clerks for filing and copying to include professionally trained staff who were able to offer 'comment and advice in minutes or to draft memoranda and instructions to post abroad in the form of despatches and telegrams'.[46] A further major reform had come in 1918, when the Diplomatic Service and the home Foreign Office staff were amalgamated. Even so, by the late 1920s it had little more than 200 members, of which 70 served in the Foreign Office at home, with the rest in embassies and missions abroad. In addition to the Permanent Under Secretary, who was head of the office, there were two Deputy Under Secretaries, one of whom was the Chief Clerk and responsible for all administrative matters, and three Assistant Under Secretaries. In London the balance was made up of 12 Ministers/Counsellors, and 24 First, 12 Second and 15 Third Secretaries.

Overseas there were 49 diplomatic missions, staffed where appropriate in similar proportions to those in London. The consequence of the service being so small was that it was a 'tightly knit body with a strong esprit de corps'.[47] Members of the service nearly all knew each other well and were often close friends. The work was divided into several departments, varying in size but normally each with fewer than half a dozen officers. There were technical departments, dealing with administration, communications and routine matters such as passports and visas, and political departments, which were organised on a geographical basis, dealing with a country or region.

Makins joined the Foreign Office in October 1928.[48] As was the custom at the time, a new entrant was on probation for two years before being confirmed as a Third Secretary. As top of the list Makins was offered the choice of joining a department immediately, or learning one of the 'hard languages' such as Russian

---

[45] *Oxford and Beyond*, p. 48.

[46] Makins Papers, MS Sherfield 523, *Foreign Service Handbook*, p. 3.

[47] Bodleian Library Oxford, Patrick Reilly Papers (Henceforth Reilly Papers) MS Reilly 6917, Memoirs, p. 2.

[48] Ernest Makins Papers, MS Sherfield 195, letter Makins to father, 24 October 1928.

or Chinese. Makins, now aged 24, had studied enough and he instantly chose the first option and was assigned to the American Department, which at that time dealt with relations between the United Kingdom and the United States, the whole of Latin America, the Arctic and the Antarctic. Makins was responsible for monitoring and reporting on the affairs of Mexico, Brazil, Argentina and Chile. During his first week he told his father that 'already the work is interesting and I enjoy doing it'.[49]

The head of the American Department in 1928 was Leslie Craigie, an officer who had served in Washington and had an American wife. His deputy was Thomas Snow, a Winchester classical scholar who had joined the office some 15 years before Makins. Snow remained a lifelong friend of Makins. Craigie and Snow each had their own office; Makins along with the others in the department was consigned to a big room often referred to as the 'third room' or simply 'the department'. All papers coming into the Foreign Office were indexed and entered in the Registry before being sent down to the departments. Telegrams were also deciphered and circulated by the Registry. Because of this officers did not need to arrive for work much before 10 am. Lunch might take two hours, and officers rarely stayed past 6 pm. The important telegrams were sent directly to the head of a department, but most papers started at the bottom and so probationers and junior officers were able to express their views before the papers were passed up the chain. Thus, as Makins observed, 'one was made to feel, at the outset, part of the action'.[50] It was something of a surprise to Makins, who prided himself on his writing ability, that his various draft reports were returned to him 'torn to pieces and rewritten'. But as he observed 'the FO had its own style which demanded the utmost clarity and economy of language'.[51]

When he first joined the Foreign Office, Austen Chamberlain was the Foreign Secretary, and the Conservative government, led by Stanley Baldwin, had been in power for four years. Within a year of Makins joining the office, the Conservatives lost power and on 5 June 1929 a Labour government was formed under the leadership of Ramsay MacDonald. Arthur Henderson became Foreign Secretary with Hugh Dalton and Phillip Noel Baker becoming his Under Secretaries. Although too junior at the time to have any significant contact with the politicians, Makins was to work with both of these Under Secretaries at later points in his career.

He did get a chance to work with the politicians in January 1930, when the American Department became involved in the Five Power London Naval Conference called by Ramsay MacDonald. The purpose of the conference was to reach an agreement on the relative strengths of the naval powers of the five

49 Ibid.

50 *Oxford and Beyond*, p. 54.

51 Ibid., p. 51.

participating countries; Britain, the United States, Japan, France and Italy. Makins was the junior member of the delegation and was the official assigned to Wedgwood Benn, the Secretary of State for India, who had been talked into being the fourth British political delegate at the conference.[52] Makins' role was primarily administrative; he was responsible for organising the conference dinner and needed to attend the daily receptions given for the delegates where the exceptionally tall Makins served a very practical purpose. Mrs Wedgwood Benn told Makins that 'my husband and I find you so useful, whenever we get separated at one of these receptions; we always agree to meet at you'.[53] It was a role Makins, who was six foot four inches tall, played for the rest of his life: at Washington parties, couples used to say 'You go right and I'll go left and we'll meet at Roger Makins'. The Five Power Conference ended on 22 April 1930 with the signing of a treaty on naval disarmament. After the Conference Makins was sent for by Wedgwood Benn, who presented him with a silver ashtray and thanked him for his services during the conference. It was his first brush with the politicians, and it augured well for the future. Shortly after this, in the autumn of 1930, Makins' appointment as a Third Secretary was confirmed. He was now a fully-fledged member of the Foreign Service.

The relaxed pace in the Foreign Office allowed Makins to continue a full social life and he enjoyed a comfortable financial position. Unlike some other young diplomats (for example Patrick Reilly) Makins was not required to survive on his salary of £500 a year. He received a generous allowance from his father as well as his £50 per annum from All Souls. He regularly attended weekend house parties; he recalls 'picnicking with Margot Asquith and playing a set of tennis with Arthur Balfour'.[54] He visited country houses such as Birkhill (Jim Wedderburn's home), Ardgowan (Lady Shaw Stewarts' home), Howick (Evelyn Baring's family home) and Forse (William Bairds' home) every year. During the winter Makins would ski at Klosters, on one occasion joining a party which included Archie Clark Kerr (later Lord Inverchapel and the Ambassador in Washington 1946–1948), a man who Makins would subsequently serve under in Washington. In London where possible, he mixed with the same group of friends he had gained at Oxford including Kit Steel, Dick Heathcoat Amory and Jim Wedderburn. He joined the Travellers Club, the main Foreign Office club and often lunched there.

Makins remembers that by 1929 he was on the dance lists of most London hostesses. 'Every evening in the summer, the footman laid out my white tie, tails and gloves and I went to one or more dances, after being asked to a dinner

[52] The others were Ramsay Macdonald, Arthur Henderson and First Lord of the Admiralty, A.V. Alexander.

[53] *Oxford and Beyond*, p. 56.

[54] *Oxford and Beyond*, p. 59.

for 8 or 10 beforehand'.[55] At this time Makins had a number of female friends including Lady Mary Cecil Grey (Molly Grey) eldest daughter of the fifth Earl Grey (she later married Evelyn Baring), Miriam Rothschild, 'an attractive, brilliant and athletic girl', who became a distinguished zoologist and Fellow of the Royal Society, and Phyllis Spender Clay. Makins became 'deeply attached' to Phyllis, who was the daughter of Herbert Spender Clay, a Conservative Member of Parliament. His suit was encouraged by her parents, but she rejected him in favour of an older diplomat, Sir Phillip Nichols, the man she subsequently married.

In April 1931, Makins was appointed Third Secretary at the Embassy in Washington. It was his first overseas posting and the first of three to the Washington Embassy. A posting to America did not have the same significance then as it does today. The United States, although already a significant economic power, was seen as something of a diplomatic backwater, partly because of her isolationist stance. Makins set sail in depressed mood. 'I had been unsuccessful in love, I had not yet recovered full health (he had recently had his tonsils removed) and I was sad at parting from so many friends of both sexes and from family'.[56] His mood was not improved much by the work he undertook at the Embassy. As the most junior secretary at the Embassy he was earmarked for the most laborious tasks – 'the bottle washer and maid of all work'. The main part of his work was dealing with immigration cases which were 'dull and tiresome'; there were a great many of them, and many had to be negotiated with the American authorities.[57] Makins was also responsible for drafting the weekly press summary for the Foreign Office and for dealing with scientific matters. He 'performed the functions of a Press Department and Scientific attaché rolled into one'.[58] Makins told his father 'the work here does not look like being half as interesting as work in the F.O.'.[59] Shortly after Makins arrived he wrote to his friend Kit Steel bemoaning his posting to Washington.[60] It was difficult for Makins knowing that Kit Steel had been posted to the Paris embassy, perhaps the most desirable posting at the time. But Makins made a number of contacts within the administration which were to serve him well in his future career; men such as Sam Reber, who Makins was to work closely with in Algiers, Harvey Bundy, who became the State Department's representative on atomic energy matters, and later Dean Acheson, who became Secretary of State in the Truman Administration.

---

[55] *Oxford and Beyond*, p. 61.

[56] *Oxford and Beyond*, p. 66.

[57] Ernest Makins Papers, MS Sherfield 196, letter Makins to father, May 1931.

[58] *Oxford and Beyond*, p. 71.

[59] Ernest Makins Papers, MS Sherfield 196, letter Makins to father, 28 April 1931.

[60] Makins Papers, MS Sherfield 472, letter Kit Steel to Makins, 23 September 1931.

One compensation for the drudgery of the work was that the Ambassador, Sir Ronald Lindsay and his wife were extremely well connected in Washington and took a lot of trouble with their staff and frequently invited them to the Embassy. Thus Makins was able to see at first hand how the embassy should be run. Sir Ronald and Lady Lindsay treated the Embassy staff as one big family; Makins records 'we were a small and congenial group at the Embassy in 1931'.[61] At the time the embassy would have consisted of only a handful of diplomats. The embassy building, which was designed by Luytens, had only been occupied for two years when Makins arrived. It was the first embassy to be built on Massachusetts Avenue, now known as Embassy Row.

Makins arrived in Washington at the mid-point of the Hoover Presidency, when the dominant issue in American politics was the Depression. However, Washington, or at least the section of Washington society Makins mixed in, was immune from the worst effects of the Depression and its social whirl continued regardless. Makins commented 'In Washington ... the social racket is more artificial, more intense, and more wearing than in any other capitol in the world'.[62] Washington in 1931 was a small society and consisted of four groups: politicians, diplomats, journalists and Washington's permanent residents (lawyers, bankers and old families) or the 'cave dwellers' as they were known. Young, 'well-mannered' bachelors were in great demand and Makins quickly became part of the Washington social circuit, much of which centred on Georgetown, the elegant eighteenth-century area of Washington where Makins lived, along with most other diplomats and politicians. He was invited to all the important houses in Washington and was on the invitation list for many of the political hostesses at the time. These included Alice Longworth, the daughter of Theodore Roosevelt, 'she is a most dynamic personality, a femme politique, with a very good brain and a strong sense of humour', Borden Harriman, 'a great friend of Woodrow Wilson's who marshalled the democrats in Washington' and the heiress Eleanor Patterson, a great friend of the Hearst's the newspaper family, 'she was a famous beauty ... and is extremely amusing but rather dangerous'.[63] Makins commented that 'circulating through these great houses, it was possible, even for a young secretary, to meet nearly everyone of consequence in Washington'. Makins was being reported as the 'idol of Washington though somewhat contemptuous of it all'.[64] He wrote to his mother ' My physique still continues to cause astonishment to the ladies of America, but accustomed as I am to cries of admiration, I confess I was taken

---

61 *Oxford and Beyond*, Annex Sir Ronald and Lady Lindsay, p. ii.

62 Lord Sherfield's Memoirs, *A Flying Visit to Hayti*, 1932.

63 Ernest Makins Papers, MS Sherfield 196, letter Makins to father, 12 December 1931.

64 Makins Papers, MS Sherfield 472, letter Kit Steel to Makins, 10 November 1932.

aback the other day when the wife of the Secretary of War, who socially is considered almost the dernier mot, informed me that I had hips like an eel!'[65]

Makins was attractive to women and attracted by them: they were an essential part of his life. Some relationships, however, were more suitable than others. Shortly after Makins arrived in Washington he met and became very fond of Felicia Gizycka the daughter of Eleanor Patterson. Felicia was recently divorced from Drew Pearson, the celebrated Washington columnist with whom she had had a child. She was an exotic creature and had a number of lovers. Makins must have described his feelings for Felicia to his mother because she wrote to him 'I do beg you to be careful in your dealings with her – she is both charming and determined but it [marriage] would be eminently unsuitable for you.'[66]

In the spring of 1932, Makins met Alice Davis. He was 'immediately and strikingly attracted to her'.[67] Alice, who was 23 years old, was the eldest daughter of Dwight Davis and Mrs Helen Davis (née Brooks). Dwight Davis was an American politician, he was also a very good tennis player and while at Harvard he founded the Davis Cup International Tennis Competition and donated the cup itself. He served in World War I and was awarded the Distinguished Service Cross for 'extraordinary heroism'. President Calvin Coolidge appointed him assistant Secretary of War in 1923 and then Secretary of War from 1925–9. In 1929 President Herbert Hoover appointed him Governor General of the Philippines and he was there until 1932. Due to the fact that Helen Davis, Alice's mother, was ill (she died in 1932) it fell to Alice to act as the hostess for her father in Manila in 1929 and 1930.

The Davis family wintered at their Plantation near Tallahassee, Florida and in early 1933 Makins spent a week there with the family. Although Makins continued to see other women. including Felicia, the relationship with Alice must have developed because in the summer of 1933, on a beach at the Davis's summer cottage in the Southamptons, Long Island, Makins proposed to Alice and she accepted. They decided not to announce the engagement at the time but to wait until Makins had a clearer idea of the plans the Foreign Office had for him. He did, however, drop heavy hints to his mother: 'it would not be a bad idea if you were both to practice getting used to the prospect of an American daughter in law. I rather think you may get one – but please practice complete secrecy.'[68]

As early as February 1933 Makins heard, through his father, that the Foreign Office were thinking of transferring him from Washington. In a turnaround from his first reflections on Washington, Makins commented that 'there were

[65] Ernest Makins Papers, MS Sherfield 205, letter Makins to mother, 23 June 1932.

[66] Makins Papers, MS Sherfield 430, letter mother to Makins, 26 June 1933.

[67] Makins Papers, MS Sherfield 947, Draft Memoir of Alice by Roger vol. I, 1985.

[68] Ernest Makins Papers, MS Sherfield 204, letter Makins to mother, 14 July 1933.

not many jobs open to me in the service which I should like more than the present one'.[69] A year later in February 1934, Sir Ronald Lindsay confirmed that Makins was indeed to be moved from Washington. Makins wrote at once to the Foreign Office and asked for Berlin, mentioning Cairo as a 'safe second choice'.[70] Makins would find out in due course just how difficult a posting to Berlin in the 1930s would have been. Resigned to a move Makins concluded that 'Washington is the worst place in the world to begin married life, it's provincial and there's no privacy'.[71] In the event Makins heard in March 1934 that he was to return to the Foreign Office to work on League of Nations Affairs in the Western Department. At least he had been able to experience the first year of the Roosevelt administration and meet some of its officials. In November 1932 Roosevelt had won a landslide victory of 22,800,000 votes to Hoover's 15,750,000 votes and he took office on 4 March 1933. (This was the last Presidential election where the winning candidate had to wait five months before taking office.) The Democrats had secured the White House and they were to remain there until Eisenhower's inauguration in 1953.

Once Makins' departure from Washington was confirmed, he and Alice announced their engagement and prepared for the wedding. The announcement received considerable publicity in Washington; Alice's picture was on the front page of most of the Washington newspapers. On 30 April 1934 Alice and Roger were married in the Episcopal Church in Tallahassee. It was a small occasion with only a few members of the family and close friends attending. Makins' father made the journey out with Dick Heathcoat-Amory who was the best man. After a ten-day honeymoon spent on the plantation, Alice and Roger made their way to New York and on 12 May 1934 set sail for England.

The marriage to Alice was perhaps the most significant event to have come out of Makins' first posting to America. There is little evidence that he made a significant impact other than on the social scene, but the connections he made were to prove invaluable for his future career. However, Lady Lindsay wrote to Alice and Roger after they had left for England. 'I doubt if anyone has ever been as much missed as you have been both personally and officially … I might also add that one of the ties between you and me is my own conviction that you will one day be British ambassador in Washington.'[72] Marriage came at a time that suited Makins; he confided to a friend that if he was to do serious work in the

69 Ernest Makins Papers, MS Sherfield196, letter to father, 24 February 1933.

70 Ernest Makins Papers, MS Sherfield 196, letter Makins to father, 24 February 1934 (24/2 is a coincidence).

71 Ibid.

72 Makins Papers, MS Sherfield, letter Elizabeth Lindsay to Makins, 9 February 1935.

Foreign Office it was time to settle down and dispense with the distractions of a single life.

After a brief temporary posting to Oslo, Makins returned to London on 6 September 1934 and took up his position in the Western Department as the third member of the team responsible for League of Nations affairs. The team's two other members were William Strang, who subsequently became Permanent Under Secretary, and Ralph Stevenson, who later became the Ambassador in China and then Egypt. By the time Makins joined the Department the League's authority was already in decline. It had failed to find an adequate solution to the Japanese invasion of Manchuria and in March 1933 Japan gave notice of withdrawal from the League. Hitler, who became Germany's Chancellor in January 1933, also frustrated the League's efforts by withdrawing Germany from the Leagues' Conference for the Reduction and Limitation of Armaments held in October 1933. Germany left the League in the same year.

There was no permanent UK representation at the League in Geneva; the team responsible for its affairs travelled to Geneva as and when necessary. Within two days of arriving back in the Foreign Office, Makins left for Geneva for his first Council Meeting of the League. Alice remained in London to look for a house. She was successful and in November 1934 the Makinses secured their first house, buying a Crown lease on 30 Chester Terrace, Regents Park, and gathered together a household: a cook, a parlour maid and a housemaid. These were joined by a nanny and nurserymaid when Alice gave birth to twin girls, Mollie and Cynthia, on 28 July 1935. Life for the young married couple must have been difficult, for one thing, physical separation was to be the story of the first ten years of their marriage. Although on occasion Alice travelled to Geneva, much of the time she was alone in a new city, without her friends and her immediate family, and even with somewhat limited access to the children thanks to the English tradition of leaving most childcare to a nanny.

The League consisted of the Assembly, which met for about a month once a year and was attended by all member nations, and a Council which met for a week or so two or three times a year and was effectively controlled by the great powers. The real work, however, was carried out by seven committees which produced reports for the Assembly. All meetings took place in Geneva. Makins was attached to the 'second committee', which dealt with economic and financial questions, and the 'fifth committee' which dealt with social questions, such as the traffic in opium, slavery and child welfare. He noted that 'as a junior member of the delegation, thrown in at the deep end, the work was very tiring and often tedious'.[73] The Council and the Assembly work, was more interesting: it was Makins' job to make notes and draft a report of the day's discussion. He describes a typical day

[73] Lord Sherfield's Memoirs, *September1934–September1939 Geneva and Foreign Office* (Henceforth *Geneva and the Foreign Office*), p. 5.

in one of his letters to Alice '– a meeting of the Assembly – a sub-committee (2.5 hours) on Russian Women – a lunch party – a meeting of Dominican delegates – a committee meeting on economic questions (3 hours) and then miscellaneous questions with a short interval for dinner'.[74] In an earlier letter Makins had written 'I suppose the first impression of this place is bound to be one of unending verbiage leading to no practical or useful result'.[75]

Working at the League gave Makins his first opportunity to work with Anthony Eden, who attended the 1934 meetings as one of the Parliamentary Under Secretaries. At that time Eden was 'emerging as a rising star, debonair, charming, mercurial, vain and already displaying a talent for skilful negotiation'.[76] Later Eden attended as Minister of State for League Affairs and then as the Foreign Secretary from June 1935, until his resignation in February 1938. During this period Eden developed a high level of respect for Makins' abilities and came to rely on him as the pace of diplomacy in that pre-war period increased. One example was the time Eden delegated the drafting of a policy document concerned with immigration into Palestine to Makins. Eden forwarded the document to the Cabinet virtually unchanged; only adding 'This is important. I have great confidence in Makins' judgement and little doubt that he is right'.[77]

While a great deal of the work undertaken by Makins at the League was that of 'bag carrier' and 'bottle washer', towards the end of his period in the Western Department, there was one area where Makins took a more leading role. Since its inception the League concerned itself with the issue of refugees. It had achieved some success in dealing with refugee problems resulting from the First World War, and one of its achievements was the introduction of the 'Nansen Passport' which afforded stateless persons some legal status and gave them identity papers. As the persecution of the Jews in Germany escalated with the rise of Hitler, the anti-Jewish Nuremberg laws of 1935, growing commercial and employment restrictions on the Jewish population, and the German annexation of Austria and the Sudetanland, the League attempted to address the increasingly acute issue of Jewish emigration. Makins became the Foreign Office's principal official representative in this area both inside Whitehall and at the Evian conference.

In March 1938 President Roosevelt proposed that there should be an international effort to deal with the issue. The result was the convening of an international conference to consider the matter at Evian on 6 July 1938. Makins, in a memorandum prepared in May 1938, warned that the American proposals were unlikely to have been 'thought out before they were launched' and were

[74] Makins Papers, MS Sherfield 438, letter Makins to Alice, 17 September 1934.

[75] Makins Papers, MS Sherfield 438, letter Makins to Alice, 13 September 1934.

[76] *Geneva and the Foreign Office*, p. 9.

[77] Lecture given by Martin Gilbert to Miriam Rothschild and John Foster Human Rights Trust, *British Policy Towards Jewish Refugees, 1933–1946.*

'apt to be wild and impractical'.[78] It was, therefore, more important than usual for the British government to define its own position. Makins appears to have been in favour of assisting Jewish emigration by suggesting allowing emigration to certain colonies. He also proposed that financial assistance should be offered to penniless émigrés who had had their assets confiscated by the German authorities, and were therefore not attractive prospects to countries which might otherwise have accepted them.. He acknowledged that the proposal would represent a change in policy, but argued that the reward would be the 'sympathy and support of World Jewry' and further that such an initiative would have 'a striking effect upon world opinion and particularly opinion in the United States'.[79] His memorandum also noted that the British Government should welcome and encourage the fact that the United States Government had 'departed from its policy of non-intervention in European matters'.[80]

The immigration question, however, was not one for the Foreign Office alone. At a number of interdepartmental meetings with the Home Office, the Colonial Office and the Treasury, each Department put up their arguments. The result was to severely limit emigration into Britain, the Colonies or indeed elsewhere. Makins' suggestions to assist immigration were not taken up. As he pointed out 'the main difficulty throughout ... was that though the Foreign Office was in the lead the refugee problem was not its prime responsibility; on the domestic front it was the Home Office, and on the overseas front it was the Colonial Office'.[81]

The Evian Conference, which was organised jointly by the British, American and French governments, met over the summer months of 1938; there were over 200 representatives from 30 countries. Makins was part of the British delegation which was headed by Earl Winterton. The conference was to have no real practical effect on the problem. 'A great deal of hot air was ventilated, there was a profusion of verbal sympathy, but no country showed any disposition to take more than a token number of refugees, or put up any money.'[82] In the closing session of the conference a resolution was adopted which established an Intergovernmental Committee in London (to which Makins was appointed Secretary) to 'continue and develop' the conference's refugee work such as it was. The task of the committee 'was to attempt to obtain from the German government better conditions for the orderly emigration of Jews and "non Aryans"; and secondly to persuade the Governments of the "countries of refuge"

[78] Sherman, A.J, *Island Refuge: Britain and Refugees from the Third Reich 1933–1939*, Berkeley: University of California Press, 1973, p. 100.

[79] Ibid., p. 102.

[80] Ibid., p. 102.

[81] *Geneva and the Foreign Office*, p. 44.

[82] Ibid., p. 44.

to develop opportunities for the permanent settlement of refugees'.[83] In fact few governments did confront the Germans, and this reluctance to do so can be seen as a part of the general policy of appeasing Hitler's regime.

Makins in his memoirs suggests that 'the handling of the conference and its aftermath was the first occasion on which I was able to perform as a principal rather than a bottle washer'.[84] It was also an occasion where he was able to move around other parts of Whitehall by attending a number of interdepartmental meetings. There is a sense that 1938 was the year in which he came to be noticed by senior members of the Foreign Office. By 1938, aged 34, he had been in the Foreign Service for 10 years and yet he had only achieved the rank of Second Secretary. Within the next two years, however, he was to rise to the rank of Counsellor. His talents were beginning to be recognised.

---

83 Reilly memoirs, p. 26.

84 *Geneva and the Foreign Office*, p. 48.

Chapter 2
War and Diplomacy

It is battles won and lost which tend to form the headlines of the Second World War. In reality the war was waged not merely by the armed forces, but also by industrial workers, politicians, diplomats and other civil servants. During wartime, alliances with other countries are of paramount importance and the diplomatic work includes assisting allied governments in exile, inducing countries to remain neutral, or seeking to harness the power of other nations. This chapter considers the part played by Makins and the other diplomats he worked with.

Alliances with other European countries were important during the Second World War, but the most significant international relationship for Britain was her association with America. It might be argued that the so-called special relationship between the two countries was forged during the war. It was not based solely on the bond between Churchill and Roosevelt, but also on a myriad of Anglo-American relationships across the world: in London, Washington and the theatres of war. Makins, working with Dwight Eisenhower and others, played a central role in building the close links between Britain and America in the North African and Italian campaigns. His work is a good example of how the Anglo-American relationship was built in practice.

On 3 October 1938 Makins boarded a train bound for Berlin having been sent there to report on events taking place at the British Embassy. Senior members of the Foreign Office were concerned about the behaviour of the British Ambassador in Berlin, Sir Neville Henderson. They felt that Henderson, who had been appointed in 1937 and who was totally committed to a policy of appeasement, was not properly representing his instructions. Sir Robert Vansittart noted that 'Henderson's despatches were ill thought out and above all contrary to the policy of HMG'.[1] By the time Makins became involved Henderson's telegrams were becoming 'increasingly hysterical'.

The Embassy was under considerable pressure and Makins was welcomed by Ivone Kirkpatrick (the Head of Chancery at the Embassy) as a fresh pair of hands without enquiring too much as to why he had been sent. Makins pitched in and made himself useful to Kirkpatrick who he found to be completely

[1] Johnson Gaynor (ed.), *The Foreign Office and British Diplomacy in the Twentieth Century*, Abingdon: Routledge, 2005, p. 117.

exhausted.[2] The pressure on a diplomat working in a totalitarian regime is immense and Makins must have considered himself fortunate that his request for a posting to Berlin, made four years earlier, had been turned down. He found that notwithstanding the stance taken by Henderson, the Embassy had abandoned practically all hope of peace. Staff and papers were being sent away and the remaining diplomats were preparing for the worst.[3] Makins recalls one incident, indicative of the near panic within the Embassy at the time, when four fire engines drew up at the door in the belief that the place was on fire. The false alarm had been raised because smoke was bellowing from every chimney as the staff were frantically burning all of the papers.[4]

It is interesting to note that this was taking place only a few days after Chamberlain had returned from Munich declaring 'peace with honour' and 'peace in our time': there was a considerable contrast between what Makins saw on the ground in Germany and what the Prime Minister was saying in Britain. Makins noted that 'At home the PM is talking about the new era of peace and friendship ... but in Berlin the atmosphere is as bellicose and unconciliatory as ever'.[5] Makins, who only remained in Berlin for four weeks, returned to the Foreign Office to report his findings. He concluded that the Ambassador was a very tired man and that the situation was 'very black indeed'.

In early 1939 Makins was appointed to the Central Department which had recently been created in place of the Western Department. The new department was headed by William Strang with Ivone Kirkpatrick, who had returned from Berlin, as the second in command. The Central Department at that time dealt with the affairs of Germany, Poland, Czechoslovakia, Hungary, France, Holland, Belgium, Switzerland, Spain, Portugal and Morocco. So Makins was at the centre of events as the country edged towards war and he took part in the numerous diplomatic exchanges of the months which preceded war. It gave him the opportunity to work closely with both Sir Alexander Cadogan (Permanent Under Secretary 1938–46) and with Lord Halifax who had replaced Anthony Eden as Foreign Secretary in February 1938. As well as assisting with the drafting of various telegrams he also acted as one of Halifax's speechwriters.[6] Like Makins, Halifax had gained a First in history at Christ Church and had won a Prize Fellowship to All Souls, so there was a bond between them which served Makins well, both then and later when they were both in Washington.

---

2 Makins Papers, MS Sherfield 438, Letter Makins to Alice, 5 October 1938.

3 Ibid.

4 Makins Papers, MS Sherfield 438, Letter Makins to Alice, 7 October 1938.

5 Makins Papers, MS Sherfield 438, Letter Makins to Alice, 5 October 1938.

6 British Oral Archive of Political and Administrative History, London School of Economics and Political Science Archives (Henceforth British Oral Archive) Lord Sherfield interviewed by Anthony Seldon, May/June 1980, p. 18.

The first few months of 1939 saw the government and the Foreign Office wrestling with largely insoluble problems. However, a decisive moment arrived in March 1939 when Hitler, contrary to all previous agreements, occupied the whole of Czechoslovakia. It led to the British government issuing a guarantee to Poland which sought to underwrite the Polish border and to intervene if Poland became the victim of aggression. The guarantee became a treaty which was signed on 25 August 1939 and Germany invaded Poland on 1 September 1939. Although futile at the time Britain stood by her guarantee.

On Sunday 3 September, the day that Britain declared war on Germany, Makins made his way into the Foreign Office. He arrived at around 9.00 am and watched events unfold. The final German proposal that Herman Goering should come to London to discuss an armistice was rejected, and Chamberlain's scheduled radio broadcast informing the nation that Britain was at war went ahead. Makins, who rarely wrote a diary, did record the events of that day. He noted that a 'small crowd [gathered] in Downing Street but [with] no enthusiasm [and then] an astonishing number of barrage balloons appeared in the sky ... at 11.20 am an air raid warning was sounded – most dramatic – we all trooped down to the Foreign Office shelter and after about half an hour the all clear sounded'. After Makins emerged from the shelter he returned home to Chester Terrace where he found the servants 'pale as sheets'. After lunch Makins made a speech to the household and persuaded them to stay. It is interesting to note that while he managed to keep the household in London he had arranged for Alice and his three children (a third child, Virginia, had been born on 15 January that same year) to go and live in the Cotswolds to get away from the bombing that was anticipated in London. Summing up his position on that day, he records that he 'felt the war was a confession of failure, but that it was quite inevitable'.[7]

Where did Makins stand on the broad question of appeasement? The word appeasement is now a pejorative term, but this was not always the case. Appeasement appears in diplomatic reports of the time in a matter of fact way; it was used in the sense of being a mechanism to make concessions which then might lead to a general easing of European tension. It was not a term exclusively used in the context of aggression or the actions of dictators. Appeasement, at least in the old sense of the word, was the policy being pursued by the Prime Minister. The Foreign Office, however, was rather less enthusiastic.[8]

Makins took the broad Foreign Office line. He suggested that his 'whole approach all through the period 1938/1939 was anti appeasement', adding 'I think I'd come to the conclusion that unless we took the strongest possible

---

[7] Makins Papers, MS Sherfield 337, Diary 3 September 1939.

[8] For more on this see Craig, Gordon and Gilbert, Felix (eds), *The Diplomats 1919–1939*, Princeton: Princeton University Press, 1994.

opposition to Hitlerism that there was bound to be a war'.[9] Oral history testimony is, of course, always suspect especially years after the events, but it appears that on this occasion there is evidence to support Makins' contention. Apart from the evidence in the Foreign Office files there are the accounts of those involved at the time. Oliver Harvey, Halifax's Private Secretary, noted in his diaries that Makins would come in and help 'stiffen up' draft replies to Hitler's proposals.[10] Makins, of course, had first-hand experience of the Nazi regime, having served, albeit for a short period of time, in the British Embassy in Berlin. His correspondence during this period supports the view that he was against making further concessions to Germany: 'a policy of peace at any price costs a great deal more than is bargained for.'[11] Further he had direct knowledge, gained through service at the League of Nations on immigration matters, of the brutal and deceitful way the Nazi regime treated the Jews. Makins had no illusions regarding German intentions. Interestingly he is also supportive of the line taken by some historians that Halifax was 'unfairly dubbed an appeaser'.[12] As noted above, Makins was close to Halifax and Makins suggests that Halifax felt it was 'his duty, certainly his inclination to do everything he could to avert a war', hence Halifax would meet various emissaries from Germany and respond to a variety of approaches. But Makins adds that any idea that Halifax was taken in by them was a mistake.[13]

Shortly after war broke out William Strang was appointed an Assistant Under Secretary and Makins stepped up to the number two position in the Central Department. In the same year, on 11 September, Makins was promoted to the position of First Secretary. It would not be long before he was running the Department. In May 1940 Ivone Kirkpatrick moved to the Ministry of Information and Makins took the number one slot and in August 1940 he became an acting Counsellor (all wartime appointments were acting). Makins wrote to Alice 'This is really very handsome of them indeed considering that a year ago I was a Second Secretary'.[14] The outbreak of war had led to the need to set up a number of governments in exile in London, including Polish and Czechoslovakian bodies. Makins was also involved in attempts to persuade the representatives of Belgium and Holland to enter into discussions which might aid Britain's war effort. At the time these efforts proved to be fruitless since both of these nations were reluctant to compromise their neutrality. During

---

9 British Oral Archive, Lord Sherfield, p. 16.

10 Harvey, John (ed.), *The Diplomatic Diaries of Oliver Harvey 1937–1940*, London: Collins, 1970, p. 306.

11 *Geneva and the Foreign Office*, p. 73.

12 British Oral Archive, Lord Sherfield, p. 17. See for example Roberts, Andrew. *'The Holy Fox': The Life of Lord Halifax*, London: Phoenix, 1997.

13 British Oral Archive, Lord Sherfield, p. 18.

14 Makins Papers, MS Sherfield 438, Letter Makins to Alice, 31 July 1940.

this period he continued as the Foreign Office representative at the League of Nations and attended meetings at The Hague and at Geneva.

The German invasion of the Netherlands, Belgium and Luxemburg on 10 May 1940 marked the end of the Phoney War. On 7 May Churchill succeeded Chamberlain as Prime Minister and formed a coalition government which included members of the Labour Party. Clement Attlee, who had refused to serve under Chamberlain, joined the Cabinet as Lord Privy Seal. Halifax was to remain in post until the end of the year when, under pressure from Churchill, he reluctantly moved to Washington to become the British Ambassador, a move which would benefit Makins considerably at the end of the war. Anthony Eden, with whom Makins had worked closely at the League of Nations, was appointed Foreign Secretary on 23 December 1940.

The Low Countries fell quickly: the Dutch surrendered to the Germans four days after they were invaded, and the Belgians followed suit shortly afterwards. Alec Cadogan commented 'The blackest days I have ever lived through. But there are undoubtedly worse to come'.[15] He was right. The German army attacked through the Ardennes and reached the Channel coast on 20 May 1940. The British Expeditionary Force which was in France was severed from the main French armies to the south. The evacuation of Dunkirk began. On 5 June the Germans began pushing through the French lines on the Somme, and by 14 June they had entered Paris. The events of May and June were in themselves bleak enough, but for Makins they also led to separation from his family.

The evacuation of Dunkirk showed Britain's weakness, and rumours of an imminent invasion by the Germans were rife, and indeed plausible. Dwight Davis, Alice's father, was not disposed to let his daughter and three grandchildren remain at risk. He, unilaterally it seems, telegraphed Makins to inform him that he had arranged passage for Alice and the three children on a relief ship which was being sent to Ireland, to pick up the dependents of American officials and other American citizens who were in Western Europe. Makins in his memoirs suggests that 'we were not consulted and were faced with a hard choice'.[16] He may or may not have been consulted, but he had certainly discussed the possibility a year before war broke out. In September 1938 he had told Alice 'I would be much happier if you and the children had a place in the country ... the alternative is to go to the US. You might talk it over with the family and I will discuss it with your father if he comes here'.[17]

---

[15] Dilks, David (ed.), *The Diaries of Sir Alexander Cadogan 1938–1945*, London: Cassell, 1971, 16 May 1940.

[16] Lord Sherfield's Memoirs, section entitled *The Phoney War* (Henceforth, *The Phoney War*), p. 63.

[17] Makins Papers, MS Sherfield 438, Letter Makins to Alice, 13 September 1938.

The dilemma for Makins was obvious. While his family would be safe, assuming they crossed the Atlantic without incident, it could mean a separation of many years. Further, there was the question of how a British government official, who no doubt aspired to high office and who was also the son of a Member of Parliament, should behave in these circumstances. After all, it was Makins who on the day war broke out made a speech to his servants, who were clearly anxious about remaining in London, persuading them to stay. As Makins noted in his memoirs 'there was an uncomfortable feeling that they were running away',[18] which, of course, is exactly what they were doing.

In the end Makins did not raise any objection to his family leaving the country, and in his memoirs he justified the decision by suggesting that it enabled him to 'concentrate exclusively' on his work.[19] Irrespective of the merits of the decision, it was a dark period for Makins. The weekend after the family left Makins travelled down to Overbrook, the house in the Cotswolds, where Alice and the children had previously taken refuge.

> It was May time and in the glorious sunshine of the 1940 summer the Cotswold scenery was supremely beautiful. It was a solemn moment in my life. The decision to let the family go had disturbed and upset me, even though I knew it was inevitable and in their best interests, the immediate future was sombre, it was more than ever unclear whether and if so how we could win the war. But in those three days of solitude in that incomparable countryside I resolved my doubts and summoned up my energies for the tasks ahead.[20]

As noted above, one of the primary functions of the Central Department at this time was the setting up of Allied governments in exile. By the time of the Blitzkrieg Polish, Czechoslovakian and Norwegian governments had been established. It now fell to Makins to assist with the setting up of Dutch and Belgium governments. This led to Makins' first run in with Hugh Dalton. The Belgium King was in German hands; therefore the formation of a government was complicated, especially since some ministers were dispersed throughout France. Hugh Dalton, 'the dreadful Doctor' as Makins called him, had taken over as the head of the Ministry of Economic Warfare (MEW) and began 'throwing his weight around'. Dalton wanted the Belgium Minister for the Colonies, Albert de Vleeschauer, an ardent socialist, to be recognised as the head of the Government. Makins managed to resist this and to hold the position until Henri Spaak (Belgium Prime Minister, 1939 and 1946–9) arrived from the continent and with his help installed Hubert Pierlot, the Foreign Office's

[18] *The Phoney War*, p. 63.

[19] Ibid.

[20] Ibid.

preferred candidate, as the Prime Minister of the Belgium government in exile. This would not be the last time Makins crossed a Labour Minister. By mid summer of 1940 all of the relevant governments were established and Ambassadors had been appointed to deal with them. France, of course, was an exceptional case and was dealt with at Cabinet level by Alex Cadogan. Makins had begun to turn his attention to the Iberian Peninsular.

With the advent of war, both Spain and Portugal became much more important and Makins, who had hitherto spent little time on these two countries, became more concerned with them. The Ministry of Economic Warfare began life on 2 September 1939. It sought, among other things, to put in place measures which would restrict the trade between Germany and countries which were likely to be neutral during the war, including Spain and Portugal. In effect this meant introducing a blockade against selected countries in order to stop them importing certain goods and then re-exporting them to Germany. This was achieved by reaching agreements with the neutrals on what they could and could not import.

A central question which needed to be answered before implementing a policy of restricting imports into a neutral country, was whether or not the country would remain neutral or whether it would side with Germany. If the latter, then imports would be banned, if the former then agreements could be reached with, for example, the Commonwealth countries to supply food and other raw materials. There was a fundamental disagreement between the MEW, headed by Dalton and the Foreign Office. Dalton believed that General Franco would, sooner or later, join Hitler and the Spanish should be starved; the Foreign Office, including Makins, believed that the best way to keep Franco neutral was to provide economic aid and allow imports. The issue was crucial because if Spain turned toward the Axis powers then Germany would have the facility to attack Gibraltar and close the Mediterranean.

David Eccles, a close friend of Makins who was at Winchester and Oxford with him, was brought in to advise the MEW. Eccles had business interests in Spain and considerable experience and knowledge of the country. He headed the delegation which was sent to Spain to draw up an agreement that would regulate the economic and financial relations between the two countries. There was a constant tussle between the MEW and the Foreign Office over the trade agreement. The MEW wanted to severely restrict imports into Spain, while the Foreign Office favoured a less restrictive policy. Makins was the Foreign Office 'anchor man' for the project and as such 'enjoyed the powerful support and encouragement of William Strang, Alec Cadogan and Halifax'.[21] The Foreign Office's view of Spain prevailed and The War Trade Agreement was concluded in March 1940. Throughout the process Eccles was in conflict with his own

[21] *The Phoney War*, p. 69.

department, the MEW, and later he noted that 'again and again I was saved by the steady support of Roger Makins and William Strang, with Churchill in the background'.[22]

So successful was Eccles in his dealings with the Spanish that he was drafted in to help with Portugal and, as with the Spanish, he developed strong relationships with the Portuguese, in particular António de Oliveira Salazar (Prime Minister of Portugal 1932–68), which were of considerable benefit to Britain at that time. Makins acted as a 'guide, philosopher and friend' to Eccles throughout his time in Spain and Portugal, and worked hard in the Foreign Office to present Eccles' points of view. In part through his friendship with Eccles, he was an important influence on the events which kept Spain and Portugal neutral throughout the war. The Makins/Eccles relationship is a very interesting example of how informal networks can operate inside government. There was considerable personal correspondence between Makins and Eccles, and indeed, Eccles' wife, and this communication outside formal channels was effective, both in constructing policy and in subverting the wishes of certain ministers.

By 1941 the work in the Central Department had become less interesting. The Allied governments in exile had been established, each with British diplomatic officials looking after them as Ambassadors. Relations with France were the concern of the newly created French Department, and while Spain and Portugal continued to have high priority, much of the work was led by Eccles with Makins working in the background. After the outbreak of war the League of Nations continued to function normally, until the Blitzkrieg when it began to wind down its activities. The rump of the Leagues' activities was transferred to London and Washington under the aegis of the League Supervisory Commission.[23] The Commission continued to meet and Makins attended these meetings. In July 1941 it held a meeting in Montreal,the principal purpose of which was to try and keep the league alive during the war. At that time it was felt important to keep the framework of the League in place, so that the accumulated experience of 20 years of international cooperation and administration was not lost. At the meeting the Commission settled the budgets for the League's HQ and other League bodies. After attending the meeting Makins then took several days' leave and visited Alice and the children who were vacationing in Southampton, Long Island with Dwight and Pauline Davis. It had been over a year since Makins had seen his family. Makins' recollection of that time was hazy but it must have been a very welcome diversion from his Foreign Office duties. Time passed quickly, however, and on 9 August Makins returned to Montreal. The next day and

---

[22] Eccles, David, *By Safe Hand Letters of Sybil and David Eccles 1939–1942*, London: The Bodley Head, 1983, p. 16.

[23] *The Phoney War*, Diversions section, no. 2, p. 1.

with some trepidation he boarded a Liberator bound for Prestwick, flown by a young Australian pilot. Makins' nervousness was justified as on the very next mission the pilot lost his way in cloud approaching Prestwick and crashed onto a Scottish hillside killing himself and all his passengers.[24]

It was not long before Makins was offered a second opportunity to cross the Atlantic. Earlier in 1941 Ernest Bevin, then Minister of Labour, suggested to Eden that there should be a meeting of the International Labour Organisation (ILO). The idea gradually gained momentum and was given an additional boost by the explicit support of President Roosevelt. The ILO was the only fully international organisation of which the USA was a member, and Bevin and Churchill thought it was important to engage with America at every opportunity. Clement Attlee, then Lord Privy Seal and Deputy Prime Minister, was appointed to lead the British delegation. Although the conference was primarily a Labour one and therefore staffed by officials from the Ministry of Labour, the delegation also required a Foreign Office representative, and Makins was chosen to accompany Attlee.

After arriving in New York where Attlee gave a press conference, he and Makins travelled to Washington by train. Makins took Attlee to the Embassy where he was rather embarrassed by the contrast between Halifax's greeting of him and that of Attlee. Makins was met with 'Oh Roger, how splendid to see you' and Attlee with the rather flatter tone 'Hello Attlee, how are you?' The greater part of the conference was taken up with delegate speeches on the ILO and post-war reconstruction, but Roosevelt himself attended the final session. Makins wrote a full despatch of the Conference for the British delegation which was fully approved and later published almost unchanged as a White Paper. However, the ILO was destined to be overtaken by events. After Pearl Harbour in December 1941 the US became much more belligerent, and the importance of the ILO as an instrument of US policy became much reduced. While the Conference itself may have amounted to little, the sequel of the visit for Makins, was that his first son Christopher, was born in July 1942.

There was another consequence of Makins' visit: he had managed to cross yet another Labour Minister, this time it was Attlee. When Attlee returned he informed Dalton that he had had trouble with Makins in America. 'He was supposed to be my Secretary but he tried to run me on a Foreign Office string. I wasn't having it.'[25] During the Conference a resolution was passed in favour of setting up a special commission to study post-war problems. A few days later, Makins brought Attlee a draft for a communication from him to the Foreign Secretary proposing that this commission should be presided

---

24 Ibid., p. 8.

25 Dalton papers, London School of Economic and Political Science, Diaries, 22 December 1941.

over by Paul Guillaume Van Zeeland (Belgium Prime Minister 1935–8) and that the British government should be represented by Sir Frederick Leith Ross (Chief Economic Advisor UK government 1932–45). Attlee asked Makins why he had produced the document without first discussing it with him. Makins told Attlee that it was only a draft and that he had been discussing it with the Embassy and the State Department while Attlee had been away for a few days. Attlee informed Makins that he had no authority to enter into such discussions and that the communication should not have been sent to the Foreign Secretary first, but rather to Arthur Greenwood, the Minister in charge of post-war planning. He told Makins that he had no use for Van Zeeland, who had been a member of a most reactionary government in Belgium, and that there should be three British representatives on the commission, not just one, and one of them should be a 'good trade unionist'.[26] He tore up Makins' draft and summoned a meeting of the British delegation, sending his own draft off to Greenwood. Dalton concludes his diary entry with 'It is quite clearthat M. showed great ineptitude in his handling of the LPS [Lord Privy Seal]'.[27]

It is difficult to know what to make of this incident as Makins in his memoirs claims that Attlee was always cordial to him and never gave any hint of the above, but then goes on to suggest that Attlee was tired and that Dalton was exaggerating. In the same diary entry Dalton refers to his encounter with Makins, noted above, regarding the setting up of the Belgium government in exile. Dalton's conclusion was 'It had then become clear to me that, so far as Makins exercised any influence on this subject, it would be directed to frustrate the wishes of the Labour Ministers'.[28] Makins regarded Dalton as 'a nasty piece of work', so he was certainly fortunate that Dalton was not sent to the Foreign Office, as was expected, when Labour formed the post-war government. Further, there has been speculation that Attlee vetoed Makins for the Washington Ambassadorship in 1948, when Oliver Franks was sent to Washington. However, it is difficult to discern any lasting damage to Makins' career as a result of these incidents, particularly since Makins worked so well with Bevin when he was Foreign Secretary, a point taken up in Chapter 4. It does, however, indicate Makins' ability to, on certain occasions, irritate ministers.

In May 1942 the Cabinet decided that a senior minister should go to West Africa to coordinate the war effort in the four colonies. The post was offered to the former Colonial Secretary, Lord Swinton, and given that West Africa was a significant source of raw materials, it was considered very important to the war effort. Now its importance was elevated by the imminence of Operation Torch, the proposed allied landings in North West Africa. Swinton established his

[26] Ibid.

[27] Dalton Diaries, 19 November 1941.

[28] Ibid.

headquarters in Accra, Ghana (then known as the Gold Coast). He assembled a small private office to take with him and asked for somebody from the Foreign Office to join him. Initially there were no takers but as soon as Makins heard about it he volunteered. 'I surprised everyone, myself included, by offering to go ... the desire to leave the Whitehall war for a time and do something which seems at all events to be more directly related to the organisation of the war effort, became – at this moment – almost overpowering.'[29]

Makins left London in July 1942 bound for Accra. The essence of the work in West Africa was to coordinate the various requests for assistance which came up through the Colonial Departments, deal with various telegrams from outside the Colonies, accommodate a constant stream of visitors, and organise meetings of the West African war council. It was the sort of work at which Makins excelled. In addition to his regular duties Makins also embarked on a number of tours and visit to other parts of Africa including Madagascar (where he was sent by Eden to sort out a misunderstanding between the French and the British), all the West African colonies and the Belgian Congo. It was on one of these tours that Makins first met and developed cordial relations with General De Gaulle.

Makins' work in Africa was only temporary, and it is difficult to see how he made much of an impact other than through supporting Swinton. William Strang began agitating for Makins' return and his replacement was appointed by the end of October, but he did not actually replace Makins until the end of the year. Makins left Africa on 12 December 1942 bound not for London but for Washington. It was the third time in 18 months that Makins had managed to cross the Atlantic to be with Alice. Quite how Makins managed to secure this third visit is something of a mystery, as passages across the Atlantic were in very short supply and there were no doubt many others who were separated from their families at this time who might have also benefitted. Makins arrived in Washington on 16 December, and he saw his son Christopher for the first time. He also made a point of maintaining contact with Halifax, briefing him on his African adventures.

In London another briefing was taking place. On 22 December Churchill summoned Harold Macmillan to Downing Street and outlined his views on the position in North West Africa. Operation Torch, the joint allied assault on Vichy French territory in North Africa, which was launched in November 1942, had been a success. The Allies under the leadership of General Dwight Eisenhower were established in Morocco, Algeria and the greater part of Tunisia. Churchill briefed Macmillan on the military and the political situation in the region. The military position was encouraging, but the political side was 'distressing and confusing'. Churchill accepted that the North African expedition was American led, but he felt he had a right, even

---

29 Makins Papers, MS Sherfield 441, Letter Alice to Makins, 3 July 1942.

a duty, to express British opinion in the political sphere. While there was already a Foreign Office official on Eisenhower's staff, it was felt that he was not senior enough and lacked influence. Churchill was determined to appoint someone of ministerial rank to represent Britain at Eisenhower's headquarters. Macmillan was to be that man and he was appointed Minister Resident at the Allied Force Headquarters North Africa, located in Algiers. The position was of Cabinet rank and it was a promotion for Macmillan, who had been a junior minister in Churchill's government since it was formed in May 1940.

The importance of the appointment was heightened by the fact that, for the first time in history, the command structure of the two national forces responsible for the Allied landings in North Africa was unified. In the past allied armies had fought side by side, as in the First World War, but Eisenhower's command, AFHQ as it was called, was unique in that there was a completely integrated staff in which British and American officers served not as representatives of their own nations, but as members of a single team. It was, however, American led and although political officers were embedded in this structure, Churchill wanted his own man outside of it. As Makins pointed out, the appointment of a Resident Minister was an attempt to get both 'stronger representation and a responsible source of information'.[30]

Makins' part in this was to go to Algiers and become Macmillan's adviser and deputy. In wartime the distinction between a Minister and a civil servant, particularly in a posting such as this, becomes less sharp. The party political dimension is largely removed, and with a common objective in sight there is a greater commonality of interest between the minister and the civil servant, and so the word deputy has more meaning. Makins did not arrive in Algiers until the end of January, by which time Macmillan had already left to attend the Anfa Conference near Casablanca, a summit organised between Roosevelt and Churchill to discuss the general strategy of the war. It was also an occasion when the leaders made an attempt to reconcile the 'warring' French factions, one of the major political problems which Macmillan and Makins would wrestle with. Macmillan returned to Algiers on 25 January and met up with Makins.

Macmillan's staff at the time consisted of John Wyndham, his private secretary, two Colonial Office typists and Makins. The office accommodation, although cramped, had the merit of being situated in the same building as the American civilian officials, who were advising Eisenhower. It meant, as Makins put it, that the British and Americans were 'working together at close quarters in the same building and in similar conditions of discomfort'.[31] An idea of the conditions can be gleaned from an entry in Macmillan's diary:

---

30 Lord Sherfield's Memoirs, *Life and Times in North Africa and Italy* (Henceforth *North Africa*), p. 12.

31 *North Africa*, p. 15.

> I have been very much impressed by the high standard of performance – under most disadvantageous physical conditions – of our British team. It is one thing to get through a lot of work in a Government office in London, with all its equipment of messengers, files, boxes, telephones, secretaries and the like. It is another altogether to do the same with one telephone ..., without typewriters, paper, pen or even ink, and situated with one chair and a desk formed of a piece of packing-case delicately poised upon a housemaids sink.[32]

The American civilian team, with whom Macmillan and Makins needed to work if they were to be successful, was headed by Bob Murphy, who was Roosevelt's special envoy. Murphy had been in Algiers before the Allies had landed and knew a great deal about the region and its background politics. Murphy was, in effect, Macmillan's opposite number in Algeria. He was assisted by Sam Reber, a career diplomat from Washington, who Makins knew from the time he worked in the embassy there. If the British were to make any significant contribution to the political situation in North Africa, it was essential to build an effective working relationship with the two Americans.

Eisenhower resented being concerned with a range of non-military problems. These problems included political reform in the region, the fusion of the various French forces and factions, the implementation of import controls, the administration of internment camps, and dealing with visiting dignitaries. He wanted out of the day-to-day political and economic issues, and turned to Murphy and Reber to deal with such matters. Makins' achievement was to ensure that Macmillan's office was consulted by the Americans and had at least an advisory status on all political and economic matters in the region. He achieved this by developing such a close relationship with Reber, Murphy's deputy, that he effectively integrated the back offices of the American civilian and the British civilian sides. This, in turn, meant that it was difficult for the Americans to take any action without the British being consulted, or at least being aware of what was happening.

Makins describes how, in Reber, he could not have wished for a better opposite number. Makins and Reber worked jointly on the same level and shared the tasks, but equally as important was that they 'shared the same approach to the donkey work of diplomacy'. As Makins wrote 'we seldom had to alter more than a word or two of each other's drafts, minutes and records of conversations'.[33] This close relationship between Makins and Reber resulted in daily meetings between Macmillan and Murphy. Thus a working relationship on the political side was assured. Makins commented 'The confidence built up in this way was never broken down. Until the end we were able to exercise, in the field, a joint

---

32 Macmillan, Harold, *The Blast of War 1939–1945*, London: Macmillan 1967, p. 289.

33 *North Africa*, p. 37.

Anglo-American political control, all the stronger for being unofficial and unformulated'.[34]

The relationship between the British and American civilian missions was strengthened further by the four of them serving together on a number of committees. A Political Council was formed at AFHQ which was chaired by Eisenhower and was attended by his Chief of Staff, Walter Bedell Smith. This committee met two or three times a week and included Macmillan, Makins, Murphy and Reber. Other bodies were formed, including the North African Economic Board, and again the four civilian political administrators attended. Of course Makins was not the sole person responsible for good relations between the two sides: Macmillan, with his charm and intellectual strength, was also instrumental to developing relationships with the Americans, but it was Makins who effectively institutionalised it by the simple mechanism of ensuring joint administration and this secured his place as Macmillan's number two.

His first letter to Alice from Algiers was written the day after his 39th birthday. 'This is the toughest job. I work hard and I have to do it all almost single handed. Fortunately Harold Macmillan is really excellent, he has all the right ideas, good judgement and a keen sense of humour and he never gives me a moment's anxiety!'[35] Macmillan recorded in his diary that Makins 'is an invaluable assistant, absolutely tireless, very scrupulous and a splendid draftsman. He is really a great help. He has also a keen sense of humour'.[36] Macmillan and Makins took to each other from the start and developed a mutual respect and trust in each other which ultimately was to shape Makins' career.

Algeria was technically a part of Metropolitan France, but the European population amounted to only around one million with the Arab population accounting for over six million. There was also a significant Jewish population running to about 140,000.[37] Algiers, the capital, was already a crowded place in 1943 but became more so with the arrival of the army and its attendant administration. AFHQ mushroomed to over 6000 personnel, most of whom remained in Algiers for over 20 months. There were certain places during the war which tended to become 'nodal points' through which anybody who was anybody tended to pass. Lisbon was one; Accra was another for a time, as were Cairo and Naples. In 1943 Algiers was one such point which only added to the congestion.

Having worked out a modus operandi, the British and Americans set about addressing some of the political problems Algeria presented. This entailed

[34] *North Africa*, p. 38.

[35] Makins Papers, MS Sherfield 441, Letter Alice to Makins, 4 February 1943.

[36] Macmillan, Harold, *War Diaries: The Mediterranean*, London: Macmillan, 1984 (Henceforth *Macmillan War Diaries*), 27 April 1943.

[37] Murphy, Robert, *Diplomat Among Warriors*, London: Collins, 1964, p. 202.

dealing with the French, who ran the civil administration in the region. In February 1943 the civil side was reorganised and the Haut Commissariat – Civil and Militaire – was created, and General Giraud was installed as the High Commissioner. According to Makins the creation of the Haut Commissariat was, in fact, a bloodless coup d'état. 'It was a new regime established by local fiat, and constituted a formal break with Vichy and the Petainist authority.'[38]

Dealing with the French was no easy matter: there were several factions, with tussles between the supporters of Giraud and de Gaulle. Harold Macmillan summed up the difficulties in his diary.

> Friday, 2 April 1943
> 9 a.m Saw General Eisenhower.
> 11 a.m Political and Economic Council – weekly meeting.
> 1 p.m Lunch. Deputy Chief of Staff [General Whiteley].
> 3–7 p.m Continual stream of French callers:
> (a) Giraudists
> (b) Gaullists
> (c) Neutrals
> (d) Giraudists, with sympathy for de Gaulle
> (e) Giraudists, without sympathy for de Gaulle
> (f) Gaullists, with sympathy for Giraud
> (g) Gaullists without sympathy for Giraud.
> I just sit and murmur from time to time – *"Oui, monsieur – comme vous dites, l'union français est insispensable"*.[39]

During the early part of 1943 Makins was largely concerned with persuading the French authorities to implement reforms, including the removal of Vichy officials from the administration, the repeal of Vichy legislation, including the removal of racial discrimination laws, the release of allied sympathisers from prisons and internment camps and the introduction of a freer press. An agreement on a reform package was reached, and in the spring of 1943 Giraud made an address outlining the package and announcing a number of decrees. It was during this period that Makins first encountered Jean Monnet the French economist and diplomat who subsequently became associated with the formation of the European Community. Even at the time Monnet was advocating a Federal Europe; a notion which Makins would have been suspicious of. Makins and Reber were brought in to ensure that the translation of the address and the decrees were accurate and that the whole package was presented in the most favourable light to Anglo-Saxon opinion.

---

38 *North Africa*, p. 34.

39 Macmillan, *War Diaries*, p. 55.

As the year progressed Macmillan and Makins also became embroiled in efforts to effect a unification of the French forces. There were severe disagreements between General Giraud, the incumbent leader in Algiers, and General De Gaulle, the leader of the Free French forces. However, after long and protracted negotiations an agreement was put in place and in June 1943 the French Committee of National Liberation was formed, a committee which was ultimately headed by General de Gaulle.

Algiers was a place of many factions and of competing interests. Makins noted

> My life here is almost that of a diplomatist of fiction. I move in a maze of intrigue, plot and counter plot ... French [functionaries] come and see me every day and I send messages for them in every direction ... and I give advice to an Anglo American medley of economic experts, propagandists and what have you. We entertain continually and I seldom eat a meal alone. I never have a moment to myself.[40]

As part of his workload Makins met and worked with the key players in Algiers. These included not only the French, such as General De Gaulle and General Giraud, but also the Allied commanders, such as General Alexander, Admiral Cunningham, General Eisenhower and later General (Jumbo) Wilson.

Whilst the political difficulties with the French were being resolved the military were achieving significant successes. On 7 May 1943 the Allied forces had taken Tunisia and Bizerta, and the end of the North Africa campaign was marked with the surrender of the German forces in the region on 13 May. Macmillan and Makins flew up to attend the victory parade at Tunis: 'The march past lasted nearly two hours and was a very impressive sight. French troops came first, mostly Colonial troops, including the famous Goums, whose uniform consists of dirty dressing gowns and who look, as if they would gladly skin their grandmothers. Then came the American infantry, and then units of the first and eighth armies. Finally came the British artillery ... The bearing and morale of the British troops was most magnificent.'[41] One cannot help but wonder what Makins' thoughts were as the army marched by. Was there an element of regret that he had not volunteered to fight in the war, perhaps regret that he had not followed his father footsteps? Did he recall Churchill's phrase 'There is no man who does not feel diminished in the presence of a soldier'. The post-war generation was divided by those who had fought and those who had not. It was perhaps a feeling of inadequacy which never left one.

Macmillan and Makins' work in Algiers is a good illustration of the importance diplomacy can have in wartime and it was a difficult job, as

[40] *North Africa*, p. 34.

[41] Ernest Makins Papers, MS Sherfield 197, Letter Makins to father, 21 May 1943.

Macmillan's quote indicates. Diplomats are in the middle of these conflicts and, as we have seen, Makins was closely engaged in attempting to resolve them.

The successes in North Africa were a prelude to an Allied attack on Italy. On 10 July 1943 the Allies invaded Sicily. Within ten days Mussolini had resigned and on 3 September the Allies were landing on the Italian mainland. Although the Italians surrendered on 8 September, the Italian campaign, given the fierce resistance of the Germans, took longer than anticipated and Rome was not taken until early June 1944. The military advances entailed changes for both Macmillan and Makins. By the summer of 1943 Macmillan's original staff had grown. Makins, who was described by Macmillan as his 'chief adviser', was joined by Harold Caccia to look after Italian affairs, John Rooker to deal with the French and Tom Dupree joined as the Press Attaché. The support staff were also increased: Makins gained his own secretary, a Miss Joan Eden, for the first time since he arrived in Algiers.[42] It was around this time that Macmillan decided to establish himself in a forward position in Tunis, where he would be near the Operational Commanders including Eisenhower, who had a villa there. This inevitably meant more responsibility and work for Makins who was left in Algiers to run the operation there.

In December 1943 both Macmillan and Makins attended the Cairo conference. Its central purpose was for Churchill and Roosevelt to brief Chiang Kai-shek (the leader of the Chinese Nationalists) on their plans for the invasion of Japan. However, the two leaders also took the opportunity to amalgamate the Cairo and the Algiers command structures under General Wilson, after Eisenhower was earmarked to lead the allied offensive in Europe. This new command also took over responsibility for the Italian campaign. Macmillan's influence grew further, until ultimately he was formally appointed as the political authority over the whole area. The end of 1943 brought more changes: Macmillan handed over his French duties to Duff Cooper, the first Ambassador to the provisional French Government. For Makins all of this meant less direct contact with the French, but increasingly more work on Italian and Balkan issues.

In March 1944 Macmillan moved from Tunis to Caserta, near Naples and established himself with the forward section of the AFHQ. However, the Mission's base remained in Algiers. Makins recalls that it was rather a 'restless period'. Macmillan was away a lot of the time, including spending a month in the UK recuperating from exhaustion. By this time Makins was 'battle scarred' and had learnt to take apparent crises in his stride. It was during this period that Makins, with Macmillan frequently absent, developed a relationship with General Wilson. Makins would often take telegrams up to AFHQ in order to

[42] Makins formed a life-long friendship with Miss Eden as he did with several of his other secretaries. Miss Eden subsequently joined Makins' staff while he was the Ambassador in Washington.

discuss them with Wilson. He commented that Wilson was always calm, shrewd and easy to deal with; it was a relationship which was to prove very useful for Makins when both he and Wilson ended up in Washington at the end of the war.

On 21 July 1944 the whole of AFHQ moved from Algiers to Caserta. His time in Naples was short lived; by the end of September Macmillan was hosting a leaving party for Makins in the Palace at Caserta. Over a hundred people attended the party, and it was 'a great tribute to the position which Roger had won for himself at Allied Force Headquarters'.[43] The party was followed by a dinner given in Makins' honour by General Wilson and his staff. Makins and Macmillan had developed a considerable affection for each other during the previous 18 months:

> It is naturally a great loss – even a great grief – to lose Roger. He has been a most loyal supporter in all my difficulties and a most agreeable companion and friend. I think it is a tribute to both of us that we have lived together for nearly two years, like subalterns in a company mess, without quarrelling (and Roger's temperament is more highly strung than mine). The inspiring thing about him is his standard of work. He is never satisfied with the second best. And this goes through the office and inspires the other ... Roger [is] such a unique figure in the public service.[44]

Makins in a letter to Alice said of his leaving 'My great regret is leaving Harold Macmillan ... but I hope to work again with Harold in the future'.[45]

It is difficult to know what precipitated Makins' return to London. He was being replaced by his old university friend, Kit Steel, who was 'better qualified' to deal with Balkan problems which were beginning to dominate the work at that time. On the other hand, while Macmillan thought Steel might be 'agreeable and efficient', he acknowledged that Steel did not have the 'rapier like brain' that Makins had. It is also the case that Makins, during his absence from the Foreign Office, had acquired a reputation for 'independence of outlook' and possibly they wanted that brought to an end. Macmillan and his team reported to the Prime Minister and were, therefore, funded by the Treasury; this always caused some angst in the Foreign Office. Makins told Alice that he was 'in the dog house with the Office' and that he might 'get the sack at any moment'.[46]

The most likely explanation for his move, however, is that he was sent back to England on compassionate grounds, possibly even arranged by Macmillan. By September 1944 Makins was near exhaustion and quite possibly on the verge of a breakdown. While he had returned to England on a couple of

---

43 Macmillan, *Blast of War*, p. 552.

44 Ibid.

45 Makins Papers, MS Sherfield 441, Letter Makins to Alice, 24 September 1944.

46 Makins Papers,MS Sherfield 441, Letter Makins to Alice, 1 September 1944.

occasions to brief the Foreign Office, he had been working without a break in difficult circumstances for over 18 months. On 15 September he wrote to Alice complaining that he was in decline and that he had been sleeping in for the last few days, adding that he had taken Monday off altogether to 'avoid a complete collapse'.[47] Further, the rapid progress of the war had led Makins to contemplate his future. He suggested that he would not get much of a job with the Foreign Office, and even dwelt upon the difficulties of reuniting the family in a post-war world. It was a bleak period for him.

While he was in this state of exhaustion he received the news that his brother Geoffrey had died. Geoffrey, 12 years younger than Makins, was an officer in the Army and had served for much of the war in the Middle East. He died from wounds received in France. Makins, who had encountered his brother several times during the war, last saw him in April 1944 when they were both, for a short period, at 180 Queens Gate. While Makins was, no doubt, saddened by his brother's death the more immediate concern to him would have been the condition of his parents. Geoffrey's death was a slow and painful one and Ernest and Florence's angst was compounded by the fact that they visited Geoffrey on a daily basis for the last weeks of his life and witnessed his pain and his emaciated condition.

Margaret Eden, the mother of Makins' secretary and, by coincidence, the wife of a doctor in the hospital where Geoffrey died, took it upon herself to write to Makins.

> They [the parents] have been careful not to let you know themselves quite what a heavy toll this last month has taken on them. The strain has been very long and very heavy of those daily visits to the hospital, with no real gaining of ground to sustain them, no real relief from deep anxiety from day to day ... We have not known which to admire the most – the desperate brave fight which Geoffrey made for life or their fortitude which watched ... Underneath their magnificent courage they are all shot away ... they are very stricken not only by this tragic loss but by something like shock at seeing him so pitifully reduced by illness by the time he got back to this country ... the fact is they have been spared nothing.[48]

Although, of course, there were many sad stories to be told in the theatre of war, Macmillan, who himself had had to return to England to recuperate from exhaustion, would have felt compassion for Makins, and could quite possibly have arranged his return to England. Whether he did or not, Makins was back in England by the end of September. He had been told to report to Ivone

47 Ibid.

48 Makins Papers, MS Sherfield 441, Letter Margaret Eden to Makins, 4 September 1944.

Kirkpatrick, who was to be responsible for German reconstruction after the war. Kirkpatrick told him that there was not enough work for him, let alone another person, and told Makins to go away. He did, and within a week he was in Washington, reunited with Alice and his family and ready to embark on a new phase in his career.

Chapter 3
Washington and Atomic Energy

In the immediate post-war period politicians, civil servants and diplomats were almost overwhelmed by the number of tasks needed to be undertaken on both the international and the domestic front. This put considerable pressure on the machinery of government. Against this background Britain elected a new government. In the summer of 1945 the Labour Party won a stunning victory, and for the first time came to power with an overall majority. Whilst some Labour ministers had served in the war coalition there were many who either had not served in government before or were serving in a ministry for the first time. The combination of an increased need for the conduct of international relations and the limited experience of certain ministers led to a greater reliance on civil servants and diplomats in the development of policy.

This effect was felt as much in Washington as elsewhere, and given that the focal point of the Anglo-American relationship was in Washington, the diplomats there played a central role in the development of that relationship. In addition, with the breaking of the Roosevelt–Churchill relationship, a vacuum was left in the prosecution of Anglo-American relations, a vacuum which was often filled by officials rather than politicians. Furthermore, there were areas of Anglo-American policy which were completely new to ministers, and of which they had little knowledge – atomic energy was one such area. Due to a concatenation of circumstances diplomats in Washington played a significant part in the conduct of policy in the post-war period.

Makins arrived in Washington in October 1944. He was officially on leave and without a post, and he waited anxiously to discover his fate. The Washington Makins returned to was a very different place from the one he had left eight years earlier. The Embassy had mushroomed to a staff of over 400, and its atmosphere had changed completely. It now felt like a large organisation, rather than a small family business, as it had in the days of Sir Ronald and Lady Lindsay. Washington was also the centre of gravity of the management of the war. Its population had been swollen, not only by Americans drafted in to conduct the war, but also by a range of foreign civil servants and administrators sent from overseas to assist in coordinating the war effort.

Even though it was growing fast, Washington in the 1940s and 1950s still felt like a small town with one main industry – government. Politicians, officials, journalists, diplomats and even the military top brass, were all in the same business, and constantly met and networked at social events. There was little cultural life, art or theatre or music: people went to New York for that. But there were any number of parties. The Makinses were particularly well placed to plunge into the social whirl; Makins had made many friends in his previous posting there. Alice had grown up in Washington, and had acted as hostess for her father, Dwight Davis, who had been Secretary for War in the Coolidge cabinet, and then governor of the Philippines. She had a quieter charm, and was an excellent, and unobtrusive hostess, and good at looking after people who might be overwhelmed by her sometimes daunting husband. Both were very good at making lifelong friends, and their Georgetown house in Kalorama Road was firmly on the social map.[1]

The official British contingent in Washington amounted to over 9,000 officials. During the war a 'mini Whitehall' had been established, with almost every government department represented. The Lend Lease Acts in 1941 had led to the formation of a number of British missions created to coordinate the supply of products to Britain. Further Combined Boards were established with the Americans and the Canadians to decide the allocation of resources required for the war effort. These included the Combined Production and Resources Board, the Combined Food Board and the Combined Raw Materials Board.[2] There were also various military representatives and the scientific boards which were concerned with weapons, particularly the production of the atomic bomb. All these bodies were, in theory, under the umbrella of the British Ambassador, Lord Halifax, and one of Makins' early roles in Washington was to liaise between them and Lord Halifax.

Halifax had been appointed by Churchill in 1941 and Makins had a good relationship with him, having known him both from his time at All Souls and from his wartime work in the Foreign Office. Alice was also popular with the Halifaxes. She worked as a cipher clerk at the Embassy and was often a dinner guest of the Ambassador and his wife, and she got on particularly well with Dorothy Halifax. Lord and Lady Halifax often stayed with her father and stepmother, Dwight and Pauline Davis, at their estate in Tallahassee.

After a couple of months Makins discovered his fate. He was to be appointed Minister Counsellor designate to the British Embassy in Cairo. It was a heavy blow. He did not like what he had seen and heard about Lord Killearn, the Ambassador to Egypt, and felt that Cairo was no longer an important international centre. Further, he thought a posting to Cairo would have been unsuitable for the family, and so he faced another long period of separation from Alice and the children. He also felt that he had been appointed to the Cairo position without being consulted. But the appointment was a promotion

1 Correspondence with Virginia Makins.

2 Wevill, Richard, *Britain and American after World War II: Bilateral Relations and the Beginnings of the Cold War*, London: Tauris, 2011, p. 11.

and therefore difficult to refuse. Halifax had asked for Makins to be posted to Washington as a minister, but Jock Balfour, the number two at the Moscow Embassy, who had been earmarked for the Washington post was given the position instead. Balfour was senior to Makins, and probably preferred because of his knowledge of Russia and the Eastern Bloc. Soviet-American relations would be an important element in international affairs in the post-war world, and Balfour had served in Moscow, Sofia, Budapest and Belgrade.

Makins, aggrieved at not getting a Washington posting, wrote to his father:

> I know my capacity well enough by this time. I believe I would have made a success of the job, and it would have finally decided me to stay on in the Foreign Service for keeps. Cairo is a very different proposition: whilst I was prepared to devote all my energy and resources to the Anglo-American cause, I have no such desire or ambition as regards Anglo-Egyptian relations, and in modern conditions the importance of the Cairo job can be very much exaggerated. I regard the appointment as a kind of kick across the hall, if not upstairs. I have reached a moment where I need a job of my own or one in which there is some say in the formulation of policy.[3]

The end of 1944 was an important moment for Makins. He was 40 years old, he had reached the rank of Counsellor after 16 years of service, and while he was admired by Macmillan, at that time a rather junior figure in the government, he was concerned that Eden had taken against him. Makins confided in his father 'I have little doubt that I was not given the Washington job largely owing to my close association with Harold Macmillan, which made me rather unpopular with the Foreign Office and probably particularly so with Anthony [Eden] who, as you know, is unfortunately rather small minded in these matters. From this point of view Cairo is a convenient place to put me out of the way'.[4] It may also have been the case that Makins was suggested for Cairo because it was a posting he could afford. Cairo was something of an 'honorific posting' where one needed to spend considerably more than one's salary and allowances. Compared to others in the Foreign Office, it was a posting Makins, or at least his wife and family, could afford.

Makins was due to leave Washington for Cairo on 20 December 1944. The night before, however, Makins received a telephone call from Halifax. 'I have just heard', he said, 'that my new Minister cannot arrive for some months, how would it suit to join my staff'.[5] Makins, of course was delighted, even if it was only a reprieve: Jock Balfour had been delayed by matters in Moscow

3 Ernest Makins Papers, MS Sherfield 197, Letter Makins to father, 28 January 1945.
4 Ibid.
5 Lord Sherfield's Memoirs, *Washington October 13th December 19th, 1944*, p. 6.

and Makins was to fill his position on a temporary basis. The posting to Cairo still hung over him, but at least he could delay it and set about working at the Embassy in a more established position from the beginning of 1945.

It was during these first few months of 1945, while waiting to be sent to Cairo, that Makins contemplated leaving the Foreign Office. He even outlined the timing, suggesting to his father that he could leave when the war in Europe was won. His tentative plan was to inform the Foreign Office that there would be no point sending him to Cairo since he would have to be replaced in a couple of months when he left, and therefore they might as well send someone else now. It is difficult to know how serious Makins was about leaving the service. On the one hand, he was astute enough to recognise that 'diplomats as a whole are so remarkably unsuccessful in other walks of life', on the other, he suggested to his father that he might enter politics, even possibly taking over his father's seat in Knutsford. Ernest Makins had already decided that he would leave Parliament at the end of the war and he retired from Parliament at the July 1945 election.

In the event Makins' dilemma was solved for him. By early April there were indications that his appointment was to be made permanent. It was decided that there was too much work in Washington for just one minister and so Halifax split the role into Minister Political and Minister Economic, with Balfour taking the former position and Makins the latter. Halifax had clearly been working on Makins' behalf: it was a solution which suited Makins admirably. The appointment was only expected to last for a year or so, but it was secure enough to enable Makins to abandon the plans to send the family back to England. His appointment was confirmed on 13 May 1945. He was now a minister with a salary of £2,000 a year.

It has been suggested that Makins' work in Algiers with Macmillan was the crucible of his career: this is debatable. What is not in dispute is that with the Washington appointment, Makins became identified, rightly or wrongly, with two policy areas. The first was economics; the second was the fledgling subject of atomic energy. The role Makins developed as the diplomat in Washington responsible for liaising with the Americans on atomic energy collaboration, placed him at a pivotal point in post-war Anglo-American relations. Furthermore, the expertise and contacts he developed in the field were to put him in the unprecedented position, once he had returned to England, of directly advising the Prime Minister on atomic energy matters. Ultimately it was his work in this area and the expertise he gained which led to his appointment as the Chairman of the UK Atomic Energy Authority in 1960.

The part Makins played in the field of atomic energy while he was a minister in Washington from 1945 to 1947 is discussed in some detail below, but first we turn to his work in the 'economic' field. His job of Economics Minister in Washington is sometimes said to have qualified him for the work he subsequently did, both at the Foreign Office in their economic departments and at the

Treasury. But his title was something of a misnomer, and the economic content of the role should not be exaggerated. Indeed, the most significant economic event at the time, and one which was Washington based, was the negotiation of a £3.75 billion loan from America to Britain precipitated by the ending of Lend Lease. It was an event in which Makins barely participated. The real economic work in Washington was undertaken by the Treasury Delegation, mainly by Bob Brand and Frank Lee. Even within the Embassy itself, the commercial work was carried out by John Magowan, the Commercial Minister. Most of Makins' work dealt with fairly routine liaison or organisational issues.

He did undertake more general diplomatic work, such as a speaking tour of the Mid West in 1945. The tour was organised by the British Information Service based in New York. It lasted from 11–23 March 1945 and included Colombus, Cleveland, Chicago, St Louis and Louisville. As Makins recorded in his diaries, the tour was hardly an overwhelming success: it was the first time he was called upon to make a speech in public.[6] It was a daunting experience, but one he needed to undertake if he was to progress in the diplomatic service. Makins recalls 'I had been too diffident at Oxford to speak at the Union, on my feet at the Canning Club my remarks were hesitant and halting and, apart from one English Speaking Union appearance at Baltimore in 1933, I had managed to reach the age of 41 without having made a speech in public or having to speak on my feet'.[7] Although 'overcome with nervousness akin to terror', Makins did manage to muddle through. Whilst he managed to overcome nerves on future occasions, Makins never became an accomplished speaker.

On 12 April 1945, shortly after Makins had completed his mid-west tour, Franklin Roosevelt died and Harry S. Truman succeeded him as President. Roosevelt's death stunned the American people, but it was no surprise to Makins and others who had seen him in recent months and knew how ghastly he looked. Makins, like Halifax, was an early supporter of the new President. Writing to his father he commented 'Roosevelt was always the constant in this country, a little above and aloof – a sort of Whig peer though still in the American tradition. Truman is also in the American tradition but in a different way; he is the haberdasher who gets to the White House, the success story which has constant appeal ... He is extremely popular with Congress and is by all accounts shrewd, friendly and a man of principle. He also believes in Roosevelt's foreign policies, so if he chooses the right advisers he will do well'.[8]

Makins' so-called economic role was divided into three areas: liaison with the various wartime UK missions in Washington outside the Embassy, the diplomatic work associated with the founding of the Food and Agricultural

---

6 Makins Papers, MS Sherfield 337, Diary of Midwest Speaking Tour, March 1945.

7 Lord Sherfield's Memoirs, *Washington January 1st-May 15th 1945*, p. 12.

8 Ernest Makins Papers, MS Sherfield 197, Letter Makins to father, 15 April 1945.

Organisation (FAO) and that associated with the United Nations Relief and Rehabilitation Administration (UNNRA).The first, entailed rethinking the British wartime arrangements in Washington, and required Makins to 'make proposals as to staffing and mechanism which would ensure a smooth transition from the war organisation to the peace time embassy'.[9] The British wanted their numbers in Washington reduced, in part because they desperately needed to preserve dollars. Makins must have worked fast: by early 1946 Halifax wrote to the Foreign Office that 'in six or seven months time there will not be sufficient work for two Ministers in the economic field and both the organisation and the nature of the work will call for a single supervisory head'.[10] Most of the combined boards which had managed Anglo-American cooperation during the war were closed down. The various Whitehall outposts in Washington were also either closed down, or had some of their functions, transferred to the Embassy.

The process of adjusting to the post-war situation inevitably brought the control of the residual British bodies in Washington into question. During the war many of these bodies had reported directly to their Whitehall Departments. Makins felt strongly that this practice should not continue. 'As was their wont Departments chafed at being under diplomatic control, and there was a move to set up independent departmental missions in Washington. I vigorously contested this notion pointing out that it was essential to an orderly conduct of national business in a foreign capital that all British representation should be under the Embassy umbrella.'[11] Makins' view was accepted.

As mentioned earlier, the British General Election of July 1945 saw the Labour Party sweep to power. For the first time nationally, Labour had gained an overall majority. The Conservatives lost over 180 seats and Labour gained over 239. It was a remarkable result and one which was to have implications for Makins. Ernest Bevin was the new Foreign Secretary, and in the coming years Makins would develop a strong relationship with him, becoming one of his confidants and trusted advisers. He appears to have been more circumspect than many in his circle. At the time he wrote 'The election results gave us all a surprise; though Anthony [Eden] told me when he was here [April 1945] that he did not think he would be Foreign Secretary much longer. I can't help thinking that the Conservative campaign was very badly conducted. However, it is not a bad thing that there is a clear cut situation and, in the long run, it may turn out to be the best for the country. I am glad Bevin is Foreign Secretary. I think he is the best we can get'.[12] The Bevin appointment was yet another piece

---

9 The National Archives (Henceforth TNA), FO 366/1516, Minute UK Government Machinery in Washington, p. 3 para 17.

10 TNA, FO 366/1707, letter Halifax to Bevin, 29 January 1946.

11 Lord Sherfield's Memoirs, *Washington June –December 1945*, p. 36.

12 Ibid., p. 20.

of luck for Makins: Hugh Dalton had originally been earmarked for the top Foreign Office job but Attlee, possibly in response to Foreign Office lobbying, decided to make Dalton the Chancellor of the Exchequer instead. It was a narrow escape; Dalton, as noted in the previous chapter, had very clear views on Makins.

The second aspect of Makins' economic work related to the Food and Agriculture Organisation. The idea of an international body for food and agriculture emerged early in the twentieth century. In June 1905 an international conference held in Rome led to the creation of an International Agricultural Institute. The concept was developed by the League of Nations in the 1930s and was given a more permanent footing by Roosevelt, who in 1943, called a conference in Hot Springs, Virginia which was attended by over 40 nations. The result of the conference was the establishment of a commission with a brief to put in place plans for a permanent organisation. By the time Makins became involved in early 1945, most of the detailed work had been done in terms of developing a constitution and modus operandi for the new body. This new entity became known as the Food and Agricultural Organisation, and one of its aims was to reconcile the often conflicting objectives of food producers and food consumers. Its inaugural conference was held in Quebec and was chaired by Lester B. Pearson, a career diplomat, who later became Prime Minister of Canada from 1963–8. Lester Pearson was a friend of Makins; they had first met when they were both diplomats in Geneva before the war, and continued to work together in Washington during post-war discussions about atomic energy. The FAO was the first organisation of the newly founded United Nations to be set up. Its objective was to defeat hunger and, more practically, to allow a forum for the negotiation of agreements concerned with food and nutrition.

Makins, together with 25 other British representatives, attended its inaugural conference which was held at the Chateau Frontenac, Quebec. The British delegation was led by Phillip Noel Baker, Minister of State for Foreign Affairs from 1945 to 1946. While there was always tension between the food producing and the food importing countries, the conference was a success and the FAO was permanently established, initially with its headquarters in Washington, but subsequently in Rome, where it remains today. According to Makins 'There was ... a genuine feeling among the delegation that they were blazing a trail as the first organisation of the UN to be constituted'.[13] It does not appear that Makins played any incisive part in this conference; he was just one of many delegates. Its chief value for him was probably a chance to get to know Noel Baker, and an opportunity to further cement his relationship with Lester Pearson.

---

13 Lord Sherfield's Memoirs, *Washington 1944–1947 Annex 2, The Interim Commission and the Founding Conference of the Food and Agricultural Organisation of the UN*, p. 9.

The third part of Makins' economic work related to the United Nations Rehabilitation and Relief Administration (UNRRA). UNRRA was founded in 1943 and its principal role was to plan, coordinate and administer relief for the victims of the war. It was particularly active in 1945 and 1946 but was disbanded in 1947, falling victim to Soviet excesses and an aversion in the US Congress to committing more money to an organisation over which it had little control (America was by far the largest contributor of funds). UNRRA was nominally controlled by the Council which consisted of representatives of all the signatories and which met twice a year. The executive authority rested with the Director General who reported to the Central Committee which consisted of representatives of the four great powers, America, Russia, Britain and China. Makins occupied the British seat on the Central Committee as a deputy firstly to Sir Ben Smith, Attlee's first Minister of Food, and then to Phillip Noel Baker.

The Central Committee was Makins' first experience of negotiating with the Russians; he found it, as everyone else did, a tedious and time wasting experience. In addition to attending meetings of the Central Committee Makins was also a part of the British delegation sent to the fourth UNRRA Council meeting which took place in March 1946 in Atlantic City. By March 1946 the world food situation had deteriorated considerably; in particular there was a heavy shortfall in wheat production. Makins commented that there was a marked contrast between the optimism and enthusiasm at the first FAO Conference in Canada, and the pessimism and bitterness at Atlantic City.[14] He ended his association with UNRRA having attended the sixth meeting of the organisation, which took place in Washington in December 1946 and was, according to Makins, uneventful. Again, it is difficult to discern any significant impact Makins may have made during his association with UNRRA, and he seems to have spent his time performing basic diplomatic functions, such as agreeing agendas, liaising with the representatives of other missions and briefing his political masters.

So, even though Makins' title was Economic Minister, his job was very little concerned with economics. His role was diplomatic in character and rather perfunctory at that. One has a sense that Halifax, who thought a great deal of Makins, was keen to carve out a place for him in order to keep him in Washington. Having failed to secure him as his Political Minister, Halifax may have concocted the role of Economics Minister to keep Makins in Washington. What is certainly the case is that the job was abolished after Makins returned to London. Certainly the routine diplomatic work associated with the Missions, UNRRA and the FAO were hardly opportunities to stand out. The chance to become more widely noticed within Whitehall came from his work on atomic energy.

14 Lord Sherfield's Memoirs, *Washington 1944–1947* Annex 3 UNRRA, p. 3.

Makins took over responsibility for the Embassy's work in relation to atomic energy when Sir Ronald Campbell returned to the Foreign Office in London in March 1945,[15] Sir John Anderson, the Cabinet Minister responsible for atomic energy matters, wanted to appoint an official from the Ministry of Aircraft Production rather than Makins. However, as Campbell pointed out, the work in Washington was 'acquiring a more and more political aspect' and therefore would become more 'diplomatic in character'.[16] Campbell added 'the sort of person needed for the work is one with a diplomatic training and background'. Campbell's view prevailed.

The atomic energy aspect of Makins' work is significant, and it is perhaps worth dwelling a little on the background and the framework for Anglo-American cooperation in the area. In April 1940 the British had set up the Maud Committee to report on the feasibility of an atomic bomb. Based on Niels Bohr's paper on uranium fission published in the previous year, and on the work of Frisch and Peierls at Birmingham University, which demonstrated the possibility of a nuclear explosion, the committee concluded by the summer of 1941 that an atomic bomb was feasible. The Maud Committee's report was shared with the Americans who then began to take the prospect of an atomic bomb more seriously. They set up their own atomic energy project and forged ahead with it.

Soon the British saw that a technology gap was opening between themselves and the Americans. They sought to introduce themselves into the American project on equal terms. The Americans working on the project, in particular Dr Vannevar Bush, Director of the Office of Scientific Research and Development and Major General Leslie Groves, Director of the Manhattan Project (the American code name for the project to develop a nuclear bomb), saw little merit in a joint project. By March 1943 the exchange of information on atomic energy between the British and the Americans was virtually non-existent and the British fell further behind. This led Churchill to intervene, and he persuaded Roosevelt to instruct his team to cooperate with the British. Sir John Anderson and Vannevar Bush drew up an accord, which after approval by Churchill and Roosevelt; was called the 'Articles of Agreement Governing Collaboration between the Authorities of the USA and the UK in the Matter of Tube Alloys' (Tube Alloys was the British code name for the atomic energy project). It soon became known as the 'Quebec Agreement'.

This agreement was signed in August 1943. It set up the Combined Policy Committee (CPC) which was responsible for ensuring 'full and effective

---

[15] The section in this chapter relating to atomic energy owes a very significant debt to Chapter 3 Atomic Energy Collaboration 1945–1946 as contained in Wevill, *Britain and America.*

[16] TNA, Campbell Papers, FO800/524, Minute produced by Ronald Campbell, 21 February 1945.

collaboration between the two countries'. A further joint body, the Combined Development Trust (CDT) was established in June 1944. Its objective was to gain control of and develop the production of uranium and thorium supplies (crucial to the production of atomic weapons) in certain parts of the world, in particular parts of the British Empire. The final piece in the arrangements to govern the Anglo-American relationship in this area was the so-called 'Hyde Park Agreement'. This document, based on a conversation between Churchill and Roosevelt and only 150 words long, contained the sentence: 'Full collaboration between the United States and the British Government in developing Tube alloys ... should continue after the defeat of Japan unless and until terminated by joint agreement.'

It was within this framework that Makins was introduced to the subject and took over the day-to-day embassy work in relation to atomic energy cooperation. Although Campbell had been a member of the CPC, Makins was not immediately designated to take his place, possibly because at that time Makins' appointment as a Minister in Washington had not been confirmed. He did not join the CPC until July 1945, and then only as a Joint Secretary when he replaced Denis Rickett, a Treasury official seconded to Washington and a personal assistant to Sir John Anderson.

At the July 1945 meeting of the CPC the British formally gave their approval (as was required under the Hyde Park Agreement) to the use of atomic weapons against Japan. At that time the Manhattan project was under the control of the Secretary of War, Henry Stimson, and was led by General Groves. Although membership of the CPC was fluid, the two American members of the CPC in July 1945 were Stimson and Vannevar Bush with Groves in attendance. The British member at that time was Field Marshall Sir Henry Maitland Wilson, who was the Head of the British Staff Mission in Washington and who Makins knew from his time in Algiers. The Ambassador Lord Halifax and Sir James Chadwick (Chief Scientific Adviser to the British government on Atomic Matters) attended the meetings. The Canadians were represented by C.D. Howe, the Canadian Minister for Munitions and Supply.

The Committee met infrequently and the day-to-day cooperation was managed by the Secretariat. Makins records 'Here I fell on my feet, my American colleague [i.e., the American Joint Secretary] was my old friend Harvey Bundy whom I got to know well when he was Assistant Secretary of State in the 1930's'.[17] Makins was assisted by Donald Maclean, a First Secretary at the Embassy at the time, but who was later identified as a Russian agent and defected to Russia in May 1951, when once again Makins was his boss (see Chapter 4). The mechanism of the CPC and the CDT worked successfully during the war,

[17] Lord Sherfield's Memoirs, *Washington 1944–1947, Annex 1 Atomic Energy*, p. 4 (henceforth *Washington 1944–1947 Atomic Energy*).

but it was to become less effective afterwards, and the difficulties of post-war cooperation, when the Americans became increasingly reluctant to share control and technical knowledge with the British, consumed large amounts of Makins' time and energy.

Makins' work with the atomic energy project was administrative and political. In his memoirs he makes a point about his lack of scientific training (something he had in common with most of his diplomatic colleagues), but this was essentially irrelevant. His role was not to comment on the science, but on strategies to improve Anglo-American cooperation in the field. The scientific work on the atomic project was in the hands of the various scientists who had been sent to the US to work on it. The leader of the team was Sir James Chadwick who was not only the Chief Scientific advisor but also had general oversight of all the British scientists working in America, including William Penney who worked in Los Alamos. Chadwick also played a huge part in securing American cooperation because he had built up a very good relationship with General Groves. Makins benefited considerably from Chadwick's relationship with Groves and accompanied him on several meetings with the General. Later, Makins claimed that any science he knew was thanks to the time Chadwick and Penney had kindly spent briefing him.

Campbell, Makins' predecessor, had recognised that with the ending of the war the atomic energy issue would become more politicised, whereas during the war it had been the province of the military. The change in the political landscape in Washington, with Truman inheriting the Presidency and his appointment of James Byrnes as Secretary of State introduced a further element of uncertainty. Attlee, when he succeeded Churchill as Prime Minister in July 1945, was determined that cooperation should continue and wrote to Truman in August 1945 indicating that he was 'strongly of the opinion that means should be sought to enable ... collaboration and exchange of information to be continued'.[18] Makins, aware of the strength of Attlee's interest, echoed earlier messages from the Washington Embassy and warned:

> Although full recognition was given in the United States to the British contribution, American public opinion is inclined to look on the bomb as an American possession and Congressional opinion will certainly incline to the view that it should remain one. It is important to act quickly before the American views have crystallised and while the machinery of the Combined Policy Committee and of the [Combined Development]Trust is still in active operation. President Truman ... said that he will make a decision about atomic energy ... in the interests

[18] TNA, Bevin Papers, FO 800/512, Attlee to Truman, 16 August 1945.

> of the United States and its foreign policy. We can only influence that decision by putting in our ideas at once.[19]

It was a prescient remark. With James Byrnes and General Groves in the vanguard, the Americans were already seeking to distance themselves from further collaboration with Britain. This was serious for the British since, even though there had been collaboration between the scientists during the war, Groves had run the operation on a need to know basis and compartmentalised different aspects of the project. Only the Americans had the overall picture and, indeed, knew how to produce the bomb.

In addition to warning ministers of the changing attitude of the Americans, Makins produced a list of points where a decision was required 'as soon as possible if we are to have a serious chance of maintaining our position as an effective partner with the United States'.[20] This list included estimating the amount of plutonium and thorium which Britain might require in the future. Makins knew the allocation of raw material would be a contentious issue. He also noted that Britain would need to decide what form of atomic control Britain would employ if it developed its own project and the part the Commonwealth might play in any future nuclear programme. At this point Makins was trying to instil a sense of urgency in London that was essential if Britain was to secure continued collaboration with the Americans. The minutes of the CPC meeting held in October 1945 show the significance of Makins' comments. Halifax informed the meeting that Britain had decided to set up an atomic Research Establishment, with a nuclear pile that would need raw materials. As Makins predicted, the Americans immediately asked if this would result in modification to the raw material allocations which had already been agreed by the Combined Development Trust. At this stage there is clear evidence that Makins understood American attitudes and informed London appropriately.

In addition to Anglo-American concerns over collaboration and raw material allocation, a broader issue needed to be discussed – the international control of atomic energy. Attlee had secured a summit between himself, Truman and Mackenzie King (the Canadian Prime Minister) to discuss the subject of international control as well as continued collaboration between Britain and America. The summit became known as the Washington Conference. The Conference, which only lasted a few days, dwelt mainly on the issue of international control and resulted in the 'Washington Declaration', agreed by Truman, Attlee and Mackenzie King. It recommended that a commission be set

19 TNA, CAB 134/7, Cabinet Advisory Committee on Atomic Energy, *Relations with the United States*, Note by Makins, 24 September 1945.

20 Ibid.

up under the United Nations with the objective of finding ways to control the use of atomic energy.[21]

Makins was a part of the delegation attending the summit, but had little input into the drafting or formulation of the Washington Declaration. He played a more significant role on the second issue, continued Anglo-American collaboration. Notwithstanding Truman's purported support for continued collaboration, in practice the British were encountering resistance from the Americans. Both Chadwick and Neville Butler (Assistant Under Secretary of State at the Foreign Office responsible for the American Department) were indicating that the Americans were not particularly forthcoming in terms of collaboration.[22] Butler also noted a conversation with J.G. Winant, the American Ambassador to London, when Winant told him that 'General Groves wanted to keep the inner secrets from us'.[23] It was against this background that the British were seeking to reignite atomic energy collaboration.

The talks between the three leaders over international control were so 'long and arduous' that there was little time left for consideration of continued collaboration.[24] The consequence was that the task of agreeing a basis for future collaboration was delegated to Anderson and Makins representing the British, and Groves and Patterson (the US Secretary of War) representing the Americans. 'The main discussion of this group centred on collaboration with regard to raw material supplies which the Americans needed and the complete exchange of information which the British wanted.'[25] These discussions led to two documents: The first was the 'Washington Memorandum' a document signed by Truman and the two Prime Ministers, which called for full and effective cooperation and the continuation of the CPC and the CDT; the second was the 'Anderson Groves Memorandum', which gave guidance to the CPC to be used when drawing up a replacement document for the Quebec Agreement.

John Anderson led the discussions and Makins was also present at the meeting. Makins claims that it was his intervention which led directly to the production of the Washington Memorandum: 'In desperation I intervened strongly and produced a single sentence providing specifically for the continuation of collaboration in the uses of atomic energy.'[26] If this was true it was an impressive intervention from the Embassy Minister. The American version of events was, however, different. Their record suggests that it was Groves who suggested that

21 TNA, Bevin Papers FO 800/438, Text of Communiqué on Atomic Energy, 15 November 1945.

22 Memorandum dated 4 November 1945, by N.M. Butler sent to Sir Alexander Cadogan as reproduced in Bullen and Pelly, DBPO Series 1 Vol. II, p. 580.

23 Footnote No. 4 in Bullen and Pelly, DBPO Series 1 Vol. II p. 580.

24 *Washington 1944–1947 Atomic Energy*, p. 16.

25 Wevill, *Britain and America*, p. 122.

26 *Washington 1944–1947 Atomic Energy*, p. 16.

there should be a short directive, the Washington Memorandum, signed by the President and the two Prime Ministers, and a longer statement, the Anderson Groves Memorandum. Their record states that 'Mr Rickett and Mr Makins did not dissent from this view' although it does acknowledge that the Washington Memorandum was prepared by the British'.[27] Given the American record there must be some doubt as to whether or not Makins did intervene in such a decisive manner. The most significant intervention during these meetings came not from Makins, but from General Groves who, during the negotiation of the Anderson Groves Memorandum, persuaded Anderson to accept the words 'in the field of basic research' after the words 'full and effective cooperation'. Groves persuaded the British that if 'full and effective cooperation' was used before the wording providing for the exchange of technical information then it would cause great difficulties if the wording ever came before the eyes of the Senate.[28] The Anderson Groves memorandum provided for ad hoc arrangements with regard to collaboration in respect of the design, development and construction of nuclear plants. This was the area that was of most importance to the British. Only Denis Rickett, who had been Secretary of the CPC and was then an Assistant Secretary in the Cabinet Office and Secretary to the Advisory Committee on Atomic Energy put up the 'bitterest of opposition' to Anderson's concession'.[29] Apparently Makins was silent on the matter. Truman would later use this clause as justification for ending collaboration with Britain.

'The Washington Conference resulted in three documents, the Declaration, which was published, and the Washington Memorandum and the Anderson Groves Memorandum, which were not published. Attlee returned to London believing that he had secured a start to the process of the international control of atomic energy and that he had entered a new era of atomic energy collaboration with America.'[30] These hopes were to prove optimistic. The first meeting of the CPC after the Washington Conference was held on 4 December 1945. A subcommittee consisting of Groves, Makins and Lester Pearson was set up with a view to drafting a replacement document for the Quebec Agreement. The subcommittee's work was to be based on the Anderson Groves Memorandum and the Washington Memorandum. It met on 14 December and Makins reported that 'it went unexpectedly well, and there was not, as I at one time

---

27 FRUS,1945, Vol. II, *Negotiations with the British and Canadians, 1–16 November*, Memorandum by Captain R. Gordon Arneson to the Secretary of War (Patterson), 17 April 1946, p. 63.

28 TNA, GEN 106/2, Record of the Anglo American Discussions on Atomic Energy, 12 December 1945. For more background information on this see HSTL Oral History Interview with R. Gordon Arneson by Niel Johnson 21 June 1989.

29 Paul, Septimus, *Nuclear Rivals: Anglo-American Atomic Relations 1941–1952, Ohio: Ohio State University, 2000,* p. 82.

30 Wevill, *Britain and America*, p. 123.

feared, any apparent difference of intention between us'.[31] By the end of January 1946 Makins was able to report that the negotiation of the new agreement was going along fairly smoothly, but warned that 'there is a good deal of disarray in the American camp on the whole question of atomic energy, and unless we get these agreements through very soon we may miss the market altogether'.[32] By early February 1946 the subcommittee had produced draft reports for the CPC. These included a replacement for the Quebec Agreement and a revised version of an agreement regulating the CDT. In seeking approval for these documents Makins advised London not to seek too many amendments to the drafts he was sending them, sensing that the American attitude to atomic collaboration was changing and believing that if an agreement was to be reached it needed to be reached quickly.[33]

The CPC met on 15 February 1946 and considered the draft reports. There was no dissenting voice. However, two days before the meeting of the CPC Groves sent a report to James Byrnes (by then Chairman of the CPC and US Secretary of State) which completely undermined the sub committee's work. The report denied that the British had played a significant part in the development of the atomic bomb, and listed a number of arguments as to why there should be no collaboration with the British.

At the meeting of the CPC on 15 February Byrnes, now suitably briefed, took cover behind Article 102 of the United Nations Charter. This provided that all international agreements had to be registered with the United Nations, and therefore made public. Because of this provision the committee decided that each of the three governments should reconsider the form of the agreements proposed by the subcommittee and consider the desirability of making them public.[34] The effect was to shelve any continued atomic energy collaboration. As Gowing pointed out in her official history of Britain's atomic energy programme, if the Americans were seeking to avoid further collaboration then the 'discovery of Article 102 seemed a blessing and deliverance'.[35]

Makins had been outmanoeuvred; Halifax protested to Byrnes. The Secretary of State was unmoved, but said he would talk to the President. A mere two weeks before the CPC meeting Makins had written to London saying that 'since this draft is based on a proposal by Groves, he will be committed to make it work. Furthermore, it is altogether probable that unless there is some basic change of US policy, a unanimous recommendation of the sub-

---

31 TNA Butler Papers, FO 800/541, Makins to Rickett, 15 December 1945.

32 TNA, FO 115/4305, Makins to Rickett, 1 February 1946.

33 TNA, Campbell Papers, FO 800/527, Minute to Prime Ministers from Sir John Anderson, 9 February 1946.

34 FRUS, 1946 Vol. I, Minutes of CPC Meeting, 15 February 1946, p. 1213.

35 Gowing, Margaret, *Independence and Deterrence Britain and Atomic Energy 1945–1952 Volume I Policy Making,* Basingstoke: Macmillan, *1974*, p. 98.

committee is likely to go through the Combined Policy Committee without difficulty'.[36] The question then is was there a change in American policy or had Makins been duped?

It is difficult to discern a fundamental change in American policy. There were events, however, which may have made the Americans more reluctant to conclude a deal with the British. The Gouzenkou spy case was about to break,[37] the momentum behind the McMahon Act (see below) was building in Congress, and the atomic issue was now well and truly politicised.[38] These factors could have made the Administration nervous about entering into a secret agreement with the British. Or it may be that Groves had been playing the British along with a view to increasing the amount of raw material coming into America and persuading the British to include the recently discovered South African supplies within the provisions of the Combined Development Trust. Makins was alive to this possibility, and was already aware that Groves' main objective was securing raw material supplies.[39]

It seems more likely that the changing sentiment in America, coupled with the move of the atomic issue from the War Department to the State Department, afforded Groves the opportunity to head off a policy that he had always been reluctant to pursue. Makins recognised both the threat from the changing mood, and also the consequences of moving the atomic issue into the State Department. He reported in January 1946 that 'the whole trend of Byrnesian foreign policy is away from exclusive Anglo-American arrangements'.[40] However he does not seem to have been aware that Groves would use the changing climate to subvert the decisions of the subcommittee and the earlier negotiations on which its work was based. In his memoirs Makins describes General Groves as a 'hard negotiator, but essentially a good hearted and fair minded man', and he indicates that he got on very well with Groves.[41] Perhaps this was an instance where Makins was too close to and too trusting of the Americans – a criticism which was to be levelled at Makins several times during his career.

---

36 TNA, FO 115/4305, Makins to Ricket, 1 February 1946.

37 Igor Gouzenkou was a lieutenant in the Soviet Army posted as a cipher clerk to the Soviet Embassy in Ottawa. He defected in the autumn of 1945 and disclosed that the Soviets had penetrated the Manhattan project and revealed amongst other things that Alan Nunn, a British atomic scientist working on the project, was a spy. This information became public on 19 February 1946.

38 Churchill Archives Chadwick Papers, *Embassy Report on Congressional and Public Opinion in the U.S.A. on the Use and Control of Atomic Energy*, No. 13, Period February 1 to 18 February 1945.

39 TNA, Campbell Papers, FO 800/527, Makins to Butler, 22 January 1946.

40 Churchill Archives, Chadwick Papers, Makins to Butler, 22 January 1946.

41 *Washington 1944–1947 Atomic Energy*, p. 6.

Attlee protested, and suggested ways around the apparent obstacle of Clause 102. A further meeting of the CPC was convened for 15 April 1945.The American attitude was unchanged and Byrnes suggested that the CPC did not have the authority to decide the matter and that the issue needed to be referred back to the three leaders who had attended the Washington conference. Attlee wrote to Truman suggesting that the Washington Memorandum signed in the previous November 'cannot mean less than full interchange of information and a fair exchange of material'.[42] Truman responded that while the Washington Memorandum refers to full and effective cooperation in the field of atomic energy, clause 5 of the Groves Anderson Memorandum, drawn up only a few hours later, specifically states that:

> There shall be full and effective cooperation in the field of basic scientific research ... In the field of development design and construction, and operation of plants such cooperation ... shall be regulated by such ad hoc arrangements as may be approved from time to time by the Combined Policy Committee as mutually advantageous.

The Groves intervention gave Truman his get-out clause. It was a clause which Makins made no attempt to alter.

As well as failing to achieve atomic collaboration with the Americans, Britain's negotiating team in Washington also failed to obtain the raw material allocation which it was seeking. Raw materials such as uranium ore were required both for the American nuclear programme and the planned British nuclear plants. At the time it was believed that there would be a shortage of raw material by the end of 1947. The Americans wanted virtually all the raw material that would become available, for that year and the next to be allocated to themselves. Makins offered a compromise which was rejected by General Groves. It took the intervention of Dean Acheson, then Under Secretary of State, who felt the British had been badly treated, to settle the issue. In the end the Americans kept all the raw materials received in America up to 31 March 1946 and the allocations for the remainder of the year were split equally between the British and Americans. Given the availability of raw materials in the Commonwealth and Britain's access to them, the raw material allocation was a strong card in British hands; it was, however, one which they failed to play effectively. The subject of raw material allocation and atomic energy collaboration in general was opened up again in late 1947, and Makins would also play a prominent part in these negotiations after he returned to London.

While Groves and Byrnes were seeking to shut down collaboration with the British, the US legislature was considering a bill which would effectively

[42] FRUS 1946, Vol. 1 Attlee to Truman 16 April 1946.

make collaboration illegal. The bill, soon to be known as the McMahon Act, became law on 26 July 1946. It made the interchange of atomic energy information with any other country virtually impossible 'and so the door that had already become closed to Anglo-American cooperation was now locked'.[43] The Embassy's (and therefore Makins') failure to respond to the passage of the MacMahon bill through Congress has drawn some criticism from, among others, Margaret Gowing. In March 1946 the Embassy wrote to London advising that there was no need to worry about the bill.[44] Makins suggested that the Americans had not agreed the way forward, and that there would be changes to the bill. The Embassy did send a revised bill to London but with no comment. It appears that it was Chadwick, rather than Makins, who was alive to the possible impact the bill might have, or at least Chadwick was the only one who communicated his concerns to London. He wrote to John Anderson on 17 April suggesting that the bill 'seems to exclude the possibility of collaboration with us except by the express approval of ... Congress'.[45] Anderson minuted on this letter 'this is very serious and shd. be considered at once by the Depts concerned. It is odd that we have apparently had nothing from the ambassador'.[46] Chadwick, in fact, wanted to talk to Senator McMahon, but was dissuaded from doing so by Makins.

It is difficult to know whether an Embassy intervention would have made any difference to the McMahon Act; Makins remained convinced that it would not. In his memoirs he wrote:

> The Embassy has in retrospect been criticised for not finding out the contents of the McMahon Bill and trying to intervene to get it altered. McMahon himself is said to have told Churchill some years later that if he had known about the Quebec Agreement he would not have introduced the bill with the same clauses on exchange of information. I have always regarded this, if true, as an example of esprit d'escalier ... Even if we had intervened or even leaked a copy of the agreement to a member of Congress, we would only have embarrassed the Administration without affecting the results. There was nothing to hope for from the State Department as Byrnes was strongly anti British.[47]

At least by the time the Act was passed in July 1946 Makins seems to have been aware that the Administration was against collaboration – something he clearly had not realised six months earlier.

---

43 Wevill, *Britain and America*, p. 131.

44 Gowing, *Independence and Deterrence*, p. 108.

45 Churchill Archives, Chadwick Papers, Chadwick to Anderson, 17 April 1946.

46 Footnote to the above letter reproduced in Bullen and Pelly DPBO series 1 Vol. IV, p. 252.

47 *Washington 1944–1947 Atomic Energy*, p. 19.

Many years after the events of 1945/46, Makins, in his memoirs, tried to play down the failed attempt to seek collaboration with the Americans. He wrote 'These two documents [the Quebec and the Hyde Park Agreements] formed a weak basis for the contention that the US Government was committed to collaboration with Britain'. Makins further suggests that 'the American contention that the Quebec agreement was valid for the duration of the war and had fulfilled its purpose was, in my opinion, juridically correct'.[48] Other than possibly wanting to take a defensive position it is difficult to understand why Makins makes these points. As Dean Acheson, who at the time was the Under Secretary of State and who attended the February 1946 and April 1946 CPC meetings, noted in his memoirs 'Our Government, having made an agreement [the Quebec Agreement] from which it had gained immeasurably, was not keeping its word and performing its obligation'.[49] Even at the time Makins reported that Acheson was apologetic about the American behaviour and understood that the American action represented a volte face on their part.[50]

Makins also suggests in his memoirs that the twin aims of the Washington conference, the international control of atomic energy and the reaching of a secret agreement with the Americans on atomic energy collaboration, were incompatible and therefore unachievable, although there is no evidence that he made this point at the time. While they may have been incompatible, it does not follow that these goals were not achievable. Indeed at the same time as calling for international control of atomic energy the Americans and British entered into a secret agreement on the allocation of raw materials. It is perhaps not the first time that a government has been cynical enough to call for one action in public and take a different action in private.

Makins did play a significant part in the atomic energy discussions in Washington in 1945/46, but it is important not to exaggerate his role or to lose sight of the fact that Makins failed to identify, at least until it was too late, the biggest single threat to collaboration – General Groves. Makins did play a part in the Washington conference in November 1945 and was a member of the delegation, but his role was subordinate to John Anderson, the politician. 'It has been suggested that Makins had a "major influence on the formulation and execution of British policy". If he did it was not at this time.'[51] Arguably, he was too trusting of the Americans. The following quotation from Septimus Pauls' study of Anglo-American cooperation seems appropriate.

---

48 Ibid., p. 15 and p. 17.

49 Acheson, Dean, *Present at Creation My Years in the State Department*, New York: Norton, 1987, p. 64.

50 TNA, FO 115/4306, Makins to Rickett, 6 March 1946.

51 Wevill, *Britain and America*, p. 139.

> The British approached these discussions with a naiveté that would have been appropriate to a world governed by the chivalric code of a bygone age but not to the diplomatic arena of the twentieth century, where the primacy of national security and national interest took precedence over questions of principle. It was a naiveté based on the understanding that a gentleman could be taken at his word. ... time and time again over the next few years the British would place their trust in the vague words of the Americans and be disappointed. They even attempted to rationalise the Americans behaviour.[52]

One consequence of the failure to reach agreement was that there was less work to be done in the field of atomic energy. The CDT remained active, and Makins attended these meetings until his work was taken over by Gordon Munro, Financial Minister at the Washington embassy in July 1946. Most of the work on the international control of atomic energy moved to the UN under the supervision of Alexander Cadogan, the British UN representative at the time. The attempt to negotiate an international treaty to control atomic energy was doomed to failure and came to nothing; the process was abandoned in 1947. The US Atomic Energy Commission set up after the McMahon Act under the Chairmanship of David Lilienthal took over responsibility for guarding the 'American secret'. The re-opening of the issue of collaboration and the part Makins played in negotiating with the AEC in late 1947 is discussed in the following chapter.

The loss of collaboration in the field of atomic energy, together with the diminution of Makins 'economic work', meant that Lord Inverchapel, who had replaced Lord Halifax in May 1946, could no longer justify keeping Makins' in Washington. The job of Economics Minister at the Embassy was abolished, and Makins returned to the Foreign Office in early 1947.

---

[52] Paul, *Nuclear Rivals*, p. 83.

Chapter 4

The Whitehall Elite

When Ernest Bevin became Foreign Secretary he thought British Foreign Policy should be constructed around three main areas, the Commonwealth, Europe and the United States. Echoing a Churchillian idea, these three areas were viewed as interlocking circles with each area contributing something towards Britain's status: in turn Britain would maintain a commitment to each area. Officials, and Makins in particular, did not see any symmetry in the approach to each of these areas and decided that Britain's status was more likely to be sustained by focusing on its relationship with America. The Atlanticist approach came to dominate and this led to a repudiation of a more significant commitment to Europe, and also to the Commonwealth.

Life in England was very different to life in Washington. One of Makins' first tasks when he arrived home was to go to Reading to collect the family ration cards. In February 1947 Britain was in the midst of a fuel crisis leading to large parts of British industry being shut down. She was suffering from an acute dollar shortage which limited her ability to import food. Britain's decline was also evident on the international front. India was to gain her independence; Britain's proposed solution to the Palestinian problem was rejected by both the Arabs and the Jews; and the government was forced to inform the Americans that Britain could no longer afford to honour her commitment to keep troops in Greece. It is striking to recall that in 1938 Britain's Gross Domestic Product per capita was 90 per cent of America's; by 1948 it was half.[1] In the Foreword to the 1947 *Economic Survey,* published in the month of Makins' arrival back in the United Kingdom, Attlee declared that 'the accomplishments of the country during the first eighteen months of peace were accomplishments of which we can justly feel proud'.[2] That may have been the case, but the fact was that Britain's position was precarious.

It was against this backdrop that Makins took up his position as Assistant Under Secretary responsible for the Economic Departments.[3] A vacancy for the post of Assistant Under Secretary had arisen in early 1946, and the Promotions

[1] Young, John, *Britain and the World in the Twentieth Century*, London: Hodder Headline, 1997, p. 141.

[2] Command Paper, 7046, *Economic Survey for 1947*, p. 3.

[3] The position of Assistant Under Secretary is sometimes referred to as Superintending Under Secretary, as indeed it is in the Official List.

Board at the Foreign Office reached the conclusion that 'by far the most suitable candidate would be Makins'. In May 1946 the Foreign Office wrote to Inverchapel, who had taken over as the Ambassador in that month, and told him that 'Both from the point of view of the needs of the Office and from that of Makins' future we should very much like to get him back here as soon as this can reasonable be arranged'.[4] It was to take a further eight months before Makins was released.

Makins' immediate superior in the Foreign Office was Edmund Hall-Patch, the Deputy Under Secretary in charge of the 'functional' departments which included the Economic Departments which Makins took over from Hall-Patch. The Economic Relations Department advised the Secretary of State on general economic and financial questions affecting relations with foreign countries; the role of the Economic Intelligence Department was to collect economic information relating to foreign countries and present it to missions abroad, other government departments, and within the Foreign Office; and the General Department dealt with Foreign Office interests in civil aviation, shipping transport and other political economic questions including atomic energy matters.[5]

Makins, as Assistant Under Secretary of State, was now only two levels down from the top position in the Foreign Office. However, a great deal of his work lay outside of the Foreign Office. The fragile state of Britain's economy demanded very close interdepartmental consultation on the economic side. As Edwin Plowden, Chief Planning Officer and Chairman of the Economic Planning Board, pointed out: 'most economic policies have some impact on foreign affairs' and the Treasury should 'know the Foreign Office view while policies are being planned.'[6] As a consequence Makins, representing the Foreign Office, joined the Whitehall economic team. This put Makins at the heart of events in Whitehall. It was also at this time that Makins developed a good relationship with Robert Hall who in 1947 became the Director of the Economic Section of the Cabinet Office. Later when Makins moved to the Treasury in the mid 1950s he came to rely heavily on the advice of Hall.

In addition to participating in Britain's post-war economic planning, he also continued to play a part in Britain's atomic energy programme. In February 1947 Makins joined the Advisory Committee on Atomic Energy which was chaired by Sir John Anderson, with whom Makins had worked at the Washington Summit in November 1945. The Advisory Committee had been set up by Attlee, shortly after the Hiroshima bomb was dropped, to advise

---

4 TNA, FO 366/1707, David Scott to Inverchapel, 29 May 1946.

5 TNA, FO 366/2314, Foreign Office Organisation, April 1946.

6 Plowden, Edwin, *An Industrialist in the Treasury: The Post War Years*, London: Andre Deutsch, 1989, p. 26.

the government on the implication of atomic energy and the uses, military and industrial, to which it might be put. Initially, the committee was productive, but with the passage of time there were feelings that it was unsatisfactory, not least because its Chairman sat on the opposition front bench and could not attend ministerial meetings. The last meeting of this committee was held in May 1947 and it was disbanded at the end of that year.[7]

Another committee, the Atomic Energy Official Committee, had been set up in August 1946, and gradually became the principal forum for the discussion of atomic energy policy in Britain. Makins joined this committee when he returned to the Foreign Office in February 1947. By the time he joined it the Committee had become the principal forum for interdepartmental discussions of atomic policy as they concerned Anglo-American, Commonwealth and other foreign relations. Margaret Gowing, the official historian of Britain's immediate post-war nuclear project commented, 'The Committee had not been very dynamic during the first six months, but it underwent a marked change when Roger Makins ... took over the Chairmanship'. Gowing points out that for a short time Edward Bridges (Permanent Secretary to the Treasury and Head of the Civil Service) was the Chairman but in practice Makins always chaired the committee.[8] In this capacity Makins did not report up through Orme Sargent his Permanent Under Secretary or even through Bevin the Secretary of State, but rather he reported directly to Attlee. Gowing commented 'Makins carried a heavy load, for atomic energy was only one of his many duties'.[9] It is not surprising that Makins, commenting on his return to the Foreign Office, wrote 'This place is a regular madhouse ... and I do not believe I shall be able to function here effectively unless I go mad myself'.[10] The fact remains, however, that under Makins 'the Official Committee became a real focus of power: several civil servants of long experience found it one of the most effective committees they had ever known'.[11] Makins' work on this committee is considered in more detail below, but first it is necessary to turn to his economic work.

As Makins arrived at the Foreign Office preparations were under way for the fourth post-war Conference of Foreign Ministers, which was held in Moscow in March 1947. One objective of the Conference, at least from the West's point of view, was to resolve the differences between the big four powers over the future of Germany and Austria. It is not necessary to detail the negotiations here, but by the end of the Conference George Marshall, the recently appointed American Secretary of State, had concluded that the Soviets would never accept

7 Gowing, *Independence and Deterrence*, p. 29.

8 Gowing, *Independence and Deterrence*, p. 31.

9 Ibid.

10 Zametica, John. *British Officials and British Foreign Policy, 1945–50*, Leicester: Leicester University Press, 1990, Chapter 1 Roger Makins: 'Mr Atom' by Jill Edwards, p. 19.

11 Gowing, *Independence and Deterrence*, p. 31.

any agreement on Germany that did not result in their controlling the country. 'Germany, formerly Europe's greatest industrial nation, had been unable to rebuild its industry and the population was operating at the subsistence level. Marshall, aware of the difficulties being faced by Britain and the rest of Europe during the early part of 1947, made the connection between the stagnation in Germany and the failure of the European recovery'.[12] It was this connection which led to the Marshall Plan, outlined in the now famous Harvard Speech which Marshall made in June 1947. The speech eventually led to the passing of the Economic Co-operation Act by Congress in 1948 and the subsequent allocation of $13 billion worth of aid to Europe over the following four years. Marshall's speech had two consequences for Makins; firstly, he sat on the London Committee which was set up to coordinate the British response to the Marshall Plan and, secondly, it led, indirectly, to his promotion to Deputy Under Secretary.

The response to Marshall's initiative, which consisted of detailing the production plans and financial and other requirements for 16 European countries, was led by Britain and France. In order to put this into effect the Committee of European Economic Cooperation was formed, based in Paris and consisting of representatives from the European countries. This committee in turn appointed an Executive Committee, chaired by Oliver Franks (subsequently appointed the British Ambassador to Washington, 1948–52), which carried out the detailed work. Bevin was keen to retain control of the process and, fearing that the Treasury might see itself as being in the vanguard of the operation, sent Hall-Patch to Paris to liaise with Franks' committee and keep Whitehall informed. This left Makins in London as the Foreign Office's principal representative on the committee set up in Whitehall to coordinate the British response. The purpose of the London Committee, as it was called, was to ensure that the proposals for European aid were successfully implemented, and to extract maximum advantage for Britain vis-à-vis other European countries. In this context Makins demonstrated Atlanticist rather than European credentials. During the process of putting Marshall aid together there were several suggestions that any ultimate agreement with America could be on a European-wide basis. Makins, keen to secure a direct link with America rather than one subsumed in a European response, promoted a bilateral approach which in the end prevailed.[13]

While Britain was coordinating her response to the Marshall Plan proposals, the need for aid was exacerbated by the requirement for Britain to move to

---

12 Wevill, *Britain and America,* p. 187.

13 For more detail on this see Zametica, John, *British Officials and British Foreign Policy,1945–50,* Leicester: Leicester University Press, 1990, Chapter 1 Roger Makins: 'Mr Atom' by Jill Edwards, pp. 26–7. See also TNA, FO 371/62567 and GEN 188/35.

convertibility of sterling (at least in respect of current account transactions) by 15 July 1947. This was one of the provisions of the Loan Agreement which Britain had entered into the previous year. One of the first minutes Makins wrote when he returned to London in February 1947 was to report a conversation he had had with Will Clayton (the American Under Secretary of State for Economic Affairs) before he left Washington. Makins reported that 'Mr Clayton went out of his way to say to me that if we were likely to run into difficulties over the loan [e.g. convertibility] we should be well advised to discuss these difficulties with the Americans as soon as possible and not leave it until a late stage'.[14] Makins was ignored.

Notwithstanding the fact that the proceeds of the loan were declining rapidly as the government drew on them to support sterling as Britain moved towards convertibility on 15 July, the Treasury did not raise the problems they were having, particularly the rapidly dwindling reserves, with the Americans until the eleventh hour. This failure to consult with the Americans at an early stage was to cost Britain dearly, both in terms of currency and reputation. On the evening of 20 August 1947 Hugh Dalton, the Chancellor of the Exchequer, announced over the radio that external convertibility of sterling had been suspended because of an unacceptable drain on external reserves. In the first half of 1947, the balance of the loan had been reduced by $1,630 million and in just under two months, from 1 July to 23 August, a further $930 million had disappeared.[15]

Makins was always mindful of the Americans' position. Even on the morning of the announcement of the suspension of convertibility Makins wrote to Bevin outlining three alternatives 'a) not to suspend convertibility b) to take action on American terms c) to take action unilaterally without any agreement with the Americans'. Makins concluded that 'the second course seems to be the least bad alternative but it involves immediate consideration of very important issues with the Americans'.[16] It is interesting to note that when Makins wrote this note there was already a team of Treasury officials in America negotiating the terms of a suspension of convertibility with the Americans. Clearly Makins was not, as yet, in the inner circle. The successful conclusion of the Marshall Plan proposals was perhaps about to change this.

The Economic Co-operation Act was passed on 2 April 1948, and Europe was called upon to put in place a body to supervise, in tandem with the Americans, the European Recovery Program as Marshall Aid was now called. Europe responded by forming the Organisation for European Economic

[14] TNA, FO371/62263, Minute by Makins, 19 February 1947.

[15] Newton, C.C.S., 'The Sterling Crisis of 1947and the British Response to the Marshall Plan', *The Economic History Review,* 37.3 (Aug 1984), p. 398.

[16] TNA, FO 371/62270, Minute Makins to Secretary of State, 20 August 1947.

Cooperation (OEEC). The Executive Committee was the most powerful body within this hierarchy and its first Chairman was Edward Hall-Patch. The consequence of Hall-Patch's appointment was that it created a vacancy at the Foreign Office, and Makins was well placed to fill it. He had had sufficient time to establish himself in Whitehall and more importantly he had gained the confidence of Bevin and, indeed, had become one of Bevin's closest advisors. In April 1948 Makins was appointed Deputy Under Secretary in charge of the Functional Departments. It was rapid promotion for Makins; it is interesting to reflect that it was only four years earlier in 1944 that he went to Washington as a mere Counsellor and now he was only one level below the Permanent Under Secretary.

Makins, reflecting upon his promotion several years later, suggested that Hall-Patch's promotion was 'an astonishing stroke of good fortune ... and it marked another major turning point in my career'.[17] Hall-Patch was 'dug in' as Bevin's principal economic advisor and 'guarded his position rather jealously'. Makins added 'For me, the difference between playing second fiddle to Hall-Patch and moving to the top post on the economic side of the Foreign Office enormously increased my influence and authority in the Office and in Whitehall'.[18] Shortly after his promotion Makins purchased Sherfield Court, a large and attractive, but not particularly grand, house with a beautiful garden situated near the village of Sherfield on Loddon. The house came with 300 acres and was described as 'unquestionably one of the most attractive medium sized estates in the Basingstoke area'.[19] It was to remain the Makins' home for over 30 years. Shortly after moving into Sherfield Court Makins was made a Knight Commander of the Order of St Michael and St George (KCMG) (he had been made a Companion of the Order in 1944). The Order is the main one given to Foreign Office officials, since it is mainly conferred on those who provide loyal or important service (other than military) in respect of British interests overseas.

Britain continued to receive aid under the European Recovery Program up until 1951 and Makins continued to work on the project being 'much involved' in policy and usually accompanying Bevin on his numerous visits to Paris to meet with the American representatives of the aid programme. In addition he was involved in several other areas. These included Commonwealth Relations; he was a member of the UK delegation to the Colombo Conference in 1951 and the Commonwealth Conference of 1952. He also served on several of Britain's bilateral economic relations committees. He chaired the Anglo-Norwegian, the Anglo-Italian and the Anglo-French committees, and was a member of the Anglo-Scandinavian committee. In addition he was called upon to deal with

17 Lord Sherfield's Memoirs, section entitled, *Marshall Plan*, p. 7.

18 Ibid.

19 Makins Papers, MS Sherfield 821, Sherfield Court, John D. Wood Property Details.

various political/economic issues such as the devaluation crisis of 1949. Each of these areas is discussed further below.

There were several interdepartmental committees which coordinated policy at the official level, but the most important was the Overseas Relations Committee. Makins was the Foreign Office representative on this committee and he 'spent hours in the airless sub ground of the Treasury thrashing out recommendations to Ministers'.[20] Edwin Plowden was the most influential member of the team and he was a close ally of Robert Hall. Makins recalls how he and Plowden worked together to coordinate the advice on economic questions which was being given to both Cripps, who had succeeded Dalton as Chancellor of the Exchequer in November 1947, and Bevin 'thus minimising the effect of possible misunderstanding or even conflict between these two powerful ... contrasting characters'.[21] Makins recalled how this process worked:

> Edwin Plowden was quiet, cautious and rather self effacing, but he was highly intelligent, shrewd and decisive with good judgement, firm in his opinions and clear in his objectives. He and I and Robert Hall were usually in broad agreement with each other and therefore tended to prevail [over other officials] not to speak of Ministers.[22]

There was clearly mutual respect between Plowden and Makins. Plowden recalled that Makins 'had an acute mind and a robust view of where British interests lay'.[23] Plowden was also aware of Makins' strong Atlanticist views:

> His experience as Economics minister in Washington and, before that, as assistant to the resident minister at Allied Forces Headquarters, Mediterranean, strengthened his [Makins'] conviction that it was essential to keep the United States in Europe if Europe was to recover economically and be defended in the long run . He made us all especially conscious of the danger of a retreat into Fortress America.[24]

The implementation of the European Recovery Plan usually entailed discussions between the executive of the OEEC and the American European Co-operation Administration (ECA), both Paris-based organisations. This process tended to overshadow more direct Anglo-American bilateral negotiations. Aware of this, officials sought to resume dialogue with the Americans, outside of a European

[20] Lord Sherfield's Memoirs, *The Foreign Office 1947–1952* (Henceforth *The Foreign Office*) Chapter 1, p. 10.

[21] *The Foreign Office*, Chapter 1, p. 9.

[22] Ibid.

[23] Plowden, *An Industrialist at the Treasury*, p. 26.

[24] Ibid.

forum, and direct talks were resumed. These discussions covered the International Monetary Fund (IMF), convertibility issues, and the dollar sterling position. One result was the suggestion from the Americans that Britain might consider a devaluation of sterling as a way to address Britain's dollar shortage, at least in part. The suggestion was initially resisted by both officials and politicians but eventually, after a year or so and with the dollar drain showing few signs of improvement, the possibility of devaluation had to be faced. It was suggested that there should be high level Anglo-American talks to be held in Washington at the time of the annual meetings of the IMF and the International Bank for Reconstruction and Development (IBRD) due to be held in September 1949. Makins was brought into these discussions.

On 27 July 1949 Edward Bridges gave a dinner at the Athenaeum Club at which the group of officials who were pushing for devaluation attended. It was a group which had considerable influence on ministers, influence which was greatly increased by their collective approach. The group included Oliver Franks (the British Ambassador in Washington who was on leave in London), Edwin Plowden, Robert Hall, Frank Lee (Permanent Under Secretary Ministry of Food) and Treasury heavyweights such as Wilfred Eady, Richard Otto Clarke and Leslie Rowan. Makins was also invited to the dinner and in his memoirs he commented on the occasion 'though I had become a major player in the still somewhat esoteric field of atomic energy, it is clear in retrospect that I was now accepted as a player in the first Whitehall eleven and had become a member of the "circuit"'.[25] Makins was now firmly in the Whitehall elite.

The rest of July and most of August was taken up preparing briefs on devaluation for ministers prior to the Washington talks, the Cabinet having taken a decision to devalue sterling in early August 1949. Makins in one of his briefings suggested that the September talks would be the last chance for Britain to secure a role as America's global partner.[26] Bevin, Cripps, Plowden, Rowan and Makins, together with private secretaries, set sail for New York on the RMS Mauretania on 31 August. Bevin and Cripps were different characters; Cripps being somewhat austere rose early, worked with officials until late afternoon, and then, as a rule, retired. Bevin did not emerge from his cabin until early evening and then worked with officials up to and including dinner. Eventually with some coaxing from Plowden and Makins Cripps 'sat up long enough and Bevin got up early enough to meet each other'.[27] The result was that the ministers, both of

---

25 Lord Sherfield's Memoirs section entitled *The Devaluation of Sterling 1949* (Henceforth Memoirs *Devaluation*), p. 3.

26 TNA FO 371/75594 Anglo-American Canadian Talks. General Considerations. Minute by Makins 26 August 1949.

27 *Devaluation* p. 5.

whom were unwell, arrived in New York on 6 September rested and in agreement on the strategy for the talks.

The talks themselves got off to a shaky start. However, once the British declared their hand and told the Americans that they were prepared to accept devaluation, they became much more productive. As the date for the announcement of the devaluation approached, the officials who had agreed the rate of $2.80 to the pound amongst themselves needed to persuade Bevin and Cripps.[28] The Treasury officials worked on Cripps; Makins was deputed to persuade Bevin of the merits of $2.80. He was successful and on 18 September the Chancellor announced that sterling was to be devalued.

During these talks Robert Schuman, the French Foreign Minister and Maurice Petsche, the French Finance Minister, were also in Washington for talks with both the British and the Americans. Throughout these talks, which included discussion on the economic relationship with the 'new' Germany (Konrad Adenauer had recently been elected as Germany's first post-war Chancellor), the British never once mentioned that they were about to devalue, although devaluation would have significant repercussions for France. The first the French heard of it was on the evening of 17 September shortly before a public announcement was made. It was regarded as a Foreign Office matter to inform the French and so Makins was 'handed the poison chalice'. Makins, in what he described as 'the most distasteful and invidious task I had to undertake in my whole diplomatic career' went to see Petsche and informed him of the British decision. Makins reported that the French expressed consternation. Petsche described it as 'une decision brutale' and according to Makins Hervé Alphand (Director of Economic Affairs at the French Foreign Ministry) became 'somewhat hysterical'.[29] Makins subsequently suggested that it was a 'grave blunder' not to have broken the news at the ministerial level and in Makins' opinion had serious repercussions for Anglo-French relations, and was even one of the factors that turned the French away from closer ties with Britain and towards a rapprochement with Germany.

Although relations with the French suffered, Makins was able to report to William Strang that the 'Americans have conclusively demonstrated that they are once more prepared to deal with us ... as their principal partners in world affairs'.[30] Makins added:

> we have a real chance of getting close together with the Americans and the Canadians over the whole range of economic policy and thereby moving towards

---

28 Hall Diaries, 11 September 1949.

29 Bullock, A., *Ernest Bevin Foreign Secretary*, London: Norton, 1983, p. 721.

30 Makins Papers, MS Sherfiled 523, Letter Makins to Strang, 16 September 1949.

> some form of closer economic union without at this stage raising any of the institutional and political difficulties with which this concept is surrounded.[31]

The difficulties Makins refers to were the effect a more open Anglo-American union would have on the governments of Europe and, indeed, on politicians, both British and American, some of whom favoured closer European integration.

William Strang succeeded Orme Sargent as the Permanent Under Secretary at the Foreign Office in February 1949; it was a positive move for Makins who was close to Strang. They had worked together during the war and they corresponded with each other, often outside formal channels, throughout their Foreign Office careers. Makins also joined Strang's newly constituted Permanent Under Secretary's Committee which was formed earlier in the year to consider long-term questions of foreign policy and to make recommendations to the Secretary of State. It was another vehicle of influence for Makins and one he used to cement the Foreign Office's view that Britain should not join an integrated, supra national European body. It was a view, of course, which never really encountered any substantial opposition.[32]

The Washington visit enabled Makins to cement his relationship with Oliver Franks and his Whitehall colleagues. As Makins pointed out in his memoirs the 'first eleven' took every opportunity to talk together and to discuss future policy and organisation. The extent to which this group was able to influence policy and appointments in Whitehall can be gauged from an entry in Robert Hall's diary:

> OSF [Franks] RM [Makins] EP [Plowden]and I [Hall] had some chat yesterday about bodies generally, and whether to move Hall-Patch from Paris. I should be sorry that this had to be done but it is very bad that he does not get on with Harriman [the American representative in Paris] ... We have decided that the next steps at home are to cut expenditure and to wake up the people at the Board of Trade doing the dollar export drive. It was also agreed by everyone ... that H[Harold]Wilson is no good, ought if possible to be shifted from the Board of Trade, and certainly ought not to succeed SC [Cripps]. If any young one is to do it, it is to be Gaitskell.[33]

Makins remained in Washington for talks on atomic energy matters while Bevin visited Canada. They met up again in New York and in early October set sail on the Cunarder *Queen Elizabeth* bound for England. It had been a gruelling six-

---

31 Ibid.

32 Strang, Lord. *The Diplomatic Career*, London: Andre Deutsch, 1962, p. 112.

33 *Robert Hall Diaries 1847–1953*, p. 83.

week visit but it was one which saw Makins' place in the first 11 confirmed by both ministers and officials.

Despite Makins' continuing emphasis on the importance of relations with America a significant part of his workload was concerned with bilateral relationships with other European countries. After the disruption caused by the war it was necessary to rebuild inter-European commercial and financial relationships. This was effected by the setting up, from 1947 onwards, of a variety of joint committees with other countries; as mentioned above these included France, Italy, Norway and the other Scandinavian countries. Typically each committee would meet twice a year: once in London and once in the other relevant capital. They continued to operate even after the European Economic Recovery Plan was put in place. In 1948 Hall-Patch chaired two of these committees, the Anglo-French and the Anglo-Italian committees, and after he was sent to Paris two vacancies occurred. Hall-Patch sought to stay on as chairman, but Orme Sargent, the Permanent Under Secretary at the time, stopped this, saying that Makins must be on the committees or he would not be able to perform his function properly.

There was also a challenge from outside the Foreign Office. The Board of Trade always felt that its representative should chair the committees but Bevin thought differently. Bevin explained to Harold Wilson, the then President of the Board of Trade, that 'so long as our trade had to be conducted on the present basis and foreign policy was so closely connected with, and indeed dominated by, trade and economic considerations, it was essential for the Foreign Secretary to claim, through his representative, a controlling influence on the handling of the negotiations'.[34] Wilson was no match for Bevin and Makins took the chairmanship of both committees. It is perhaps a testament to Makins' abilities and, indeed, Bevin's faith in them that when the Anglo-Norwegian committee was subsequently set up in 1949 he was appointed Chairman without discussion.

In the period from July 1948 to July 1952 there were seven meetings of the Anglo-French, ten of the Anglo-Italian, seven of the Anglo-Norwegian and two of the Anglo-Scandinavian committee. Makins attended all of these bar two; it was as Makins suggested a considerable element of his workload.[35] Much of the work was detailed and dull, covering issues such as French imports from the Sterling Area, negotiation of coal and tinplate exports to Italy, and Norwegian shipping contracts with Britain: it is not possible to discern any grand strategy or policy to emerge from their work. However the meetings, while overtly economic in their content, served a political purpose and were just another

---

[34] Lord Sherfield Memoirs, section entitled *Bilateral Economic Relationships* (Henceforth *Bilateral Relationships*), p. 1.

[35] *Bilateral Relationships*, p. 3.

example of how the reconstruction of post-war Europe was effected. It was also a further example of how Makins was able to extend his influence in Whitehall.

It was also a way in which he could further defend his Atlanticist ideals. In 1949 Jean Monnet (a senior French civil servant and the General Commissioner for French Modernisation Plan, 1946–52), perhaps conscious of Makins' and indeed the Foreign Office's instincts, approached Plowden to suggest joint planning of the British and the French economies over and above the structure of the bilateral committee's work. The suggestion had a political, as well as, economic one. Plowden reported that:

> Monnet explained that in his view Western Europe was a vacuum, on either side of which were the two great dynamic forces of Communism and American capitalism. He felt that this vacuum could be filled either by one of these two outside forces, or by the development of a Western European way of life.[36]

The message was clear and one that Makins did not like. Plowden sought Makins' views. Makins poured cold water on the idea, suggesting that the Foreign Office was wary of Monnet's motives. Makins knew Monnet from his days in Algiers and even at that time Monnet was arguing for a post-war Europe not constituted on the basis of national sovereignty but rather in the form of a federation of European States. Makins told Plowden 'whilst France was an extremely important ally of the United Kingdom and the Foreign Office was anxious to see a consolidation of the good relations we shared with the French Government, at the end of the day our special relationship with the United States was paramount and to be maintained at all costs'.[37] This was not the first, nor would it be the last time, that Makins turned away from the possibility of closer integration in Europe.

Makins' economic work at the Foreign Office encompassed Commonwealth affairs as well as American and European relations. Given the cards which Britain held in the immediate post-war period Bevin and Foreign Office officials could be said to have played them well. They had managed to persuade America to provide finance to Europe in the form of the European Recovery Plan, thus averting the economic collapse of Europe. Also, as a result of Bevin's leadership, the North Atlantic Treaty Organisation was formed in 1949, and the significant American involvement meant enhanced security for Europe. Britain, during Bevin's tenure, still, whether justifiably or not, retained the status of world power albeit behind the Soviet Union and America. As early as February 1949 Bevin also sought to persuade America and indeed, his colleagues that there was a danger that 'the

36 TNA, FO 371/77933, E.N. Plowden Note on four conversations with Monsieur Monnet 3 March–7 March 1949.

37 Plowden, *An Industrialist in the Treasury*, p. 74.

West's successes in Europe were being offset by an adverse shift in the balance of power in South East Asia'.[38] The victory of the communists in China, and the signing of the Sino Soviet Treaty was unless countered, bound to have an adverse effect on Britain's influence in the region.

This was the background to the Conference of Commonwealth Foreign Ministers, the so-called Colombo Conference, which took place in January 1950. It was the first Commonwealth Conference to take place outside of Britain and Makins went as the principal British Foreign Office advisor. The Conference, which was attended by the Foreign Ministers of all the major Commonwealth countries, considered a number of issues including recognition of China, the situation in Vietnam and the Japanese Peace Treaty. The overriding issue was to find the best means of countering communist influence in the region. It was decided that a formal defence pact for the region was inappropriate at that time, and that the best defence against the spread of communism was to raise the living standards of those living in the region. During the opening session of the conference John Spender, the Australian Foreign Minister, spoke strongly in favour of a coordinated economic approach to the region. That evening Bevin sent Makins to meet with Spender in order to develop the idea further. Makins discovered that Spender's ideas were consistent with those of the British. Spender had produced a paper on the subject, and Makins was able to persuade him that a new executive with a Commonwealth nucleus to coordinate the approach was needed to give the ideas full effect.

Makins was asked to chair a sub-committee of the Conference to put together a paper for consideration the following day. The committee produced an agreed text which was presented and adopted, almost without amendment, by the Conference. The paper was, in effect, the first draft of the Colombo Plan and Makins in his memoirs, with some justification, 'claimed to be its midwife'.[39] The Colombo Plan, sometimes seen as the Asian Marshall Plan, fostered economic cooperation in Asia and while the sums raised were less significant than those for the Marshall Plan it nevertheless forged an important link between the West and Asia. By the end of the decade 26 countries, including America and Japan, had joined the Plan and it still continues, in association with the UN, to operate today.

---

[38] Bullock, *Ernest Bevin*, p. 743.

[39] Lord Sherfield's Memoirs, section entitled *The Colombo Conference 9th–14th January 1950 and its Aftermath* (Henceforth *Colombo Conference)*, p. 14.

Bevin's health deteriorated rapidly over the following 12 months. Dean Acheson recorded his feeling on a visit to London in May 1950 to discuss the Schuman Plan:[40]

> I found Ernest Bevin in distressing shape when I met him and his staff in midmorning. He had recently undergone a painful operation and was taking sedative drugs that made him doze off, sometimes quite soundly, during discussion. His staff seemed accustomed to it, though I found it disconcerting.[41]

Indeed his staff were accustomed to it: they had been supporting Bevin throughout his tenure as Foreign Secretary. Makins records an incident in Colombo when he met Bevin upon his arrival and found him in 'a very poor state and speechless'. It fell to Makins to take him to his residence to revive him. Bevin was effectively forced to resign in March 1951and was replaced by Herbert Morrison. Bevin wrote to Makins:

> I cannot leave the FO without writing to let you know how grateful I shall always be for the loyal support and help which you always gave me. My task was a very heavy one but my burdens were greatly eased by your help. Our close association will always be a very happy memory.[42]

Makins never developed a close relationship with Morrison, who was regarded as less effective than Bevin.

Bevin's concern with the potential spread of communism in the Far East was soon shown to be well founded. On 25 June 1950 Kim Il Sung the leader of the North Korea (or the Democratic People's Republic of Korea) launched an attack on South Korea. The invasion was designed to 'liberate' the south and so unify the two Koreas. Two days later President Truman announced that the United States would deploy military force on behalf of the UN to defend the South. Initially the North Koreans were successful and virtually overran the South. But a counter attack by the UN forces led by General Macarthur succeeded in pushing the North Koreans back. By November 1950 the UN forces had reached the Yalu River which formed the border between China and North Korea. China then entered the conflict and loose talk by President Truman, which implied that he might use the nuclear bomb, led Attlee to cross the Atlantic to dissuade him from doing so. The meetings between Attlee

40 A French proposal to place the German and French coal, iron and steel industries under a single authority which could then be joined by other countries in effect a supra national authority.

41 Acheson, D. , *Present at Creation*, New York: Norton, 1969, p. 384.

42 Makins Papers MS 451, letter Bevin to Makins, 22 March 1951.

and Truman took place in early December 1950. Makins who was chosen to accompany Attlee took part in the discussions with the President, and attended all the subsidiary meetings. The talks were a success in the sense that Attlee was directly briefed by the Americans and he did cause the Americans to pause and reflect on their actions. Makins' interventions as such were not particularly decisive or impressive, but his presence there did much to enhance his status within Whitehall. Even though Makins had crossed Attlee during the war, he became closer to him during the post-war period largely because of his role in respect of atomic energy, and it is to this area that we now turn. In order to do so we need to go back to early 1947, the period when Makins left Washington and returned to the Foreign Office.

At the end of World War II Britain had no nuclear programme of her own and no nuclear weapons. In October 1945 Attlee decided to set up the Atomic Energy Research Establishment (AERE) at Harwell and in December of that year gave the go ahead for the building of an atomic pile to be used for the production of plutonium. By the time Makins had returned to the Foreign Office in February 1947 tension between the West and the Soviets had increased considerably. The Soviet Union was now increasingly seen as a potential enemy rather than as an ex wartime ally with benign intentions. Partly in response to this, but also because of a lack of faith in any proposals for the international control of atomic energy and Britain's unwillingness to acquiesce in the American monopoly of atomic power, ministers decided in January 1947 to produce a British atomic bomb. Attlee issued a directive that it should take priority over other government projects.

As Chairman of the Official Committee on Atomic Energy Makins played a part in certain aspects of Britain's post-war atomic energy discussions but it is important not to exaggerate his role. The individuals who played by far the most important role in the development and management of Britain's post-war atomic energy programme were William Penney, Christopher Hinton and John Cockcroft. Broadly speaking, Penney, who was a key figure in the American project during the war, was responsible for designing the weapon, Hinton, the former Head of ICI's Alkali Division, was responsible for the atomic piles which were to produce the fissile material for the bomb and Cockctoft, the pre-war splitter of the atom, headed the research laboratory at Harwell and was responsible for advising on the methods of producing plutonium. The committee Makins chaired was only one of 20 committees which considered the subject.[43]

Makins' central role was to consider the international questions raised by atomic energy. This included consideration of the part Britain might play in the international control of atomic energy, the development of a

[43] Gowing, *Independence and Deterrence*, p. 58.

Commonwealth policy, and, most important of all, the continuation of the work he undertook while he was in Washington, the consideration of Anglo-American cooperation on atomic energy matters. We saw in the previous chapter how Britain sought and failed to persuade America to share certain information on atomic energy. We also noted that Britain's only card in any negotiations with the Americans on the sharing of information was Britain's access to the raw material needed to produce atomic bombs (a significant amount of uranium ore came from Commonwealth countries). One of Makins' last acts while he was in Washington immediately before he returned to the Foreign Office in February 1947 was to visit Dean Acheson and try to break the deadlock that existed on atomic energy cooperation. The initiative failed. By the end of 1947, however, discussions regarding the possibility of continued cooperation had been resurrected; they led to the so called Modus Vivendi Agreement.

In May 1947 Dean Acheson, at the insistence of the newly formed US Atomic Energy Commission (a government agency set up to foster and control the development of peacetime atomic energy), informed the Joint Congressional Committee for Atomic Energy (JCAE) of a number of secret wartime agreements between Britain and America.[44] This included the Quebec Agreement (discussed in the previous chapter) which contained a clause requiring, in effect, British approval before America could use the atomic bomb. Acheson also informed the Congressional Committee that, as a result of existing agreements, stocks of supplies of raw material needed for the manufacture of the atomic bombs was held on a 50:50 basis with Britain. Matters were made worse by the fact that given America's atomic bomb production programme she was likely to run out of uranium ore in the foreseeable future, but Britain, which had no immediate need for such stocks, had a significant surplus. When the committee heard Acheson's statement, the 'room erupted in indignation and anger. Several members walked out at the very thought that we'd [America] have to ask anybody's permission to use these weapons'.[45] The Chairman of the Committee, Senator Bourke Hickenlooper, wrote to George Marshall (the US Secretary of State) telling him that the agreements with Britain were 'ill advised' and must be 'mutually rescinded'. As a result of these revelations Britain's friends in Washington, people such as Dean Acheson and George Marshall, found themselves in some political difficulties with Congress.

While this was taking place, and possibly in response to it, Makins presided over a meeting of the Official Committee held on 10 June 1947

---

[44] The section in this chapter which refers to the Modus Vivendi Agreement owes a significant debt to Chapter 5 of The Marshall Plan as contained in Wevill, *Britain and America*.

[45] Paul, *Nuclear Rivals*, p. 117.

which recommended that Britain should not seek to force the United States to cooperate under the secret agreements, but rather that Britain should seek a 'modus vivendi' or working arrangement with America which would replace the secret wartime agreements. This was a clear move away from the position Britain had previously adopted and was a reflection of the new realities. One reality was that Congress had the ability to thwart the Administration's ambitions, some of which included the provision of aid and support for Britain and Europe.

Makins informed Bevin on 17 November 1947 that there were signs that the Americans might be prepared to share information on their atomic energy programme, but that they needed a new agreement in order to effect this. The British Embassy then told Makins that the State Department was pressing for urgent talks. The urgency came from the fact that the Congressional hearings, which would be needed before the European Recovery Plan (the legislation containing the Marshall Aid proposals) could pass through Congress, were scheduled to begin in early January 1948. The Administration feared that certain Senators would challenge the Marshall Aid proposals if the existing wartime atomic energy agreements, including those related to the holding of raw material stocks, were not replaced. Lord Inverchapel, the British Ambassador, wrote to Makins informing him that the talks would be held within the framework of the Combined Policy Committee (CPC), and that the objective was to 'establish a new basis for cooperation in future and thereby remove the US-UK and the US-Canadian misunderstandings in this field'.[46] At the same time Inverchapel cabled Bevin informing him that the talks were sufficiently important to justify sending Makins.[47]

The Americans convened a meeting of the CPC for 10 December 1947. It was decided to send Sir John Cockcroft, David Pierson (Ministry of Supply) and Makins to Washington under different cover stories. It was felt appropriate to keep the talks secret so that the Anglo-American-Canadian grouping was not seen to be 'ganging up against the Soviets at a time of great international tension'.[48] Given that Donald Maclean, soon to be exposed as a Soviet spy, was Secretary to the CPC, such secrecy was to little avail: the Soviets were probably getting a blow by blow account. Prior to leaving for Washington the Official Committee, chaired by Makins, drew up a brief for the talks; this was approved by a meeting of ministers chaired by Attlee on 10 December. Makins attended this meeting of ministers, thereby missing the first meeting of the CPC held on 10 December. In fact Makins did not arrive in Washington until 11 December.

---

[46] TNA, AB 16/2022, Inverchapel to Foreign Office, 2 December 1947.

[47] TNA, FO 800/438, Inverchapel to Bevin, 4 December 1947.

[48] Lord Sherfield Memoirs, London 1947–1952 Annex I *Atomic Energy* (Henceforth *Atomic Energy*), p. 17.

The priorities for the Americans were to secure access to Britain's supply of raw materials and to alter the Quebec Agreement. The British saw things differently. Makins reported 'We regard it as essential that exchange of information should have at least as firm a place on the agenda as allocation of raw materials. Our objective is a comprehensive agreement on the future basis of collaboration, and our agreement on allocation would be dependent on a satisfactory agreement on exchange of information'.[49] At the meeting of the ministers on 10 December it was also made clear that 'Above all it is essential not to yield to any American demand to transfer some of our existing substantial stocks of uranium ore out of this country'.[50] As Septimus Paul pointed out in *Nuclear Rivals* the British and American negotiating teams met in Washington with different priorities. 'The Americans wanted to gain possession of a stockpile that the British were unwilling to yield. On the other side, the British sought full atomic collaboration, which the Americans could not and would not concede'.[51]

In his memoirs Makins records that he was 'much impressed by the change in the American attitude towards cooperation on atomic energy with Britain and Canada which had taken place since [he] was last in Washington in early 1947'.[52] Furthermore, Makins reported at the time 'there is now a general desire to go as far as possible to implement the intention of past agreements'. Makins put this down to a variety of motives, concluding that 'anxiety about the raw material position is certainly not the only, and perhaps not the main reason'.[53] This is something of a contrast to the American position as recorded in its official history of events. The American authorities had agreed that they would 'strive to abrogate the wartime agreements, to acquire British ore stocks, to get a much greater share of Congo production,[54] to restrict the supply of raw material in Britain to a minimum, and to obtain British and Canadian support for ore negotiations with South Africa. In return the United States would give *some* information'.[55] Yet again Makins had put too much of a generous slant on American motives.

After the formal meeting of the CPC on 10 December the informal talks began. Discussion took place over several days and centred on three areas: technical cooperation, the allocation of raw materials and the form of any

49 TNA, AB 16/2022, Makins to Munro, 3 December 1947.

50 TNA, AB 16/2022, Cabinet Offices to Joint Staff Mission, 10 December 1947.

51 Paul, *Nuclear Rivals*, p. 125.

52 *Atomic Energy*, p. 19.

53 *Atomic Energy*, p. 47.

54 The Belgium Congo was a rich source of ore and Britain, which had close contacts with the Belgium government, had managed to secure significant supplies.

55 Richard Hewlett and Francis Duncan, *History of the USAEC, vol. II Atomic Shield, 1947–1952,* Pennsylvania State University Press, 1969, p. 279.

new agreement. Cockcroft and Vannevar Bush (an American member of the CPC and the Director of the Office of Scientific Research and Development) drew up a list detailing the areas where cooperation would be forthcoming. According to Cockcroft and Makins the list was sufficient for the development of Britain's nuclear programme in the following year. Others, however, were less sanguine and felt that it fell short of what was needed, indeed, what was expected. Raw material allocation was to prove trickier. Notwithstanding ministers' insistence that raw material already in Britain was not to be allocated to America, a formula was devised by Makins and Robert Lovett (US Under Secretary of State, 1947–9) whereby Britain would transfer up to two thirds of her raw material stocks should America's build programme require it. This was in addition to America being allocated all of the uranium ore supplies produced in the Congo during 1948 and 1949. The argument Makins gave for abandoning his instructions was that when the instructions were drawn up before they left London, they did not know what the American supplies of raw material were or indeed how significant their nuclear programme was. Discussions regarding the form of the agreement involved making all the wartime agreements including the Quebec Agreement null and void. Thus Britain would lose her right of veto over America's use of the atomic bomb.

On 19 December Makins, Cockcroft and Pierson returned to London to persuade ministers to accept the deal they had negotiated. On 23 December Makins briefed the Official Committee, and he met with the Ministerial Committee early in the New Year. He recommended to ministers that they should accept the formula that had been worked out in Washington. He pointed out that:

> the moment is very favourable for an agreement which will finally wipe out the misunderstanding and bitterness of the past and put our relationship on a solid basis. It will be wise to settle the problem before the rats can get at it. No doubt there will be argument in the future and some difficulties ... but the evidence is clear that the responsible men in the United States are full of goodwill and prepared at the moment not only to accept an arrangement on the general lines proposed but to implement it.[56]

It was not to be the case as we shall see below. Nevertheless ministers accepted Makins' recommendation and on 5 January he returned to Washington to conclude an agreement on the basis of the new instructions. The agreement provided that: a) all wartime agreements were null and void except of course those related to raw material; b) all supplies of uranium ore extracted in the Congo during 1948 and 1949 were to be shipped to America; c) if the American

[56] *Atomic Energy*, p. 24.

programme demanded it then raw material supplies would be shipped to America from the British stockpile; and d) there was to be an exchange of information in a limited number of areas. It is not surprising that Senator Vandenberg, a member of the JCAE and the most senior Republican member of the Senate, told Lovett, the leader of the American negotiating team, that the 'negotiations represented a considerable accomplishment, and that more had been obtained than he thought possible'.[57]

The Modus Vivendi Agreement has been the subject of criticism by Gowing and others. The main criticism seems to be that Britain, in agreeing to nullify the wartime agreements, gave up too much. The principal example given is the loss of the veto on the American use of the atomic bomb at a time when American bombers were being stationed in Britain. Furthermore, it is argued that the areas where atomic energy cooperation was agreed were very narrow, and the broadening of cooperation which was promised at the time never materialised. Makins was very sensitive to this criticism and in an article written as a review of Gowing's book refutes much of it. However he is not very convincing. For example the argument he presents for conceding the right of veto over Americans' use of the atomic bomb is that it was 'unrealistic and unenforceable'. This may be so but it was still part of an agreement which the Americans were seeking to alter. Makins, in defending the Modus Vivendi, concedes that it did not live up to expectation, but he does argue that, as Sir John Cockcroft pointed out, some useful information was received at a critical moment in Britain's nuclear programme. An interesting question for us, however, is not so much whether the agreement was a good or a bad one, a subject which has been debated elsewhere, but the extent to which it should be regarded a 'Makins' agreement' and the extent to which Makins fully understood the American motives.

Certain historians clearly identify Makins with the agreements. For example, Saul Kelly 'he was largely responsible therefore, for Britain concluding the modus vivendi',[58] or Edwards 'Makins determination to seal the Modus Vivendi at any cost'.[59] But is it right to identify Makins with the agreement in this way? Is it not part of the exaggeration of Makins' role in this field, fuelled perhaps by his subsequent Chairmanship of the UK Atomic Energy Authority? It might possibly be argued that Makins led the negotiation, but he was not alone and, indeed, was surrounded by highly competent people, such as Sir John Cockcroft, Gordon Munro (the Embassy representative for atomic energy affairs), and David Peirson, all of whom knew the subject well. Furthermore, before

---

[57] FRUS,1948, Vol. I., Memorandum of conversation by E. Gullion, 7 January 1948, p. 678.

[58] Kelly, Saul. 'No Ordinary Foreign Office Official: Sir Roger Makins and Anglo American Atomic Relations 1945–1955', *Contemporary British History,* 14:4 (Winter 2000), p. 114.

[59] Edwards, Roger Makins 'Mr Atom', p. 33.

concluding the agreement Makins and others needed to return to London to present his arguments firstly to the Official Committee and then, to Ministers and the Chiefs of Staff. Makins did, of course, recommend acceptance of the agreement but there is no suggestion or evidence that Makins misled people, or that he did not present the arguments fairly. At the end of the day all of these people, with one or two exceptions accepted the agreement and supported it.

While it might not have been a 'Makins' agreement' one criticism which might be levelled at Makins was his failure to understand properly the American motive for wanting talks in the first place. Perhaps he was blinded by the fact that he was too close to certain Americans. 'Roger Makins was highly regarded by the American Administration for his part in smoothing the path of Anglo US relations during the Labour Administration, regarded in some American quarters as more malleable than a Conservative one ... The Americans thought his marriage to an American advantageous in making him "thoroughly familiar with American attitudes" and ranked him "a good talker", who always showed "friendliness and cooperation in dealing with U.S. officials".'[60] Makins correctly understood that the State Department contained many who were enthusiastic to support renewed atomic energy cooperation with Britain, such as George Kennan, George Marshall and Robert Lovett. But he failed to fully understand the fact that these men were using the false promise of continued cooperation as a means to extract concessions, and in particular raw materials from the British. Increasingly, he chose to believe arguments advanced by the Administration that renewed cooperation as an attempt to strengthen the West, rather than as a means of securing the passage of the European Recovery Act through Congress. Makins' friends were doing the bidding of Congress. His closeness to Americans is a theme which recurs throughout this book and one must question whether or not it was ultimately in Britain's interest to have an official such as Makins so close to the American Administration.

The Modus Vivendi worked relatively well for the first six months of 1948 and on 24 June Cockcroft was able to report to the Official Committee that satisfactory progress was being made on the exchange of technical information. However, a number of developments were to lead to further restrictions on Anglo-American cooperation in the area. One was the decision by the British to reveal the explicit existence of the atomic bomb project. Attlee had always been against any publicity for the project but was persuaded that the secrecy surrounding it was causing delays in the programme. It was decided to put the matter in the public domain by way of a planted Parliamentary question to A.V. Alexander, the Minister of Defence, on 14 May 1948. This in turn led to the existence of Britain's nuclear weapons programme being formally notified to the Americans. The confirmation that Britain had been developing its own

60 Edwards, *Roger Makins 'Mr Atom'*, p. 32.

atomic bomb was no surprise to many in America, particularly members of the Administration, but it was a surprise to others, notably Congressmen, who were taken aback by the fact that the British were developing nuclear weapons.

Senators Hickenlooper and Vandenberg learnt of the British plans and did not want any cooperation with the British on any areas concerned with weapons production. In addition, the Senators believed that the Modus Vivendi did not cover such areas in any event. In fact the agreement was silent on the matter of weapons information and deliberately so. The original intention in January 1948 was to leave it out, but hope that once Senators had become more complacent on the issue of exchange of information, the area of weapons technology could be reintroduced in due course. Makins was complicit in this ruse, which was designed to mislead Congressmen. In June, when the issue was under discussion, he wrote to Cockcroft 'You will remember that during the negotiations in January we were given the tip not to press for exchange on this topic [weapons information] as the US side were not ready to agree. Ministers, therefore, decided to leave the question on one side but to raise it later on when collaboration had made some progress'.[61]

Once the fact that Britain was working on a nuclear weapons programme became clear, the issue of continued cooperation with the British became an even greater source of friction between the various power bases in Washington. There was continued support from the Administration and most members of the AEC, but resistance on the part of Congress and the military. Furthermore, the concerns led to a tightening up of the information given under the existing provisions, and an aversion to extending the scope of the Modus Vivendi as had been anticipated.

Makins, who should have understood the politics better, exacerbated the problem by agreeing with Cockcroft that just after the Senators had been informed of the British project in May 1948 was a good time to seek an extension in the areas of cooperation. Makins' arguments were that with Congress adjourning at the end of June Senators would be distracted, and that he was keen to seek agreement before the Presidential elections in November 1948. There was at that time a fear that many of the officials with whom Makins had negotiated the agreement might not return to the Administration if Truman lost the election. On 25 August 1948 the Official Committee, with the agreement of Attlee, decided to seek further cooperation.

During August the Americans had met with Dr Woodward the scientific attaché at the Embassy and told him that the JCAE was disturbed by Britain's nuclear weapons programme: the information given under the existing arrangements would have to be carefully policed, and it was very unlikely that there would be an extension in the areas of cooperation. They suggested that

[61] TNA, AB 16/388, Makins to Cockcroft, 9 June 1948.

now was the wrong time to make the approach. This conversation was relayed to London and the conclusion on timing was strongly supported by the then ambassador, Oliver Franks.[62] The advice from the embassy was ignored by Makins and others in London. Then, unfortunately, London compounded their error by deciding to approach the military directly rather than go through the State Department or the AEC.

Predictably the military were against any extension in the areas of exchange of information, and the Joint Chiefs of Staff recorded this on 27 September 1948.[63] The American military were concerned about the security aspects of the British nuclear programme. This was related not only to the lingering doubts about the loyalty of certain Labour Party members, but also because of the strategic position of Britain with its proximity to the Soviet Union. As Makins recorded in his memoirs 'The Americans regarded Britain as vulnerable, not so much to a Soviet military invasion, but to aerial bombing, subversion and espionage'.[64] Makins, as head of the Official Committee making recommendations to Attlee, had made two mistakes. He had not listened to the advice from the Embassy, and he had decided to approach the military. Oliver Franks lodged a formal protest with the Americans, bemoaning the decision of 27 September that there would be no extension in the areas of cooperation, but the protest was to no avail. Yet again the Administration's hands were tied by both the Military and by Congress. As 1948 drew to a close, atomic energy cooperation was again in a state of limbo.

The re-election of President Truman in 1949 led to a number of changes in the Administration. George Marshall was replaced by Dean Acheson as Secretary of State and Robert Lovett was replaced by James Webb as the Under Secretary of State. They were supporters of Britain and Makins knew both men well. The new administration wanted to initiate talks with the British, both because the Modus Vivendi was coming to an end and because the Administration wanted to integrate atomic energy policy more closely with foreign policy. The administration, however, remained wary of the JCAE even though the new chairman was a Democrat. It delayed any talks with the British until it had had time to smooth the ground with Congressmen on the issue. It also wanted to wait until Congress had approved the North Atlantic Treaty, which it did in on 4 April 1949.

Talks began in the forum of the CPC on 20 September 1949. It is interesting to recall the background to these talks. The pound, as noted earlier, had been devalued only two days before and Makins was in Washington dealing with this issue as well as in Washington for the atomic energy talks. To add to the mix,

62 Paul, *Nuclear Rivals*, p. 137.

63 FRUS 1948, Vol. I, part II, Arneson to Acting Secretary of State, 27 September 1948.

64 *Atomic Energy*, p. 32.

on 19 September the Soviets detonated their first atomic bomb, the timing of which came as a complete surprise to both the British and the Americans. They had expected the Soviets to develop the bomb but not until the mid 1950s. The event galvanised the minds of those present. After considerable discussion the CPC produced an interim report which contained tentative proposals. The talks were then suspended while the Administration discussed the issues with Congressional leaders. Makins returned to London and gave an account of the talks to the Official Committee on 18 October and the Ministerial Committee on 1 November.

In essence the Americans were concerned about two points, the amount of raw material available if Britain pursued her own weapons programme as vigorously as she intended, and the advances made by the Soviets. The first point could be met by Britain reducing her nuclear programme; the second by partially integrating the British and American programmes in order to avoid duplication of effort and so speed up the West's production of nuclear bombs. Makins supported both proposals and this was his recommendation: 'Britain should reduce its program from three piles to two in return for full technical cooperation and an integrated weapons program.'[65] He justified this proposed deal on the basis that 'it did not preclude Britain building more piles as long as they did not increase the demand for raw materials during the period of the agreement'.[66] He concluded that 'if we are prepared to accept two piles instead of three and the principal of integration of weapons production, and if we are prepared to go slow in our relations with other countries, it should be possible, ... to reach a satisfactory agreement for full cooperation over the whole field of atomic energy'.[67] The ministerial committee, with some reservations, decided to sanction these recommendations.

Makins returned to Washington at the end of November 1949 to resume talks. Compromises were sought and offered by both sides and, while the Americans sought to limit nuclear activities in Britain because of her fear that Britain might be overrun by the Soviets, the British held firm and insisted on having their own fully operational nuclear programme, albeit curtailed to economise on raw materials. By early January 1950 there was some prospect of an agreement, even one which Senators would accept. Unfortunately, the Fuchs spy scandal broke and 'this completely wrecked things as far as progress towards greater cooperation between us [British] and the Americans in the atomic energy field [was] concerned'.[68] Cooperation was, for the

[65] *Atomic Energy*, p. 44.

[66] Ibid.

[67] *Atomic Energy*, p. 45.

[68] *Atomic Energy*, p. 52.

moment, at an end and it was not resurrected until the late 1950s under the Eisenhower administration.

There were, in fact, several spy scandals around this period. The first, the Julius Klaus Fuchs case, broke on 24 January 1950. Fuchs headed the Theoretical Physics Division at the British Atomic Energy Research Establishment at Harwell. He was a naturalised German who moved to Britain in 1933, and was known to have communist sympathies. Nevertheless he was part of the team of British scientists sent to America during the war, and worked at Los Alamos from December 1944 to June 1946. He was intimately involved on the atomic bomb project. The second case was Bruno Pontecorvo, another naturalised nuclear physicist who defected to the Soviet Union in September 1950. He also worked at Harwell, and during the war he worked with Cockcroft at the Canada atomic energy plants. In both these cases it was the work of the FBI and not MI6 which initially led to their discovery. The third case, and perhaps the one that convinced the Americans they could no longer trust the British at all in this regard, was the Guy Burgess and Donald Maclean case. Makins knew both Burgess and Maclean, and had a close connection with Maclean.

Donald Maclean worked in the Chancellery section of the British Embassy in Washington from May 1944 until November 1948. As well as being responsible for Embassy security Maclean, a second secretary, assisted Makins with his atomic energy work. Makins noted that 'Donald was a reserved, reticent person. He was faultlessly efficient and hardworking and meticulous in security matters ... There was nothing in his behaviour to arouse unfavourable comment or suspicion, nor were any adverse reports received from either the security service or our subordinates, or other sources'. Makins returned to London in February 1947 and in November 1948 Maclean was transferred to Cairo. Here Maclean suffered an alcoholic breakdown and was returned home in May 1950 where, after a six-month period of recuperation, he was installed as the Head of the American Department in the Foreign Office. The American Department by that time was supervised by Makins. In October 1950, shortly after Maclean's return to the Foreign Office, Makins was informed that Maclean was under suspicion for espionage and that he needed to be careful with regard to the information Maclean was given access to. Makins also knew Guy Burgess but did not work with him directly. Burgess was in Washington in the late 1940s but was sent home by Oliver Franks for a series of misdemeanours and he became the personal assistant to Hector McNeil (Parliamentary Under Secretary, 1945–50). Makins' comment on Burgess was that he 'took an instant dislike to him and avoided contact with him was much as possible. He appeared as untrustworthy as Donald Maclean appeared trustworthy'.[69] On the evening of Friday 25 May 1951 both Maclean and Burgess fled the country, ultimately ending up in the Soviet Union.

On that Friday evening at around 7.00 pm Makins 'by the merest chance' ran into Maclean in the courtyard of the Foreign Office. Maclean, who was carrying a parcel under his arm, informed Makins that he was on his way to his house in the country and would remain there all weekend. Makins says that he had no reason to doubt this story but then says that he went back to the office to see if the security officer, Carey Foster was around in order to inform him of this encounter. Makins does not say why. The security office was closed and Makins, already late for a dinner engagement, decided not to press the matter or to raise the alarm. Makins' rationale was that he thought Maclean was under surveillance by the Security Service and, therefore, there was no need to take action. Maclean was, in fact, under surveillance but only as far as the station, so when he got to the country he was free to abscond. There is clearly an argument here to suggest that Makins should have been more diligent. He obviously had suspicions but apparently decided that dinner was more important. Makins, in his account of the Maclean disappearance, also fails to mention that the Foreign Office security department got into a bit of a 'flap' on the Saturday morning when Maclean failed to show up for work. (It was normal practice at that time to work on Saturday mornings.) The issue was 'resolved by Makins' admission that he had forgotten to report that he had given Maclean, who was subordinate to him, the Saturday off'.[70] Similarly, agitation was caused on the following Monday morning when Maclean failed to turn up again; on this occasion 'Makins' had thought it possible that he had agreed to Maclean taking the Monday off as well. Consequently, it was not until Tuesday that it was thought for certain that Maclean had fled. Makins' account of these events, as given in his memoirs, might, at best, be described as selective. Also, in Makins' account he is dismissive of the damage that Maclean might have caused: 'In the Washington period I do not think he did very much harm or, indeed, that he was in a position to do so.'[71] Reflecting on his work in the American Department Makins indicates that 'Maclean's contribution [to the Soviets] could only have been of marginal value'.[72] This is not the view taken by certain others. Richard Aldrich devotes a chapter to the impact of Burgess and Maclean's espionage activities and concludes 'It is now clear that Moscow received the cream of British policy papers during the

---

69 Lord Sherfield's Memoirs, section entitled *Burgess and Maclean* (Henceforth *Burgess and Maclean*), p. 4.

70 Reilly Memoirs, p. 22.

71 *Burgess and Maclean*, p. 4.

72 *Burgess and Maclean*, p. 5.

first decade of the Cold War. Donald Maclean alone had been well positioned to deliver such material'.[73]

The Maclean affair, and Makins' connection with it, was resurrected in 1955 when Lord Reading (Minister of State, 1953–7) in response to a question about the Maclean affair, and the Foreign Office's handling of it, indicated that at the time 'Makins had been watching Maclean closely'.[74] This was interpreted by the *Daily Express* as meaning that Makins 'ran the enquiry' and 'watched, checked and cleared Maclean'.[75] Makins protested vigorously to Ivone Kirkpatrick who had taken over from William Strang as Permanent Under Secretary in 1953, 'I do not mind taking whatever responsibility was mine but I don't want to be tagged with responsibilities which were not mine and with duties which it was not my business to perform ... I thought the rule was that Ministers should suffer for the mistakes of civil servants, not vice versa'.[76] Lord Reading was made to correct the impression he had given. There does not appear to be any lasting effect on Makins' career as a result of the Maclean incidents either in 1951 or in 1955. It is ironic to note, however, that at least for a time, Makins, by virtue of his presence in Washington between 1944 and 1947, was one of the prime suspects for the source of the leaks to the Soviets.

In October 1951, four months after the Burgess/Maclean case, Attlee's second Labour government was succeeded by Churchill's Conservative government. The atomic energy policy of the new government remained largely the same, in part, because Lord Cherwell, Churchill's influential adviser, had kept in touch with the Labour government's atomic energy programme and supported it. Churchill himself, however, was out of date, still believing that the Quebec Agreement was extant and still wanting a joint project with the Americans. Cherwell managed to persuade Churchill of the merits of Britain having her own programme and how, in the end, that would lead to greater Anglo-American cooperation. Perhaps the most significant change, at least for Makins, was that the Ministerial Committee was wound up and Makins, as Chairman of the Official Committee, reported to Cherwell. With this change Makins' influence in regard to atomic energy policy declined: it was Cherwell who now advised the Prime Minister.

Makins did accompany Churchill and his party on his trip to America in January 1952 (see below) where he played a minor supporting role in the atomic energy discussions which were led by a combination of Churchill and Cherwell.

---

[73] Aldrich, Richard, *Hidden Hand Britain America and Cold War Secret Intelligence*, London: John Murray 2001, p. 422.

[74] Makins Papers, MS Sherfield MS 525, Foreign Office Telegram No. 4897 to Washington Embassy, 25 October 1955.

[75] Makins Papers, MS Sherfield MS 525, Letter Makins to Kirkpatrick, 29 October 1955.

[76] Makins Papers, MS Sherfield MS 525, a further letter Makins to Kirkpatrick, 29 October 1955.

The talks failed to secure any greater cooperation and Makins reported to the Official Committee on 23 January that Truman had 'made it clear that it was politically impossible for him to assist in Anglo-American technical cooperation by seeking further amendments to the McMahon Act from Congress before the November 1952 Presidential election'.[77] The Administration had lost the will to find ways around the McMahon Act.

Makins at least had the consolation of being Chairman of the Official Committee at the time Britain detonated her first nuclear bomb at Monte Bello, Australia on 3 October 1952. As Gowing has pointed out, the British demonstration of the success of her own atomic energy project was probably one of the factors which encouraged the much fuller American cooperation which developed in the mid to late 1950s.[78] Makins chaired his last meeting of the Official Committee in December 1952. The next chapter will consider the part he played in the continuing discussions while he was serving as the Ambassador in Washington.

The year 1952 was to be the last year in which Makins worked in the Foreign Office. It began, as noted above, with a trip to America. After their success in the October 1951 election Churchill and Eden, who had once again become Foreign Secretary, were keen to re-establish relations with the American administration. It fell to Makins, however, to warn Churchill that 'Truman is not FDR [Roosevelt] and his method of working is different'. Truman's method of operation was more formal than Roosevelt's; he also attended meetings with his advisers and did not make snap decisions.[79] Makins noted in a Memorandum entitled 'Objectives in the Washington Talks':

> The Anglo-American partnership is difficult to manage owing to the increasing disparity of power within it. We are on a difficult wicket at the moment because, however we try to disguise it we are back on the breadline for the third time in six years. The Prime Ministers' arrival in the USA will coincide with another disquieting disclosure about the run on reserves. This added to the impression already created in the USA by Persia [Iran] and Egypt that the British Empire is in liquidation.[80]

These remarks are an early indication that Makins understood the changing nature of the Anglo-American relationship, something which neither Churchill nor Eden had quite grasped.

77 *Atomic Energy*, p. 63.

78 *Atomic Energy*, p. 67.

79 TNA, FO 371/90938, Minute by Makins, 29 November 1951.

80 Ibid.

The party of over 30 people, including Makins, boarded the Queen Mary on 30 December 1951. Churchill clearly had certain reservations about Makins. At one point during the voyage Churchill turned to Eden and asked 'Tell me, Anthony, about Roger Makins, You like him? Is he good?' Eden replied 'Yes he is very able but the Prof. [Lord Cherwell] here knows all about him'. Cherwell spoke well of Makins and indicated that Makins had passed top of the Foreign Office list, had a 'brilliant first' from Oxford and was a Fellow of All Souls. Eden added 'And he's sensible in spite of that'.[81] On one occasion after the party had arrived in America the Prime Minister was putting the finishing touches to a speech he was about to give to Congress. Churchill needed to refer to the Korean War, which was still continuing. Churchill asked Makins 'If the Chinese cross the Yalu River our reply will be – what'? Makins immediately replied 'Prompt resolute and effective'. 'Excellent' said Churchill and the words became a part of his speech.[82] This trip to America gave Makins a further opportunity to cement his many relationships within the Washington establishment; it also, however, enabled Makins to raise his profile with the Prime Minister. This was important if he was to secure the post he perhaps coveted most of all.

[81] Lord Moran, *Churchill: The Struggle for Survival 1940/65*, London: Constable, 1966, p. 352.

[82] Colville, John, *Foot-Prints in Time Memories*, London: Collins, 1976, p. 234.

Chapter 5

The Ambassador and the Foreign Office

In June 1952 Anthony Eden, then Foreign Secretary, wrote a paper entitled *British Overseas Obligations.* In it he set out Britain's worldwide obligations and concluded that 'on a longer view, it must be assumed that the maintenance of the present scale of overseas commitments will permanently overstrain our economy'.[1] One of the major obligations, 'second only to Western Europe', was in Egypt and the Middle East. Eden concluded that the only practical way to remove the strain on the economy was to share the burden with the United States, the only Western country capable of assuming it. He wrote 'our aim should be to persuade the United States to assume the real burdens ... while retaining for ourselves as much political control – and hence prestige and influence – as we can'. He ended: 'the more gradually and inconspicuously we can transfer the real burdens from our own to American shoulders, the less damage we shall do to our position and influence in the world.'[2] Eden wanted it both ways – control of policy without financial commitment.

The Americans did not prove to be as malleable as Eden had hoped. While they shared similar objectives for the Middle East, their approach was different. This led to considerable tension between the two countries. Eden often felt frustrated by the American stance, and it fell to the British officials at the Embassy in Washington to try to diffuse the tension. But Eden and certain Foreign Office officials lost patience, not only with the Americans but also with the officials who were explaining the American position. This loss of confidence in his ambassador was to have disastrous consequences for Britain.

On Sunday 20 July 1952 Makins drove himself to Chartwell, Winston Churchill's country house near Westerham in Kent. He had been asked to lunch with the Prime Minister, ostensibly to do some drafting work. Afterwards he was to go on to see Anthony Eden at his house in West Sussex. When Makins arrived the Prime Minister was slumped in a chair, and did not react at all to his arrival. However, a bottle of champagne was produced and after a couple of glasses Churchill perked up. After lunch Churchill took Makins off to his study to discuss a Middle Eastern problem and to draft some telegrams. He then walked Makins around the gardens. On their way back to the house Churchill asked Makins if he would like to see some of his things. They ended up in Churchill's

1 TNA., CAB/129/53, *British Overseas Obligations.*

2 Ibid.

studio where the walls were covered from floor to ceiling with his drawings and paintings. Makins, who collected art himself, preferred the landscapes to Churchill's other paintings, and honestly said how much he liked them. After he left, Churchill telephoned Eden who, on Makins' arrival, offered him the Washington Embassy on the spot.[3]

There had been some tension between Eden and Churchill over who should replace Oliver Franks, the retiring British Ambassador to Washington. Churchill, who once said that Anglo-American relations were too important to be left to mere diplomats, wanted to appoint a public figure, someone like Lord Mountbatten, to the post. Eden disagreed. There had been three 'political' appointments to the post of Ambassador out of the previous four: Lord Lothian (1939–40), Lord Halifax (1941–6) and Oliver Franks (1948–52), Eden wanted a professional in the job,[4] and the Chartwell visit turned out to be a final inspection.

Other professional diplomats were, of course, in the frame. Speculation over Oliver Franks' replacement began as soon as he made it clear the previous April that he wanted to leave Washington. Gladwyn Jebb, the British Ambassador to the United Nations was a leading candidate. Another possible was Pierson Dixon, Deputy Under Secretary of State at the Foreign Office since 1950; he was to take over as Ambassador to the UN in 1954. A third candidate was Ralph Stevenson, Ambassador to Egypt from 1950 to 1955. But Makins was the obvious choice. As shown in earlier chapters he had considerable experience of North American affairs. He went to the North American Department when he first joined the Foreign Office in 1928; he had served in Washington twice, first under Lord Lindsay (1932–6) and subsequently under Lord Halifax and Lord Inverchapel (1944–7). He had also worked closely with the Americans both during the Second World War and afterwards, when he was a Deputy Under Secretary at the Foreign Office. His wife was an extra asset: she had grown up in Washington and spent most of the war there; she too had a considerable network of contacts. As Makins put it 'It is not always the case that at a given moment the Foreign Office can produce a couple, after all it has to be a couple, who are ideally suited to the Washington post'.[5] It is quite possible that being the obvious choice for Washington cost Makins the top job at the Foreign Office. Ivone Kirkpatrick, who was appointed to the position of Permanent Under Secretary at the Foreign Office in November 1953, wrote to Makins 'I had hoped that you

[3] Based on a passage contained in Lord Sherfield's Memoirs entitled *Mission to Washington* (Henceforth *Mission to Washington*), p. 2.

[4] Lord Inverchapel, a career diplomat, filled the position from 1946–8.

[5] *Mission to Washington*, p. 1.

would fill the "hot seat" and that I should be spared. But your elevation into the Washington Embassy wrecked that'.[6]

When Makins' appointment was announced to the public on 4 October 1952 it received wide publicity in both the British and the American press. He was well known in Whitehall but this was the first time he emerged as a public figure. Photographers from several newspapers and magazines went down to Sherfield, their country house, to take pictures of him and Alice and whichever of his six children (the two youngest, Patricia and Dwight, had been born in 1946 and 1951 respectively) were there at the time; the *Tatler* even sent Cecil Beaton. The photographs appeared in several newspapers and magazines. The press started to look into Makins' background and got hold of the fact that he had chaired the Official Committee on Atomic Energy leading to headlines such as 'Britain's Atomic Ambassador' and 'Back Room Atom Man is Envoy to US'.

It must have been a heady time for both Makins and Alice. The appointment to such a high profile role coincided with a growth in the media's curiosity about public figures. Television was about to take off. There had been 15,000 television licences issued in England in 1947. By 1952 there were nearly 1.5 million.[7] The Foreign Office had given little thought to the need for diplomats to be trained in media skills let alone how to deal with television appearances, so Makins, foreseeing the exposure, took himself off to the BBC at Lime Grove to learn the 'rudiments of the art of appearing on TV'.[8] He was also aware that in the US, he would have to do considerably more public speaking than he had been used to. Acknowledging that he was a poor public speaker, he laid on some practice sessions before he left for America.

The next few months were extremely hectic for both Makinses. Alice had to buy a suitable wardrobe that could be an advertisement for British designers and hire domestic staff: the large British Embassies such as Washington and Paris operated, in effect, as small hotels and social venues, catering for a constant stream of official visitors and many large parties and events. She was fortunate in that Joan Eden, one of Makins' secretaries from his time in Algiers, agreed to become her social secretary, and the two of them were to be a very efficient team. Joyce Wingate, Makins' longstanding secretary at the Foreign Office, also went with him to Washington.

Roger and Alice set sail for America on the morning of 31 December 1952. It was not a relaxing cruise. Their fellow passengers on the *Queen Mary* included the Prime Minister, Winston Churchill and his entourage. Makins had to be on call, and he and Alice had to attend a number of functions hosted by Churchill

6 Makins Papers, MS Sherfield 526, Letter Kirkpatrick to Makins, 5 June 1953.

7 Hennessy, P., *Having it so Good: Britain in the Fifties*, London: Penguin, 2006, p. 112.

8 *Mission to Washington*, p. 6.

including dinner on New Year's Eve.[9] The *Queen Mary* docked in New York in driving rain early in the morning of 5 January 1953. It was exactly a year to the day since Makins had accompanied Churchill on his previous visit to America. One of his first duties in America was to coax Churchill into meeting the press; Churchill was averse to early morning starts and needed some persuasion. The press were also keen to interview the new Ambassador; *The New York Times* wrote an article likening Makins to 'an affable hawk'. After the press conference Churchill stayed on for a few days in New York, where he met with President Elect, Dwight Eisenhower, and then the Makinses travelled to Washington with three days to get the Embassy ready for Churchill's stay there, and for the farewell dinner the Prime Minister was giving at the Embassy for President Truman and members of the outgoing administration.

Makins just had time to present his credentials to Truman on 6 January 1953 before Churchill arrived. He knew Truman well from his earlier posting to Washington and his time as Deputy Under Secretary. On the morning of 8 January, he met Churchill who had flown down to Washington on the President's aircraft *Independence*. Makins took the Prime Minister to meet with Truman and some of the outgoing members of the Cabinet including Dean Acheson, Bob Lovett and John Snyder, the Treasury Secretary. It was a nostalgic time for Makins as well as the politicians present. These were all people he had known and dealt with in the past and who were now about to leave office. The day ended with the Embassy dinner for Truman hosted by Churchill, which must have been a success since it ended around 1.00 am.[10,11] Makins was able to report to the Foreign Office that 'The President and his advisers, who are clearly still smarting from their election defeat, were touched by the manifest courtesy and attention shown to them by the Prime Minister in their closing days of power. I am sure that this action will be noted and remembered with gratitude in the Democratic ranks'.[12]

After Churchill left Washington Makins turned his attention to the Embassy personnel. He and Alice gave a party for all the 600 or so Embassy staff and their wives 'all of them down to the coloured messengers' as Makins put it.[13] They also gave another party for British military and civil missions which were stationed in Washington. Makins' training with the BBC in London proved worthwhile: he appeared on television three times in his first week in Washington and had good press, though he acknowledged that it was somewhat blanketed by Churchill's

9 Coleville, J., *The Fringes of Power*, pp. 613–18.

10 Colville, J., *The Fringes of Power*, p. 621.

11 The dinner guests included Dean Acheson, Averell Harriman, General Marshall, John Synder, General Bedell Smith, Kit Steel, Sir Edmund Hall Patch and Denis Rickett.

12 TNA, FO371/103495, Weekly Political Reports, 10 January 1953.

13 Ernest Makins Papers, MS Sherfield 197, letter Makins to father, 13 January 1953.

visit. Alice too had to hold a press conference with 40 women journalists, all of whom wrote complimentary articles about her.[14]

Makins now turned his attention to the new administration. Eisenhower's inauguration as the 34th President of the United States and Richard Nixon's as the 36th Vice President took place on 20 January 1953. As was customary the ceremony took place on a platform erected on the steps of the Capitol building. It was a fine cold day and the inauguration was watched by a record crowd of over 100,000 people and a television audience of several millions. Makins watched from 'reasonably good seats at the back of the platform' as Senator Richard Nixon was inducted as the Vice President and Chief Justice Vinson administered the oath to General Eisenhower.[15] The inauguration was followed by the usual procession which lasted over six hours and the evening was taken up with the inauguration balls. Makins went to the ball in Constitution Hall where he was seated in the same box as ex-president Herbert Hoover (who had been President when Makins was first posted to Washington in 1932) and the Danish-turned-American opera singer Lauritz Melchior who had acquired American citizenship the previous day. He held out his hand to shake Makins' and exclaimed in 'a strong guttural accent: "Velkom to my country"'.[16] It is clear that Makins found all this rather amusing.

A week after the inauguration there was a diplomatic party hosted by the President. There were over 100 ambassadors in Washington in 1953 and they were all there, including Makins, who, being the latest diplomatic arrival in Washington, was at the back of the line. By the time he reached Eisenhower the President was shaking hands with his head down. As Makins took the President's hand Eisenhower looked up and exclaimed 'Christ, Roger, what the hell are you doing here'. They had known each other in Algiers, and the greeting encouraged Makins to believe that he could gain access to the President whenever he needed it. 'Alice and I were in business', he wrote in his memoirs.

Closeness to the President is, of course, a considerable advantage to an Ambassador. But a good working relationship with the Secretary of State is just as important. Makins had not met John Foster Dulles (Secretary of State 1953–9) before he became Ambassador but he very quickly established a rapport with him and they became good friends. This was important, given that Eden and others at the Foreign Office thought of Dulles as something of 'a bogeyman'.[17] Makins was greatly helped in his dealings with the State Department and Dulles by his friendship with Walter Bedell Smith, until 1954 the Under Secretary of State. Bedell Smith was Eisenhower's Chief of Staff in Algiers and so they had

14 Ernest Makins Papers, MS Sherfield 206, letter Makins to mother, 17 January 1953.

15 *Mission to Washington*, p. 17.

16 *Mission to Washington*, p. 20.

17 *Mission to Washington*, p. 23.

got to know another well during the war. It also helped that Dulles' brother Allen, the Head of the CIA, and his wife were old friends of Makins. There were frequent misunderstandings between Eden and Dulles, and Makins and Bedell Smith were almost always able to clear them up.[18]

This became much harder when Bedell Smith was replaced by Herbert Hoover Jr, the ex-President's son. Makins soon came to realise that Dulles 'never took an important step or replied to representations on major issues without first consulting the President'.[19] That Eisenhower, contrary to many people's expectations, was firmly in control of American foreign policy was an important insight when conducting Anglo-American relations and one which Eden and others at the Foreign Office, who had known Eisenhower only as the military Commander in Chief during the war, found very hard to accept.

In addition to Makins' connections with the President and the Department of State he was also close to other important members of the administration, and a significant number of Congressmen and Senators. The leading journalists Joe and Stuart Alsop were friends of Makins, and so were the influential columnists Scotty Reston and Walter Lipmann, William McChesney Martin, chairman of the Federal Reserve was his brother in law and close friend. Makins was the only foreigner to be elected a member of the exclusive Burning Tree Golf Club, which was frequented by the President, Cabinet members, Congressmen and other influential members of Washington society. It was here that Makins made the acquaintance of the Vice President Richard Nixon: They were both poor golfers and as Makins noted 'we formed a bond of misery and a friendship developed which endured until he was driven from the White House'.[20]

Social networking was always useful in diplomatic and political life and was particularly important in Washington, where so many people were, one way or another, involved in the business of government, and where society hostesses liked to bring them all together at their parties. Makins' predecessor Oliver Franks and his wife Barbara preferred a quiet, academic and domestic life and did not really relish the social side of the job. The Makinses threw themselves into it: they thought it important that the Embassy should be a prominent destination on the Washington social map, and they had the means to spend more than the official allowance for entertaining.

When Makins took over the Embassy in 1953 Anglo-American relations were satisfactory. There had been difficulties during Oliver Franks' ambassadorship, with disagreements about the devaluation of sterling in 1949, the potential escalation of the Korean War and Britain's attitude towards China, but the 'special relationship' between Oliver Franks and Dean

---

18 Ibid.

19 *Mission to Washington*, p. 23.

20 *Mission to Washington*, p. 33.

Acheson, the Secretary of State from 1949 to1953 managed to dissipate much of the tension. After Churchill came back as Prime Minister in October 1951, the wartime closeness between him and first Truman and then Eisenhower returned. Nevertheless, as Makins pointed out, while America regarded Britain as her most reliable ally and Britain put the 'maintenance of good relations with America at the top of the agenda ... it does not follow that there was agreement on policy'.[21]

In 1953 there were a number of issues where there was no meeting of minds between the two countries. These were the subject of talks when Eden and Rab Butler (Chancellor of the Exchequer from 1951 to 1955) visited America in March 1953. Makins accompanied Eden and Butler to the State Department where they met with Dulles, George M. Humphrey (Secretary to the Treasury from 1953 to 1957), and others. The discussions started with economic matters; the Americans had always been wary of Britain's trading relationships with the Commonwealth and the position of sterling balances. On its side, Britain was concerned at the level of protection in some parts of the American market, especially since America was about to overtake Australia as Britain's biggest export market.

A Commonwealth economic conference in December 1952 had come up with proposals for promoting and liberalising international trade, including a move towards the convertibility of sterling. The British contingent outlined these proposals, and their arguments impressed the Americans, who were in favour of both liberalising trade and sterling convertibility. But they had reservations. The proposals required financial backing from America and the 'new administration was reluctant at such an early stage to put before Congress any radical measures which were intended either to win financial backing for the Commonwealth proposals or reduce tariffs'.[22] The American administration also doubted whether the British economy was strong enough to risk convertibility of sterling at this stage. Both the British and the Americans were reluctant to give the impression that the economic talks had failed and so the final communiqué indicated that the talks were the first in a series which would take place between the American, British, European and Commonwealth governments – a typical diplomatic ruse designed to mask disagreement.

While the economic talks were going on Dulles, Eden, his principal private secretary Evelyn Shuckburgh and Makins left for a meeting with Eisenhower. The meeting lasted an hour and focused on the issue of the Middle East, in particular Egypt, and Iran (or Persia as it was then called). Britain had a long standing connection with Egypt which went back to 1875 when she bought shares in the Suez Canal. The Canal was an important route to India and British troops had

---

21 *Mission to Washington*, p. 37.

22 *Mission to Washington*, p. 43.

been in Egypt since [1888]. The British relationship with Egypt was regulated by the Anglo-Egyptian Treaty of 1936, which provided for the stationing of British troops in Egypt among other things, but was due to expire in 1956. Successive Egyptian governments had sought revision or cancellation of the Treaty and pressure for cancellation grew with the overthrow of King Farouk in 1952. At the time of the Eden and Butler talks in Washington General Mohamed Naguib was in control in Egypt. Britain was prepared to negotiate a revision of the treaty and to agree to the withdrawal of troops, but wanted the ability to station troops there in the event of a war. Eden also had plans to try to draw Egypt into the Baghdad Pact, a defensive mechanism designed to bolster the Middle East against Soviet penetration. By March 1953, however, talks with the Egyptians had run into difficulties and Britain wanted American help with the negotiations.

The Americans had mixed views on Egypt: on the one hand, they disliked the British imperialism they saw there; on the other hand, they were in favour of British efforts to prevent Soviet influence in the Middle East. Eisenhower, in his talks with Eden and Makins, agreed to help the British in their negotiations with the Egyptians on the basis of an agreed formula, but only if the Egyptians approved of the American involvement. Notwithstanding pressure from Britain, he was reluctant to 'gatecrash the Anglo-Egyptian talks in case it exacerbated Egyptian nationalism'.[23] At a further meeting, this time between Eden, Eisenhower, Bedell Smith and Makins, a formula which would involve the Americans in the talks was agreed. 'Unfortunately, these carefully laid plans came to nought since the Egyptians quickly rejected U.S. participation and the Americans refused to insist upon it.'[24] As Eden commented in his memoirs, 'If we had been able to bring about joint Anglo American negotiations with Egypt at this stage ... the future position of the Middle East would have worked out differently'.[25]

The Anglo-Iranian oil crisis was a further source of friction between America and Britain. Since 1933 the British Anglo Iranian Oil Company (AIOC) had an agreement to extract oil and, in exchange, to pay royalties to Iran. In the late 1940s this agreement came in for criticism not only from the Iranians but also from the Americans, who felt that the level of the royalty payment was tantamount to British exploitation. Perhaps more importantly, they wanted American companies to get a piece of the oil business. On the other hand, they were concerned that Iran remained in friendly hands and did not succumb to communist infiltration. Tension was heightened when, in 1952, the Shah was exiled and Mohammed Mossadeq became Prime Minister. Shortly afterwards AIOC's interests were nationalised by the Iranian government. The British

---

23 *Mission to Washington*, p. 43.

24 *Mission to Washington*, p. 46.

25 Anthony Eden, *Full Circle The Memoirs of Anthony Eden*, London: Cassell, 1960, p. 253.

responded with a boycott of Iranian oil, and reinforced the Navy presence in the area. They were also keen to see Mossadeq removed. The Truman administration was against the use of force fearing that it might lead to Soviet involvement; the Americans wanted a negotiated settlement with Iran and, of course, access for American oil companies. By the time of the Eden/Butler talks in March 1953 the British had made proposals for a settlement to the Iranians, but Anglo-American agreement seemed a long way off.

At the first meeting of Eden and Eisenhower in March 1953 Makins reported that Eisenhower was obsessed 'by the fear of a communist take over in Persia [Iran] and he was keener, therefore, than Anthony to continue to deal with ... Mossadeq in search for an end to the oil dispute'.[26] By the end of the talks, however, the Americans agreed that if Mossadeq rejected the latest British proposals, then they [the Americans] would look for an alternative to Mossadeq. Makins had made a significant contribution to the talks, and the British thought they had achieved a successful outcome. Subsequently, Mossadeq did reject the latest proposals and Britain and America staged and financed a coup in August 1953 which led to the return of the Shah, and a new oil agreement with a consortium where American companies had a 40 per cent interest where previously they had had none.

The March 1953 talks also covered European matters: America wanted to rearm West Germany in order to bolster the defences of Europe. At a meeting of the North Atlantic Council in September 1950 the Americans insisted on West German rearmament and even threatened to pull out of NATO command if this failed to happen. The French, having been attacked by Germany three times in the previous hundred years, were wary of rearming Germany; instead, they concocted a plan for a European Defence Community (EDC), made up of a number of national contingents integrated into a European army. There would not be a German army as such but German battalions would be distributed throughout the army. Churchill described the plan as 'a sludgy amalgam', and the British were not in favour, however they supported the idea in deference to the Americans. They never intended to join the European army but said that they would work alongside it. The EDC treaty was signed by the countries concerned in 1952, but it required the ratification of participating states before it could be operational. Since it never got through the French Assembly the treaty was never ratified, but at the time of the Washington talks both Britain and America agreed to work towards it. The 1953 talks, which were intended to be 'informal and exploratory', can be viewed as a success. They were significant in that they were the first talks Eden had with Dulles since he came to office and, while the British were unable to persuade the Americans to support their Commonwealth inspired trade proposals, there were some concessions with regard to the Middle

---

26 *Mission to Washington*, p. 40.

East. Makins commented: 'The Eden/Butler talks had gone as well as could have been expected. There were no major contretemps.'[27]

After the talks, in the spring of 1953, Makins, while on a visit to New York, called on the Duke of Windsor who was spending the winter in an apartment at the Waldorf Astoria. It is the duty of an Ambassador to call upon any British royals who are staying within the Ambassador's jurisdiction and keep them informed of international events. Makins found the Duke alone with his dogs; the Duchess was out with her 'cronies'. Makins commented that 'the poor fellow had little to do but exercise his dogs around the block'.[28] He discovered that the Duke and Duchess (formerly Mrs Wallis Simpson) were planning a trip to Washington and intended to stay in a rather second-rate hotel which Makins judged to be unsuitable for royals. He invited them to stay at the Embassy, instead. It was an invitation he regretted. A piece from the Duchess's diamond bracelet fell off, and she caused a major domestic upset by accusing the staff of having stolen it. It was later found, swept into a corner, but she offered no apology. During the visit Alice saw the Duke alone, staring out of a window. She commented that she had never seen a sadder look on a man's face. Makins was glad to see the back of the Windsors. Makins wrote 'He was pathetic and she was an ill-mannered, disagreeable woman'.[29]

Makins had telegraphed the Foreign Office before the visit to make enquiries as to the correct protocol for the royal visit. The Foreign Office duly replied by telegram with a set of instructions: the Makinses were amused by the instruction that they should bow and curtsey to the Duke, but not the Duchess, but try not to do it too noticeably! Afterwards Roderick Barclay, an Assistant Under Secretary, sent an official letter saying it was presumed that the Windsors had invited themselves. In addition, the Foreign Office enclosed a set of instructions, issued by the Palace to the Foreign Office, suggesting the correct way to deal with the Windsors. These instructions had been issued in 1937 but ratified by the Palace in 1952. They stated that 'the Duke and Duchess should not be invited to stay as guests at the Embassy'.[30] Makins, rather put out by receiving such a letter from someone junior to himself, replied rather defensively, questioning whether the instructions really applied to Washington and claiming that he was not aware of them. It is perhaps typical of Makins that he did not take too kindly to being pulled up on something, no matter how trivial it might be.

[27] Ernest Makins Papers, MS Sherfield 197, Letter Makins to father, 21 March 1953.

[28] *Mission to Washington*, p. 49.

[29] *Mission to Washington*, p. 50.

[30] Makins Papers, MS Sherfield 528, Extract from a letter from Sir A. Hardinge, Balmoral Castle, to Sir R. Vansittart 2 September 1937. The instructions were confirmed by the Palace in 1952.

A different Foreign Office rebuke from the Permanent Under Secretary, William Strang, was more serious. Makins had started his mission to Washington addressing telegrams to both the Foreign Secretary and the Chancellor of the Exchequer (Rab Butler was a personal friend). William Strang the Permanent Under-Secretary wrote:

> I think it would be best not to address telegrams jointly to the S of S and The Chancellor. As H.M. Ambassador, you address the S of S and he may want to have further correspondence with you before bringing in his colleague. The financial situation is, as always, very tricky: and we are doing our best ... at the official level to keep things smooth. You can count on us to do this: we will look after the liaison,you cannot do it from Washington, even through Rickett [the Treasury representative at the Embassy]. This is really rather important. The S of S will want to feel you are his man.[31]

It is surprising that, after 25 years in the service, Makins needed to be reminded of this. It is also interesting to note that only a month into his Ambassadorship he was being warned that the Secretary of State needed to feel that Makins was 'his man'.

Britain's relations with the People's Republic of China were a continuing source of friction in Anglo-American relations in the spring of 1953. Contrary to American wishes, Britain had recognised the Communist regime in Peking in January 1950; after the Chinese entered the Korean War on the Communists' side in November 1950, this recognition became more of an annoyance to the Americans. A combination of their frustration at being unable to end the Korean War, and Senator McCarthy's focus on Britain's trade with China 'considerably distorted the popular perception of Britain's role in international affairs'.[32] McCarthy was the Junior Senator from Wisconsin and Chairman of the Senate Permanent Sub Committee on Investigations. Makins reported to the Foreign Office that trade with China is 'by far the most sensitive point in Anglo American relations at the moment and this fact is brought home to me everywhere I go in this country'.[33] In late May Senator McCarthy alleged that British-owned ships were carrying communist troops and that British trade with China had greatly increased in the first quarter of 1953. Other Senators repeated these allegations, and so Makins delivered a speech which stated that 'on all the evidence available no ship under British flag and subject to British law had transported Communist military personnel in Chinese waters'.[34] The speech

---

31 Makins Papers, MS Sherfield 527, Letter Strang to Makins, 15 January 1953.

32 *Mission to Washington*, p. 54.

33 TNA, FO 371/103495, Weekly Political Summary, 2–8 May 1953.

34 *Mission to Washington*, p. 54.

received good publicity and went some way to putting the record straight and alleviating some of the strain between Britain and America.

Makins kept London abreast of the growth of McCarthyism, and the extent to which it affected Anglo-American relations.

> During 1952 McCarthy and his supporters moved from the lunatic fringe into the position of a national political force ... The persistent Congressional investigations uncovered just enough evidence of Communist infiltration to make the administration's blanket denial unbelievable and to convince the average man that whatever the excesses, the McCarthyites were at least doing something about communism from within.[35]

The basis of McCarthy's influence was fear, 'the blind haunting fear in the American people of communism'. The problem, of course, was that the average American made no distinction between a Communist, a Socialist or a plain liberal. The effect of McCarthy's allegations went beyond Britain's China policy. Britain was also criticised for its limited efforts in fighting communism in Korea, but her part in fighting communist-inspired forces in places like Malaya was ignored.[36]

McCarthyism also affected the day-to-day work of the Embassy when dealing with the Administration. Makins noted that the US government was having increasing difficulty in recruiting high quality officials, partly due to the questioning they would have to undergo by McCarthy and his cronies. Morale in the Department of State during the McCarthy era was very low and as Makins noted 'The State posts are badly paid and bring nothing but obloquy'.[37] By the end of 1953, however, the march of McCarthyism was checked. There were a number of unproductive investigations; McCarthy attacked the protestant clergy which alienated many people and the committee was boycotted by Democratic members. By the end of the following year McCarthy was a spent force. In the spring and summer of 1954 he lost a considerable amount of credibility during the infamous 'Army hearings'. In a nasty set of allegations and counter allegations McCarthy claimed that the army of having been infiltrated by communists. The hearings were televised and reported verbatim for three months in the middle of 1954 and 'overshadowed everything else on the American political scene'.[38] McCarthy fared badly and on 2 December 1954 the Senate, by a vote of 67 to 22, passed a resolution condemning his actions. Makins reported that the

35 TNA, FO 371/103497, Report to Lord Salisbury, 10 August 1953.

36 *Mission to Washington*, p. 59.

37 TNA, FO 371/103497, Letter to Strang, 26 February 1953.

38 TNA, WO 32/499613, Letter Makins to Eden, 14 July 1954.

Senator's formal condemnation was 'an act which has only three precedents in the history of the country'.[39]

Recalling the events 30 years later, Makins, although not everyone would agree with his analysis, did rather put the McCarthy episode into context:

> McCarthyism which was often seen mistakenly abroad as being akin to Fascism, damaged the international reputation of the United States. However ... in comparison with the immense prestige and popularity of General Eisenhower and the strength of the Republican Party machine McCarthy and his associates are not much more than a pack of jackals round the legs of an elephant, even though the spotlight may be trained on the parasites rather than the pachyderm.[40]

On 27 July 1953 the armistice in Korea was announced. According to Makins the negotiation of the armistice was 'undoubtedly the Eisenhower Administration's greatest achievement in its first year'. Dulles, however, was criticised both in the House of Commons and by the British press for the way in which he handled the negotiations. The criticism reached such a pitch that the radio carried the headline that 'yesterday in London was anti Dulles day'. Not for the first time Makins asked for moderation, arguing that Dulles was 'possibly the most sincere and genuine advocate of close Anglo American cooperation in the United States today'.[41] He was aware that Dulles was a sensitive man and also rather clumsy in his dealings with the media. He also knew that, with each of these attacks on the Secretary of State from British sources, a piece of goodwill was used up, goodwill which was to be desperately needed in the years ahead.

In October 1953 there were further negotiations over Anglo-American cooperation on atomic energy. A high powered delegation visited Washington, including the Paymaster General, Lord Cherwell, usually known as 'the Prof', who had been Churchill's scientific advisor during the war, Sir Christopher Hinton, the nuclear engineer, and the physicist Sir John Cockcroft. Their objective was to try to persuade the Americans to share information on the Soviet atomic bomb test and the effects of atomic weapons, so that the British could improve their civil defences in the event of a war. Makins took Cherwell to meet with Eisenhower who, although sympathetic, was non-committal, citing the provisions of the MacMahon Act. He did, however, suggest the party meet with Admiral Levi Strauss

---

39 TNA, FO 371/109104, Letter Makins to Eden, 20 December 1954.

40 *Mission to Washington*, p. 61.

41 *Mission to Washington*, p. 58.

the new head of the US Atomic Energy Commission.[42] The meeting was a success and agreement was reached on a number of issues.[43] The most important outcome, as Makins noted, was the noticeable change in attitude towards Anglo-American cooperation in atomic energy, which stemmed from the new administration's review of its whole approach to defence policy and cooperation with allies. After the visit Makins 'learnt from Gordon Arneson (Under Secretary in the State Department responsible for atomic energy matters) that the Administration intended to ask the next session of Congress to amend the McMahon Act to allow the United States to cooperate with other countries in military and intelligence matters'.[44]

In early December 1953 the summit between the three Western leaders Eisenhower, Churchill and the French Prime Minister, Joseph Laniel, which had been planned for the previous summer but was postponed due to Churchill's ill health, eventually took place in Bermuda. Although Makins was due to attend the summit scheduled for the previous summer he was not asked to the December summit. One of the significant issues to be discussed at Bermuda was atomic energy. It is slightly odd that Makins did not attend, though he did brief the State Department in advance of the summit. On 2 December, two days before the Bermuda summit was due to begin, he met with Douglas MacArthur II, a Counsellor at the State Department. Makins indicated that Lord Cherwell would be unlikely to raise any new issues and was satisfied with the progress he had made in the Washington talks on atomic energy in the previous autumn. However, he felt that Cherwell would seek clarification on amendments to be made to the McMahon Act. Makins then indicated that he wished to 'speak on a personal and highly confidential basis about a related matter'. He said that Churchill was still very upset by the Americans reneging on the various wartime agreements about atomic energy cooperation that Britain and America had entered into, including the Quebec Agreement. Furthermore, Churchill believed that Truman had also promised continued cooperation and had also reneged on his promise. As Makins indicated 'Churchill continues to brood about all of this and is now in quite a bitter frame of mind'; he indicated that, in his opinion, it would be unwise for Churchill to take up the matter with Eisenhower particularly given, at least in Makins' view, the satisfactory way the atomic energy discussions were now proceeding. He then said he believed that the wartime agreements were just that and were for the duration of the hostilities only.[45]

---

[42] Makins Papers, MS Sherfield 528, Record of Conversation, Meeting of Makins and Cherwell with Eisenhower, 14 October 1953.

[43] Makins Papers, MS Sherfield 528, Record of Conversation, Meeting of Makins and Cherwell with Levi Strauss et al., 15 October 1953.

[44] *Mission to Washington*, p. 77.

[45] FRUS 1952–1954 Western European Security Part II, pp. 1725–6.

It is interesting to note here the extent to which Makins was acting personally and in doing so undermining his Prime Minister. Makins' view on the validity of the Quebec Agreement is debatable to say the least and this was not the first time, as was shown in Chapter 3, that Makins chose to take a 'soft line' with the Americans on the atomic energy issue. Makins suggested that the reason he did not attend the summit was because he was due to visit London for 'consultations and discussions'.[46] It is difficult to believe this since the summit ran from 4 to 8 December and Makins did not leave for London until 11 December. It is tempting to speculate whether Churchill, knowing Makins' views on previous atomic energy agreements, was keen to keep Makins away from Bermuda.

Makins returned from London on 22 December and immediately became embroiled in discussions about Egypt with Dulles. An agreement between Britain and Egypt on, among other things, the withdrawal of troops had not yet been finalised and this was causing the Americans considerable frustration. They wanted to grant aid to the Egyptians and on several occasions had only held off at the request of the British. The British believed that absence of aid would pressurise the Egyptians into an agreement. The Americans, on the other hand, thought that the aid could be used by General Naguib as a tool to sell the deal to the Egyptians. Dulles, clearly frustrated, asked Makins to get the British to put down on a piece of paper which items had been agreed, and to make proposals on those which had not. The note of the meeting records that 'the Secretary went after the Ambassador hard'. Makins, rather presciently, pointed out that 'Egypt was the most explosive current topic in British domestic politics and potentially in the realm of UK-US relations'.[47] Few people at the time realised that the Egyptian issue was a time bomb ticking under the Anglo-American relationship.

Notwithstanding the unresolved Egyptian issues Makins must have been encouraged as his first year as Ambassador drew to a close. He and Alice had happily reintroduced themselves into Washington society, their visits and tours around America had been a success, his appearances on television were seen as positive and even Makins' speeches were going down well.[48] Furthermore, his prospects for the future looked good. Sir William Strang wrote:

> I think you are in the right place now and your work is loudly acclaimed by all hands. But I hope that time will bring you to top this chair [Permanent Under Secretary at the Foreign Office] which I am now vacating. Ivone [Ivone

[46] *Mission to Washington*, p. 84. Also see Makins Papers, MS Sherfield 527, Strang to Makins, 3 November 1953.

[47] FRUS 1952–1954 *The Near and Middle East*, pp. 2181–2.

[48] Ernest Makins Papers, MS Sherfield 197, Letter Makins to father, 1 December 1953.

> Kirkpatrick was William Strang's successor] is saying firmly that three years is his limit: and that ought to be about right.[49]

During 1954 Anglo-American relations were becoming more fraught. Britain's failure to support the American position in Indo-China, her lack of support for American policies towards a communist regime in Guatemala, and her refusal to accept American proposals for security in South East Asia did, as Makins reported, throw 'a sharp strain on the relations between the two Governments'. Against this, however, a visit by Churchill and Eden in the middle of the year and Eden's deft handling of the French rejection of the European Defence Treaty, helped to ease some of the tension.

Makins began 1954 by attending the State of the Union address given by Eisenhower on 7 January. The address covered a broad spectrum of subjects; the one that was of most interest to Makins and Britain was the announcement of a probable change in America's atomic energy strategy. The following month Eisenhower asked Congress for legislation to amend the Atomic Energy Act of 1946, otherwise known as the McMahon Act. The proposed amendments included the sharing of 'restricted data' and some other measures which, if Congress accepted them, would lead to a considerable step forward in Anglo-American collaboration and give the British government substantially everything it wanted in this area. But Makins cautioned that it would be unwise to assume that the proposed changes would pass through Congress quickly or unchanged. The amended Act was approved by Congress on 30 August 1954, but Congress demanded that a new bilateral deal with the British should be put in place, and that this deal should be approved by the Joint Congressional Committee on Atomic Energy. This finally took place in 1955; in the meantime, collaboration, such as it was, continued under the extended Modus Vivendi arrangements.

Whilst Makins was optimistic about Anglo-American cooperation in atomic energy matters he was less confident about relations over the Middle East. Makins' concerns over Egypt were noted above, in early 1954, however, Makins wrote a note putting these concerns in the context of the Middle East, a note which was circulated to the Cabinet. Makins said that he thought the coming year was likely to see difficulties in the Anglo-American relationship with regard to the Middle East and set out his reasons why: he said that the American influence in the region had expanded greatly since the Second World War and that the British were suspicious about it. He then asked 'Are the Americans consciously trying to substitute their influence for ours in the Middle East? And, even if this is not their conscious policy now, is it nevertheless the inevitable conclusion to the present trend of events'. He suggested that the answer to the first question was No and that the answer to the second depended on Britain's

[49] Makins Papers, MS Sherfield 527, Letter Strang to Makins, 1 November 1953.

response to American action in the region. The Americans did not want to push the British out, he argued, because it would mean an extension to their military commitments in the region and it was not consistent with their attitude to the British. But the Americans had concerns about British behaviour in the region. 'Briefly, I should say that they [the Americans] are inclined to feel that we have cast them for a supporting role, which is to consist of switching on or off the powerful current of their diplomatic and financial influence at a word from us. Or to put it differently, they feel we are asking them to accept limitations on their activity which we do not accept ourselves.' Makins offered several examples of this behaviour, including the case where the British ignored American objections to their supply of jets to Israel, but at the same time tried to stop the Americans supplying bombers to Saudi Arabia. In short, Makins was saying that the Americans saw the British as wanting American cooperation in the Middle East but only on their own terms. Makins then took the Egyptian situation as an example: the Americans were very frustrated by the British request to withhold aid to Egypt, while at the same time the British were procrastinating over the Anglo-Egyptian negotiations for a new treaty.[50]

Makins was also dealing with another difference of opinion between the British and the Americans. In 1954 Laos, Cambodia and Vietnam were still part of the crumbling French empire. France was involved in a gruesome war in Vietnam, with over half the costs funded by the Americans. A Far Eastern Peace conference in Geneva to discuss Korea and Indo-China had been organised for the spring of 1954. Britain, France, Russia American and China were to attend. As the date for conference approached, the position of the French in Vietnam looked precarious. A division of elite French troops were trapped at Dien Bien Phu in North Vietnam and the Americans feared that if the French capitulated Vietnam would fall to the communists. To prevent this Dulles advocated a policy of 'United Action'. This would consist of a coalition of countries, which would include Britain, America, Australia, New Zealand and the Philippines, declaring that they would support the French position, if necessary by military force.

Makins was conscious that Eden would not respond well to this approach. He attempted to explain the American position and how it might be best to proceed. 'Hitherto we have agreed pretty well with the Americans on the day-to-day handling of policy in the Far East in spite of longer range differences of political appreciation. But though we continue to agree on tactics, a decision to range ourselves with the fundamental American position or dissociate ourselves from it cannot be long delayed and will have a profound effect over the whole field of Anglo American relations.'[51] The Embassy's view was that the

[50] TNA, CAB 129/66, Middle East Anglo American Policy Note by Makins, 25 January 1954.

[51] *Mission to Washington*, p. 100.

American policy of United Action was the best chance of saving the position in the area and added 'If we align ourselves with the Administration we shall be able to bring our influence continually to bear upon them'.[52] This is, of course, an Ambassador's classic advice when trying to persuade his own country to go along with another country's policy it does not agree with. Makins offered a series of arguments as to why the British should support America and the consequences if it did not. It was possible, of course, that America could have taken action alone. But Congressional leaders had made it clear to Eisenhower and Dulles that Congress would not support the action unless other allies, and at least Britain, were involved.

Makins was shown a copy of an urgent note which Eisenhower sent to Churchill on 4 April 1954. The note predicted the disastrous consequences for South East Asia if Vietnam fell (previewing the President's falling domino theory speech given a few days later) and called for the United Action. The note also confirmed Makins' point that if Britain supported the United Action then America would support British interests elsewhere.[53] Eden was against the policy, believing that the French were finished in Indo-China and that it might lead to a wider conflict.

Dulles travelled to London to seek support for his proposals. Makins met with him on the eve of his departure and warned London that Dulles would be greatly influenced by the degree of support he received in London. Dulles returned to Washington believing that he had agreed with Britain at a meeting on 19 April that she was 'ready to take part, with other countries concerned in an examination of the possibility of establishing a collective defence ...'.[54] He duly organised a meeting of the Ambassadors of the prospective coalition group, including Makins, but Eden reneged on his agreement and, in a series of indignant telegrams to Makins, refused to allow him to attend any such meeting. Britain had refused to join the Americans in military action in Vietnam to save the situation, and instead advocated the partition of Vietnam. French resistance collapsed on 7 May, marking the end of Dulles' United Action policy. The issue was settled at the Geneva Conference with French withdrawal from Vietnam and the division of the country into North and South Vietnam, with the border at the 17th parallel.

Makins felt compelled to write to Eden, 'I have been much concerned recently about the way in which our relations seem to be developing with the Americans'. In a six-page letter he described in great detail how the Americans

---

52 *Mission to Washington*, p. 101.

53 Boyle, P., *The Churchill-Eisenhower Correspondence 1953–1955*, London: Chapel Hill, 2005, p. 136, Letter dated 4 April 1954.

54 Shuckburgh, E., *Descent to Suez Foreign Office Diaries 1951–1956*, London: Norton, 2005, p. 164.

viewed the British position, and suggested that British and American interests were the same. He poignantly added 'However irritating you may find the clumsy manifestation of American diplomatic behaviour, and their failure to make more resolute efforts to find a basis for negotiation, it is important for you to know that on their side they think, rightly or wrongly, that you have gone back on the understanding which in their mind was reached in London on April 19'.[55] Eden replied to Makins in a letter which was, rather unusually, signed by his private secretary rather than Eden himself. The letter contained a rebuttal of Makins' main points and ended with 'I realise that the job of British ambassador in Washington at a time like this is far from easy and I am grateful to you for spelling out the American attitude so clearly. I hope that this account of our own position will help you in persuading more responsible Americans that we are no less aware of the dangers of Communist expansion in South-east Asia than they are. But we have, and are entitled to have, our own ideas of how this can best be done'.[56]

The consequences of Britain's failure to support Dulles' plans for united action are difficult to estimate. It is hard to imagine, however, that Dulles had forgotten the issue when Britain asked for assistance in Suez two years later. There was also a consequence for the Ambassador. Makins' comments on the American positions regarding Indo-China and the Middle East were just two examples of Makins appearing to support the American point of view. Eden had already expressed his irritation with Makins when he sided with the State Department which had accused the Foreign Office of leaking Dulles' plans.[57] It now fell to Ivone Kirkpatrick to offer a further rebuke.

> I think I should let you know that some of your telegrams and letters have been arousing some resentment here because they seem to be rooting for America and critical of H.M.G. The Secretary of State recognises that you must interpret American thought to him; and that that must be done cogently and frankly. He also says that you are doubtless doing a great deal to impress our point of view on responsible Americans. But, if so, it would be helpful with all those who see your telegrams if this could emerge in them as well as exposition of the American point of view.
>
> This is a very old problem. There is no precise formula for solving it. But if you are aware of the state of feeling here, you should be able by agile drafting to avoid adding to the exacerbation caused by Anglo-American difference.[58]

55 Makins Papers, MS Sherfield 527, Letter Makins to Eden, 21 May 1954.

56 Makins Papers, MS Sherfield 527, Letter Eden to Makins, 26 May 1954.

57 Shuckburgh, *Diaries*, p. 162.

58 Makins Papers, MS Sherfield 527, Letter Kirkpatrick to Makins, 27 May 1954.

This was a remarkable rebuke for the most senior Ambassador in the service to have received from the head of the Foreign Office. It was perhaps the beginning of Eden's loss of confidence in his Ambassador and it was to lead to Makins' disastrous recall in the middle of 1956, a recall which had significant consequences for Anglo-American relations and which are discussed later in this chapter.

One of the major events for the Ambassador in 1954 was making arrangements for the visit by Churchill and Eden in June. They came at an opportune time. While there was considerable tension between Eden and Dulles, who felt a certain amount of resentment towards Eden and the British for having gone back on the agreement over Vietnam, relations were better at the Presidential level. Makins met with Eisenhower on 27 May and was able to report that not only did the President want Churchill and Eden to stay at the White House, but he also told Makins that 'it was intolerable that one could not have an honest difference of opinion without the press talking about rifts between the two countries'.[59] Notwithstanding this Makins wrote to the Foreign Office informing them that the 'American public had been led to believe that there were rifts in the partnership and that more than the usual communiqué would be required if the visit was not to be regarded as a failure'. He recommended that the Foreign Secretary and Prime Minister should 'present firm proposals and to arrive at, if not decisions, then at least an agreed course of action'.[60] He advised Eden to tread carefully with Dulles who he said could be an awkward character, but he added 'I still think that he wants to be friends, and it is really quite important to get him out of his "pet", if you can bring yourselves to make the attempt'.[61]

A further source of friction between Eden and Dulles was Guatemala: the Americans were concerned with the pro-communist activities of its president, Jacobo Arbenze's regime and had instituted a blockade of the country. America had even demanded to board and search British ships in the region, something Eden would not allow. The tension escalated after Guatemala appealed to the UN for assistance in the wake of the CIA-inspired invasion of the country by Colonel Carlos Castillo Armas. America wanted Britain's support for the matter to be referred to the Organisation of American States, a body which the Americans could control. Dulles told Makins that 'this matter might well be a touchstone of the Anglo-American alliance. Makins warned Eden that it would be disastrous if we did not support them over the troubles in the Isthmus of Panama'.[62]

---

59 Makins Papers, MS Sherfield527, Letter Makins to Eden, 29 May 1954.

60 *Mission to Washington*, p. 108.

61 *Mission to Washington*, p. 110.

62 *Mission to Washington*, p. 113.

On the morning of 25 June, Churchill, Eden and their party were met at the airport in Washington by the Vice President Richard Nixon, Dulles and Makins. Eden, presumably having heeded Makins' warning, agreed with Dulles in the car on the way to the White House to abstain on a UN vote which would pave the way for the Organisation of American States to become involved in the Guatemalan issue. It was a good start to the talks, which continued over the next five days and covered a number of issues which had been causing tension between the British and Americans. The Americans agreed with Churchill's request to continue withholding arms and aid from the Egyptians until Britain had reached an agreement with them, and even to the cut off aid if the Egyptians broke the agreement. Furthermore, the Americans pledged support for the freedom of transit through the Suez Canal. Britain offered support for the American proposal for a South-east Asia Treaty Organisation (an organisation established for the collective defence of South-east Asia) by agreeing to encourage Commonwealth Nations to participate. There was discussion on the sharing of atomic energy information, although it was acknowledged that the amendments to the McMahon Act needed to be made before they could be implemented.

The talks not only resulted in agreement on a number of issues and a reduction in the tension between the two countries, but also in the announcement of a formal Eisenhower-Churchill Declaration of Principles, sometimes called the Potomac Charter, which stated that Britain and America upheld the principle of self-determination and that they would secure independence for all countries that desired it and could sustain it.[63] The talks were also a success from Makins' point of view. It was he who had suggested something better than the normal communiqué be issued, and Eden had taken on board many of Makins' suggestions with a view to easing the tension between Dulles and himself. While Makins did not attend all of the talks and, therefore, might not have had a significant input into them at the time, it was the case, as it often is, that the Ambassadors' input beforehand was instrumental to their success.

The Eden-Churchill talks were not the only ones Makins was involved in during 1954. The middle of that year was a busy period for the Embassy: Makins hosted visits from Duncan Sandys, the Minister of Supply, from 9–13 June, Peter Thorneycroft, the President of the Board of Trade, from 3–7 July, Lord Alexander, the Minister of Defence, from 16–21 July and the Treasury team including Rab Butler, the Chancellor of the Exchequer, and Reginald Maudling, the Economic Secretary, during September. In the midst of these visits Makins returned to London in mid August for consultations, and did not go back

---

[63] Hubard, J., *The United States and the End of Colonial Rule in Africa 1941–1968*, North Carolina: Macfarland and Co., 2010.

to Washington until 11 September. In London he attended a meeting of the Official Committee on Atomic Energy, now Chaired by Lord Plowden who had become the first Chairman of the UK Atomic Energy Authority when it was established in 1954. The Official Committee met to discuss their response to the passing, by Congress, of the Atomic Energy Act on 30 August 1954, which from then on would regulate Anglo-American cooperation. It eventually led, as was noted above, to the abandonment of the Modus Vivendi agreement, which Makins had helped negotiate in 1948.

While in London Makins was briefed on Eden's proposals to resolve the crisis caused by the French Assembly's refusal to ratify the European Defence Community treaty. In summary these were that Germany should be allowed to rearm, albeit with limitations, and to join NATO. The British offered various safeguards to placate the French. Eden's bringing together of the various European powers and America to effect this proposal was a deft piece of diplomacy, and one which did much to enhance Anglo-American relations at the time. Makins, back in Washington after the end of the nine power summit which agreed the proposals, was able to report 'The agreement reached ... has had an enthusiastic reception and a mood of sober optimism has replaced the irritation and sense of despair which followed France's rejection of the EDC'.[64]

A further development which cleared the way for more harmonious Anglo-American relations, at least in the short term, was the agreement reached between Britain and Egypt in October 1954. The treaty, which had been negotiated with Lieutenant Colonel Gamal Abdel Nasser who took over as Egypt's leader in April 1954, provided for the withdrawal of British troops, including from the Suez base, but with a right for them to return in the event of an attack by a foreign power on Egypt, on another Arab country, or Turkey. Makins reported that Dulles had described the agreement as one of far reaching importance as indeed it was,[65] but it is doubtful, however, whether Dulles realised at the time just how far reaching it might prove to be.

When Makins returned to Washington there were further signs of tension between the Ambassador and the Foreign Office. Makins wrote to Ivone Kirkpatrick expressing his concern at the number of messages which were passing directly from Eden to Dulles, thus bypassing the Embassy. This had been a source of frustration for British Ambassadors to Washington from Halifax onwards: throughout his time as Prime Minister, Churchill often wrote directly to Roosevelt, Truman or Eisenhower. However, it was more unusual for the Foreign Secretary to indulge in direct correspondence, and Eden would have known it would frustrate Makins who wrote:

---

64 TNA, FO 371/109101, Weekly Political Summary, 2–8 October 1954.

65 TNA, FO 371/109101, Weekly Political Summary, 16–22 October 1954.

> I accept that the personal correspondence between the Prime minister and President is a channel of inestimable value, provided it is not used too much ... On the other hand personal messages passing between two Secretaries of State on matters of substance effectively put me out of action, and since they are inevitably rather short, they may give rise to even more misunderstanding than verbal conversations may engender ...
>
> My relations with Dulles are sufficiently close for me to be able to see him at any time and to speak to him with complete frankness. I do not flatter myself that I have much influence on the complicated old pachyderm but as a postman I cannot do much more than pass the time of day with him![66]

Perhaps the most important event during 1954 for Makins personally was the official visit to America of Queen Elizabeth, The Queen Mother; it was the start of a long friendship. The visit began on 26 October 1954 and lasted 24 days. Its timing was perhaps not ideal, coming in the midst of the Congressional mid-term elections of 2 November 1954 which saw the Democrats secure control by the slenderest of margins of both the House of Representatives and of the Senate.[67] The Queen Mother stayed at the Embassy from 6–10 November and Makins escorted her on a number of visits, including a visit to Williamsburg, the old colonial capital of Virginia, and one to New York, where she was entertained by the Mayor.

Makins also organised a large reception at the Embassy for the Commonwealth Heads of Missions, Senators, Congressmen and other Washington notables. He avoided the problem caused on the Queen Mother's last visit in 1939 when she had come with her husband King George VI. On that occasion the Embassy decided to invite selected Senators and Congressmen, causing great offence to those who were not invited; this time Makins took no chances and invited all the Senators and most of the Congressmen.[68] While he acknowledged that the royal visit was a great success and that he had no previous experience in royal matters, he rather typically took it upon himself to write to Eden offering suggestions as to how visits might be better organised in the future. Suggestions included making proper funds available for the Royals, offering an aeroplane which could accommodate the whole rather large royal party, more consultation with commonwealth countries, suggesting revised itineraries and so on. It was a classic Makins' letter, helpful but strident in tone.[69]

The year 1954 had been a tense one for Anglo-American relations. Makins, however, felt able to report at the end of the year that relations with the Administration were closer and public feeling towards the UK was better than

---

66 Makins Papers, MS Sherfield 527, Letter Makins to Kirkpatrick, 18 September 1954.

67 TNA, FO 371/109109, Letter Makins to Eden, 8 December 1954.

68 *Mission to Washington*, p. 139.

69 Makins Papers, MS Sherfield 527, Letter Makins to Eden, 26 November 1954.

at any time since his arrival in Washington in 1953.[70] While relations between the two countries may have been good, relations between Makins and the Foreign Office were showing signs of strain, and this would have repercussions in the years ahead. But the year ended on a high note for Makins. Eden wrote to him informing him that he was to be appointed a Knight Grand Cross of the Most Distinguished Order of St Michael and St George.[71]

The tension in the Formosa Straights dominated Anglo-American relations at the beginning of 1955. After the Communists took over mainland China in 1949 the Nationalist leader Chiang Kai-Shek fled to Formosa, a large island some 150 miles from the mainland. The Nationalists also retained control of groups of smaller offshore islands including the Tachens, the Quemoy and the Matsus, some of which were only ten miles from the mainland. Britain and America had always taken differing views on China. As noted above, Britain, against American wishes, recognised The People's Republic of China in 1950 and she did not wholeheartedly support America's commitment to defend Formosa.

In the autumn of 1954 the Chinese Communists began shelling the offshore islands. The Nationalists wanted to defend the islands, and the Americans supported their position. The British, however, did not think the islands were defensible or indeed worth defending. It was, to a large extent, left to Makins to navigate through the differences between Eden and Dulles. He made it clear to the Foreign Office that Dulles' desire was twofold: 'to stop hostilities between Formosa and the mainland and to make plain that the United States will not tolerate its capture by the Communists.'[72] The Foreign Office was concerned that America, by seeking a mutual defence treaty with the Nationalists, could end up in a position where it was forced to defend the Quemoy and the Matsus islands.

In January the Communists stepped up the shelling and threatened invasion; Tachen was evacuated. The Americans, in a desire to bolster Nationalist morale, told the British that they intended to announce that they would defend Quemoy; the British thought this would be a disaster. Makins, in an attempt to seek a compromise, suggested that Britain support America in her efforts to stop communist aggression provided she dropped the idea of announcing that she would defend Quemoy,[73] and the Foreign Office supported the compromise. On 24 January Eisenhower sent a message to Congress requesting more authority than he currently possessed to use armed force if necessary in the conflict.[74] This fell short of explicitly announcing that he would defend Quemoy and dissipated

70 TNA, FO 371/114349, Makins to Eden, Annual Review 1954, 1 March 1955.

71 Makins Papers, MS Sherfield 527, Letter Eden to Makins, 30 December 1954.

72 TNA, PREM 11/867, telegram Makins to Foreign Office, 18 October 1954.

73 TNA, PREM 11/867, telegram Makins to Foreign Office, 21 January 1955.

74 TNA, PREM 11/867, telegram Makins to Foreign Office, 21 January 1955.

some of the tension between Britain and America. By May 1955 the crisis had passed and the offshore islands remained in Nationalist hands.

Makins reported 'The American attitude to the Chinese is distinguishable from their attitude to any other foreign country. They were deeply hurt when the Chinese, on whom they had lavished so much care and effort, turned away from them to the heresy of Communism; to this was added the feeling of frustration, failure and humiliation because American arms did not win an outright victory in Korea. There is undoubtedly a suppressed desire to avenge what are to many Americans shameful defeats'.[75] China, then, was a very emotional subject in America at the time, much more so than in Britain where the Foreign Office could take a rather more detached approach to the problem. Makins had recognised the impact that the China situation had on both Congress and the population as a whole, and used his skill and knowledge to help avoid a public falling out between Britain and America over the islands, and in the process reduced the potential adverse impact on Anglo-American relations.

While the tension between the Americans and the Chinese continued at a high level the American attitude to the Soviets began to mellow a little. Makins wrote, 'There seems to be a greater willingness to think out the implications of peaceful coexistence than was being shown even a short time ago. There have also been statements from the President and Mr Dulles that they will be willing to negotiate with the Russians'.[76] It appeared that the Americans were moving more towards Churchill's belief that some sort of dialogue with the Soviets was best for world peace (during Churchill's post-war Premiership he had advocated a summit meeting between the British, American and Soviet leaders). This trend towards dialogue was noticeable towards the end of 1954; by March 1955 it had gathered momentum.

In that month Makins inadvertently 'provoked a crisis at the top of the Conservative Party, indeed, at the top of the Government' by sending a telegram intimating that Eisenhower might be prepared to come to Europe on the 10th anniversary of VE day, 8 May 1955.[77] The story is revealed in a series of private letters from Ivone Kirkatrick to Makins. It was well known that Eden had been Prime Minister in waiting for many years, and that many believed that Churchill was past his best and should stand down in Eden's favour. According to Kirkpatrick's letters to Makins 'The P.M., after breaking many promises, had categorically undertaken to resign on 5 April 1955'. Eden would succeed and there would be an election in the following May. The feeling was that an election would remove the uncertainty and the government would have the benefit of a new mandate, which could relieve the pressure on sterling that had dogged

75 Makins Papers, MS Sherfield 525, letter Makins to Macmillan, 14 April 1955.

76 TNA, FO 371/109114, Letter Makins to Eden, 5 November 1954.

77 Colville, *Fringes of Power*, p. 659.

British life in the 1950s and avoid a run on the pound. So everyone – at least everyone in the know – was all set for a new PM on 5 April followed by a May election. All set, that was, until Makins' telegram arrived and Churchill took it to mean, albeit without justification, that Eisenhower was coming to Europe to take part in top level talks with the Russians. As Kirkpatrick remarked 'the Churchill cause has triumphed'.

Naturally Churchill thought that he must stay on and that there could be no May election, saying 'That would be putting party before peace'. According to Kirkpatrick, 'violent reactions followed in the Eden camp'. Eden argued that Eisenhower had no intention of travelling to Europe and the agreed succession must go ahead. Churchill was very angry, believing that he was being hounded from office by Eden's followers. Kirkpatrick even suggested that Churchill might 'tear the Tory party to pieces'. Eden was not to be 'fobbed off for the umpteenth time' and the Eden camp intended to resign en bloc if Churchill did not go. As Kirkpatrick reported to Makins, he spent the weekend constrained between the two conflicting blocks. On 14 March when Kirkpatrick wrote this letter to Makins he was unsure of the outcome: as he put it 'The air was charged with passion' and 'the typhoon may pass away. It may not'.[78]

Two days later Kirkpatrick wrote to Makins again indicating that, although there were ugly brushes in Cabinet, tempers were lower. It seems that representations had been made to the Americans, probably through Winthrop Aldrich, the American Ambassador in London, and it was now understood that Eisenhower did not intend to take part in a top level meeting with the Soviets and so the succession timetable could be restored with the proviso, however, that if the understanding changed then Churchill would stay on. Kirkpatrick ended his letter with 'please burn this letter too. You are the only man outside a very small circle in Whitehall who is informed'.[79]

The following day a further letter arrived:

> The Sec of State does not know that I have written fully to you. But he did remark yesterday – and you should be aware of this – that he regarded it as most important that it should not be on record anywhere that anyone on the British side had invoked our domestic electoral problems as a reason for stopping or delaying a beneficent American international initiative.
> Burn this will you.[80]

Clearly domestic politics and international initiatives had become confused and, rather than seek clarification formally through the British Ambassador in

78 Makins Papers, MS Sherfield 527, Letter Kirkpatrick to Makins, 14 March 1955.
79 Makins Papers, MS Sherfield 527, Letter Kirkpatrick to Makins, 16 March 1955.
80 Makins Papers, MS Sherfield 527, Letter Kirkpatrick to Makins, 17 March 1955.

Washington, Eden must have instructed his Permanent Secretary in London to deal with the matter through the American Ambassador in London, thus, no doubt, securing the outcome Eden desired.

Churchill did resign on 4 April, and the Premiership passed to Eden. Macmillan became Foreign Secretary, an appointment which cheered Makins who knew from previous experience that he could work with Macmillan and that they respected each other. Macmillan was also delighted and when writing to Makins after his first visit to Washington as Foreign Secretary added a handwritten postscript to his letter, saying 'it's fun to be working with you again'.[81] Makins regarded the appointment as positive for Anglo-American relations, reporting that the appointment was 'heartily welcomed' with Americans recalling the war time association between Eisenhower and Macmillan, and also the fact that, along with Churchill, Macmillan had an American mother.[82] The appointment was confirmed when Eden won the General Election held on 26 May 1955. The Conservatives increased both the number of seats they held and their share of the total vote.

The change of Foreign Secretary was also welcomed by Dulles; Eden and Dulles never got on well. Eden was an intuitive man, who quickly became bored with Dulles' long expositions and stopped listening. After Dulles had finished talking, Eden was in the habit of passing some remark to state his position but Dulles would not take it in. According to Makins there was 'a good deal of misunderstanding between them'.[83] The dislike of Eden, now the Prime Minister, was not restricted to Dulles. Kirkpatrick, when privately reporting the Geneva four power conference to Makins, indicated that 'Ike and all his party think that the P.M. is too much of a prima donna', and added that 'Foster Dulles and Harold M get on very well together'. The change of Foreign Secretary must have come as something of a relief for Makins, not only because they knew each other well, but because it would make Makins' professional life as Ambassador somewhat easier.

Makins wasted no time in offering Macmillan advice. He wrote to him suggesting that 'Americans are afraid of international conferences. They are always concerned that they will be out smarted by the unscrupulous foreigner'. Makins contrasted the American approach to business, where Americans are able to make snap decisions, work fast and are go-getters, with their approach to diplomacy where they move very slowly and take months to mature their decisions, which, once taken, are harder to alter. Their 'ponderous' approach is made worse by the fact that they are always aware of the need to carry Congress

---

81 Makins Papers, MS Sherfield 525, Letter Macmillan to Makins, 28 June 2012.

82 TNA, FO 371/114350, Weekly Political Commentary, 2–8 April 1955.

83 Lord Sherfield's Memoirs, *The Suez Crisis – The Makins Experience* (Henceforth *Suez Crisis*), p. 2.

and the American public on any issue. 'No government is more sensitive to public opinion than the American, and no public is harder to guide in matters of foreign policy'. Makins then suggested that the British should not push the Americans too hard on any particular issue and that 'if we are patient with them now we are more likely to win them to our view in the long run'.[84] It was a message which Makins had been projecting throughout his tenure as Ambassador and one which he largely failed to get through. As will be discussed below, one of the significant reasons for the breakdown in Anglo-American relations during the Suez Crisis was the failure to accept the slow pace of the American approach to diplomacy, and to understand the relevance of the American political timetable in foreign affairs.

A significant part of Makins' remaining time in Washington was spent dealing with Middle Eastern questions and, as noted, there was 'never really any identity of view between the British and the U.S. governments on the Middle East'. The fact was that there was never really an identity of view on a vast range of issues whether that be China, Indo-China, Europe or even how to deal with the Soviets. The Middle East was just one issue in a chain of differences which affected Anglo-American relations. The strength of the relationship was really about the way the two sides approached each other and dealt with differences rather than the way they reached agreement. The Ambassador played a significant part in easing the differences; however if he was not listened to, naturally his influence was curtailed.

In February 1955 Turkey and Iraq signed a mutual defence agreement; Britain adhered to the pact in April 1955 when it became known as the Baghdad Pact. Other countries including Pakistan and Iran joined later in the year and Makins spent a significant part of the spring and summer of 1955 attempting to persuade the Americans to join. His efforts 'came to nought'.[85] His failure to persuade the Americans was a cause of considerable frustration in London, however, as Makins made clear the issue for the Administration did not really stem from opposition to the idea itself, but was, at least in part, due to concern over the attitude of Congress to America joining an Arab pact, given the strength of the Jewish lobby. In addition Egypt was seen as a rival centre to Bagdad for leadership of the Arab world and America was keen not to alienate Egypt from the West and drive her into Soviet arms. Britain shared this ambition, but had already begun to alienate Nasser, and was less optimistic about retaining Western influence over Egypt.

A number of events contributed to Nasser's decision to nationalise the Suez Canal in July 1956 and the subsequent debacle. One was the West's withdrawal of an offer to help finance the building of the Aswan Dam across the River Nile.

---

84 Makins Papers, MS Sherfield, 525, Letter Makins to Macmillan, 9 July 1955.

85 *Suez Crisis*, p. 3.

The proposed dam was to be 365 ft high, over three miles long, and capable of holding over 45 billion gallons of water. Such was its scale that it would be able to regulate the flow of the Nile throughout the year. Makins played a significant part in the discussions with the Americans over the proposed financing of the project. Egypt had been in negotiations with the World Bank and other Western sources of finance for the project for several years. The Soviets had already in 1955 financed an arms deal for the Egyptians and it now became clear that they were considering financing the Aswan Dam project, increasing American concerns that their influence in the region was growing.

Makins was on a speaking engagement in Denver Colorado when he was informed by Macmillan of the Soviets' intentions regarding the dam. Furthermore, Macmillan told Makins that both he and Eden felt that it was essential, particularly following the Soviet arms deal, to prevent this further blow to Western prestige in the region. There was already an Anglo-Franco-German consortium in place prepared to build the dam, but it required guarantees from Western governments to underwrite the financing for the project or funding from the World Bank. Macmillan dismissed the idea of funding coming from the UK, which, given its overseas commitments and balance of payments situation, would be 'a heavy risk for us to underwrite'. He asked Makins to approach the Americans 'at the highest possible level' to ask if they might provide economic aid to the existing consortium – a consortium which excluded American firms.[86]

Macmillan and Eden's proposal was that the Americans put up the money, but that they have no involvement in the project. It was absurd, and just another example of the British government's lack of realism. It again fell to Makins to inject a sense of reality. After meeting with Gene Black, the Head of the World Bank, George Humphrey, the Secretary of the Treasury, a personal friend of Makins, and Herbert Hoover, the Deputy Secretary of State, Makins needed to inform London that 'some arrangement involving the association of American firms with, or participation in, the consortium was a sine qua non'.[87] Once again, Makins made his view clear, saying that 'Her Majesty's government cannot expect to get into the poker game unless they are willing to put up the ante'.[88]

Makins in the end persuaded London that if there was any hope of American help then London needed to make concessions including putting up some money and allowing American involvement in the consortium. This, together with intelligence reports coming out of Egypt, which confirmed that unless an offer came from the West soon then Egypt would turn to the Soviets for finance, persuaded the Americans to support a financing package. In the event

[86] FRUS Volume XIV Arab-Israeli dispute 1955, p. 633.

[87] *Suez Crisis*, p. 8.

[88] TNA, FO800/669, telegram Makins to Eden, 30 November 1955.

the British government agreed to contribute $15 million towards a first stage grant offered by the American government of $70 million, and conceded there should be competitive tendering for the contract. The World Bank also offered a loan of $200 million for the second stage of the project. The Egyptian finance minister seemed pleased with the offer, but it was for Nasser to make the final decision on whether to accept it or not.

Makins, through a considerable amount of hard work, had been able to persuade the British to change their position and to accept the American preconditions for help. But it took a number of sharp telegrams to the Foreign Office to get them to move. One, for example, contained the following passage, 'Further reflection increases my concern at the consequences of handling this matter, as we appear to be doing, by concentrating on an immediate British commercial interest to the exclusion of the wider considerations involved ... If we ram through the consortium contract they [the Americans] will undoubtedly resent it very much, and this will increase our difficulties in the future ... I understand the need for speed but not the need for haste'.[89]

Towards the end of 1955 Eden, then, of course, Prime Minister, wrote to Makins asking for his advice on a proposed visit to the United States to meet with Eisenhower. Eden outlined his plans which included a full talk with the President about international developments and a review of the Middle Eastern scene. Eden was also keen to 'demonstrate Anglo-American solidarity' in advance of a planned visit to London by the Soviet leaders in the following April. Eden ended his letter with 'Let me know frankly what you think of all this'. Makins replied to the Prime Minister welcoming the idea of a visit and made suggestions as to the optimum timing and itinerary.

By the time Eden arrived in America at the end of January1956 he had reshuffled his cabinet. For Makins this meant his third Foreign Secretary in as many years. His new master was Selwyn Lloyd who had moved from the Ministry of Defence. It was a promotion on a 'grand scale' for a man who had only been in the Cabinet for eight months. Makins' relationship with Selwyn Lloyd was brief but difficult and in the end Makins was to feel betrayed by his Foreign Secretary. The tension between them might be discerned by the following remark made by Makins on the telephone: 'Secretary of State, are you ordering me not to make this speech because unless it is an order, I intend to make it.'[90] It has been suggested that Selwyn Lloyd's appointment was an attempt by Eden to regain control of the Foreign Office; Eden always found Macmillan a prickly customer to deal with. Macmillan reluctantly moved to the Treasury and in doing so he extracted a concession from Eden that he would give an assurance that Rab Butler, Macmillan's rival in any future leadership contest, would not

89 TNA, FO800/669, telegram Makins to Caccia, 8 November 1955.

90 Correspondence with Virginia Makins.

be the Deputy Prime Minister. Macmillan's appointment as Chancellor of the Exchequer was to have significant consequences for Makins. In the interim, however, Makins was obliged to accept the substitution of a man he knew well and with whom he could work for one who he hardly knew.

Makins and Sir Pierson Dixon, the British Ambassador to the UN, met Eden and Lloyd off the boat in New York in the early morning of 30 January. The party flew to Washington in the President's plane and in the afternoon a series of meetings with the President and his entourage began. Although the question of European integration was discussed the talks focused on the problems in the Middle East. These ranged from measures to be put in place to avert an Arab-Israeli conflict, the continuing differences of opinion over the Bagdad Pact, Saudi Arabia and the Buraimi oil dispute, and Egypt. Eden asked how long the Western powers would be able to continue to cooperate with Nasser given his 'violent attacks' on Britain's allies in the area. The Egyptian leader had recently attacked Nuri es-Said, the Prime Minister of Iraq and co-founder of the Bagdad Pact, and he was continuing to fill the air waves via the radio station 'The Voice of Arabs' with anti-British propaganda. Dulles agreed, and indicated that the continuing talks on the Aswan Dam project with, among others, the World Bank, which had been facing breakdown, would show whether Nasser was willing to work with the West or not.[91] It remained the case, however, that Dulles and Eisenhower, while supporting the British, did not see Egypt as of paramount interest to the Americans in the way Eden perceived it to be for the British.

After the talks had finished Makins and Harold Caccia (Deputy Under Secretary at the Foreign Office) who also attended the talks, put together the final communiqué which, according to one commentator, was a rather woolly affair and was criticised for its vagueness. Perhaps this was unfair since not all the decisions reached at the talks could be announced. Makins then escorted Eden to Capitol Hill where the Prime Minister addressed both Houses of Congress. It was as Makins commented, 'a real personal triumph' for Eden. This triumph, however, could not hide the increasingly gloomy view American commentators were beginning to take of Britain's prospects. The Alsop Brothers, the well known political commentators, reporting on the talks, wrote 'Britain is now in very real danger of ... defeat in her courageous struggle to maintain her standing as a major world power'.[92] By the end of the year that struggle would be over.

During the early months of 1956 a number of events connected to Middle Eastern affairs, such as the undermining of British interests in Jordan and the failure of Western efforts to broker peace talks between Egypt and Israel, led to both the British and the Americans taking a tougher stance towards Egypt.

---

91 TNA, FO800/689, Record of Meeting Held at the White House, 30 January 1956.

92 TNA, FO 371/120312, Weekly Political Summary, 28 January to 3 February 1956

Again there were differences in approach between the two countries. The Americans developed a plan which would use political and economic means to isolate Nasser. Project Omega, as it was known, called for secret Anglo-American cooperation to convince Nasser of the error of his ways. This would include withholding aid, providing the Iraqis with a powerful transmitter to counteract Nasser's Voice of the Arabs propaganda, encouraging arms sales to Israel and supporting the Bagdad Pact. On top of that the Americans proposed to build up King Saud of Saudi Arabia as an alternative leader to Nasser in the Arab world. The British plan also sought to isolate Nasser, but focused more on strengthening the Bagdad Pact and taking more direct measures, such as withdrawing the finance for the Aswan Dam. Britain, of course, had reservations over promoting Kind Saud as an alternative leader, largely because the UK was not prepared to make concessions over Buriami. At this stage the Americans did not feel that Nasser was irrevocably committed to the Soviets. The British were more sceptical and in early April 1956 Makins sat down with Dulles at his Georgetown home and tried to resolve the differences. After a number of meetings and with instructions passing to and from London the differences still remained unresolved; Makins had been unable to reconcile the two approaches.[93]

Eden's frustration with the Americans and their refusal to be seen to be cooperating with the British in the Middle East, which he believed undermined Western influence, was yet again beginning to adversely affect the Anglo-American relationship.[94] Consistent with the Project Omega plan, but also influenced by the attitude of Congress towards financing the Egyptians, Dulles decided, after discussions with the President, to withdraw the offer of finance to facilitate the building of the Aswan Dam. The British were not necessarily against the withdrawal of the offer, but were more inclined to let the offer 'wither on the vine'. Dulles, however, took a different approach. On 13 July 1956 Dulles met with Makins and made clear his reservation about continuing with the finance, saying that he would make a final decision in the next few days.[95] Makins kept London informed of the way Dulles' mind was moving. On 18 July he informed London that Dulles would be meeting with the Egyptian Ambassador and that it was probable that he would withdraw the offer of American funding. The Foreign Office replied at 1.50pm (Washington time) on 19 July: 'It suits us very well if Mr Dulles speaks as you foresee. We would rather he said as little as possible about 'some future assistance' but we do not want him to think that

---

[93] FRUS, 1955–1957, Vol XV, pp. 433–5, 457–70. Memorandum of Conversation, Secretary Dulles Residence, 1 April 1956 and 4 April 1956.

[94] *Suez Crisis*, p. 21.

[95] FRUS, 1955–1957, Vol XV, pp. 830–32 Memorandum of conversation, Department of State, 13 July 1956.

there is any disagreement between us on the essential point.'[96] Britain then was clearly warned of the changing American view.

During the morning of 19 July Dulles met with Makins again and confirmed that he intended, that afternoon, to inform the Egyptian Ambassador that the offer of finance to build the dam was to be withdrawn. Makins told Dulles that the Cabinet had not yet taken a decision on the matter and the British would have preferred a further exchange of views before a definitive decision was reached. But he added that the general view in London was similar to the Americans and the offer should be withdrawn. Makins told Dulles that he or John Coulson (Minister at the British Embassy) would telephone London before he met with the Egyptian Ambassador that afternoon. Dulles, in a conversation with his brother Allen Dulles, the Head of the CIA, noted that he had not heard back from Makins and therefore assumed it was OK with London. It seems clear that notwithstanding the accounts given in both Eden's and Lloyd's memoirs Makins gave London adequate warnings of American intentions. 'The French Ambassador to the United States, Couve de Murville was the only one to predict correctly how the Egyptians would react to the withdrawal of finance. They will do something about Suez. That is the only way they can touch the Western countries'.

It was during this most sensitive moment that Dulles, on 17 July, was informed that Makins was to be withdrawn from Washington and replaced by Harold Caccia. Makins, in fact, knew he was leaving Washington in the previous April, but it had been decided not to make an announcement at the time. In a letter to his father Makins wrote:

> Its typical of our present rulers that having dithered for months and finally taken a decision they want to announce it immediately at the most inconvenient time for me. He [Dulles] took it all very much amiss, which was of course a compliment to me though hardly HMG! He first of all said "it's crazy" and then observed that it would effect Anglo American relations as they all had such confidence in me and felt that they could treat me with absolute frankness etc etc.[97]

When Nasser nationalised the Suez Canal on 26 July 1956, Makins was on vacation with Alice at Lake Tahoe. Makins returned to Washington the next day and discovered that Eden had lost patience with Project Omega and was advocating direct action against Nasser. There then followed a frenetic period of activity where Makins endeavoured to protect Britain's interests by securing tangible support from the Americans while, at the same time, dealing with

---

96 *Suez Crisis*, p. 23. See also TNA, FO 371/119056.

97 Ernest Makins Papers, MS Sherfield 197, Letter Makins to father, 18 July 1956.

the differences in approach between the Americans and the British. It was the customary role for a British Ambassador in Washington.

Makins delivered a letter from Eden to Eisenhower which called for international control of the canal to be regained by force if necessary. Eisenhower was keen to support his allies but also to defuse the belligerence of Eden and he sent Bob Murphy, with whom Macmillan and Makins had worked in Algiers, to London for talks. In the meantime Makins, with his Economics Minister Lord Harcourt, met with Herbert Hoover Jr (the Under Secretary of State) to negotiate economic measures to put pressure on the Egyptians and to protect Britain's position. These included blocking Egyptian balances in the United States, diverting canal dues, and putting in place contingency plans to secure oil supplies for Britain should the canal close.

Hoover was not entirely supportive of the British requests and Makins formed the impression that the Americans 'were weak and irresolute in the face of this crisis, and are tepid about taking any vigorous action. The State Department do not feel themselves directly involved as principals in the dispute with Egypt and are acutely aware of the domestic repercussions which strong action might have'.[98] Makins relayed these views to London and advised them that if they intended to take firm action with American support, they must make a strong impression on Bob Murphy.

In the event the Americans responded to certain British requests for indirect action against Egypt, mainly by freezing Egyptian government and Suez Canal financial assets. It did not, however, go as far as the British and French governments did. For example, the Americans excluded private Egyptian funds from the measures put in place and also continued to pay canal dues to Egypt. In the meantime Murphy was sending back reports suggesting that the British were minded to use force to deal with Nasser. On 30 July Dulles felt obliged to warn Makins that:

> the US Government would not be in sympathy with any attempt to make the Egyptian Government rescind their nationalisation decrees, or to regard them as inoperative, under the threat of force. As long as there was no interference with the navigation of the canal and no threat to foreign nationals in Egypt, there is no basis for military action and therefore no case could be made to Congress or would gain public support for US military intervention.[99]

In relaying this message to London Makins pointed out that it confirmed the pessimistic impression given by Hoover in their earlier discussions and he also suggested that no better time could have been chosen by Nasser who was, of

[98] *Suez Crisis*, p. 25.

[99] *Suez Crisis*, p. 26.

course, aware that it was election year and that Congress would have to be recalled and consulted before the Administration could use force.[100] There was no prospect that the administration would recall Congress for this purpose during an election year, even if they were disposed to use force, which they were not. As Makins pointed out in his memoirs 'this remained the American position throughout the crisis'.[101]

In an attempt to defuse the situation the Americans proposed that an international conference should be convened under the Constantinople Convention of 1888 on the Suez Canal. In an important intervention Makins pointed out that this entailed the Soviets becoming involved, and suggested a Conference of Canal Users instead. While arrangements for the conference were being put in place Makins began securing 'Anglo-American cooperation on non-military measures in case Nasser blocked the Canal', such measures included securing oil supplies and the means of transporting them.

During August Makins was on holiday with Alice and the children at a ranch in Wyoming. Consequently he was out of touch with events during the first London Conference and the Menzies Mission to Cairo. The London Conference led to proposals effectively to internationalise the Canal and it appointed Sir Robert Menzies, the Australian Prime Minister, to present these proposals to Nasser, who rejected them stating that he wanted 'complete ownership, management and operating control of the Canal by the Egyptian Government'.[102] Makins broke his holiday to return to Washington on 8 September. The next day was a Sunday and Makins met with Dulles at the Secretary's home in Georgetown. Dulles outlined his proposal to set up what became the Suez Canal Users Association (SCUA). He also asked if the British had really thought through the economic implications of using force, and proposed alternative strategies to deal with Nasser. Makins replied to Dulles that he 'entirely agreed and had already clearly represented his views in this respect to London'.[103] In relaying the proposals to London Makins, in what he refers to as his 'most important telegram' sent during the Suez Crisis, set out the underlying issues. It is worth quoting at length.

> Our relationship with the Americans is following the pattern which has appeared on previous occasions and which is becoming more and more marked. We agree upon the substance of the policy, but differ on method and timing. We press for immediate action while the Americans are inclined to move with greater phlegm and deliberation. This is the opposite of what our natural temperaments are

[100] TNA,PREM 11/1098.
[101] Suez, p. 26.
[102] Kyle, K., *Suez,* London: Tauris, 2011, p. 222.
[103] FRUS, Vol. XVI, p. 448.

> supposed to be ... Mr Dulles' statement that the Administration are determined to join with us in cutting Nasser down to size seems to me very significant and he has now produced concrete suggestions for the next stage of the process ... It is true, as the President says, that there is no support in the United States for the use of force. If we wish to retain full American support we must endeavour to ensure that the responsibility for the progressive deterioration of the situation and breakdown of the operation of the Canal lies squarely on the Egyptians ... I do not really know what your innermost thoughts are as regards military action, but as it looks from Washington, to attempt it without full American moral and material support could easily lead to disaster.[104]

At the time Eden, still minded to secure American support, decided to accept the American proposals for SCUA. Dulles travelled to London for the second conference on 17 September. Makins noted in his memoirs that SCUA was a device by Dulles to gain time until the Presidential election was over. He also suggests that Eden did not really understand Americans or American politics in the broad sense, or the constitutional difficulties of the President. He offers no evidence to support these remarks and it seems highly unlikely that Eden, who had considerable contact with the Americans during and after the war, failed to understand their difficulties. A more plausible explanation for Eden's reluctance to accept Makins' analysis was the fact that Makins had consistently taken the American line during his ambassadorship. Eden had probably lost patience with his Ambassador who, in any event, had been recalled. As his biographer put it: 'Eden did not ... entirely regret the departure from Washington of Makins, whom he felt had gone native after four years.'[105]

Notwithstanding Makins' warnings, Anglo-American relations went from bad to worse. Tired of procrastination, Eden decided, against Dulles wishes, to go to the security council of the UN. Thereafter much of the action moved away from Washington and towards New York and London. One of the final parts Makins played in the Suez affair while he was in Washington was to take Macmillan to meet with Eisenhower on 25 September 1956. Macmillan and his Treasury team had been staying at the Embassy during the annual meeting of the World Bank and the International Monetary Fund. At the meeting with the President, contrary to Makins' expectation, there was little talk of Suez 'apart from fleeting references to Nasser, Britain's draft resolution before the Security Council and SCUA, nothing of substance was raised by Macmillan or Eisenhower'.[106] There was another meeting that afternoon with Dulles where the

---

[104] TNA, PREM 11/1101, Makins to Foreign Office, 9 September 1956.

[105] Thorpe, R., *Eden: The Life and Times of Anthony Eden*, London: Chatto and Windus, 2003, p. 496.

[106] *Suez Crisis*, p. 32.

Americans again impressed on both Macmillan and Makins that they would not condone a showdown with Nasser before 6 November which was the date of the Presidential election.

At a meeting with Bob Murphy at his Georgetown house a few days later, Murphy further emphasised this point to Macmillan and Makins. He indicated that if the British government refrained from acting before 6 November the position 'would be quite different ... between us, we should be able to encompass Nasser's downfall within a few months. It was high time that Nasser's pretensions and those of the Arab states were deflated'.[107] Makins, in commenting on the meeting to the Foreign Office, pointed out that nothing Murphy had said was inconsistent with the views of Dulles and Eisenhower. He made the position clear to the Foreign Office that the Americans could not countenance the use of force before the elections. But Macmillan was giving Eden a different view; his rather optimistic message was that 'because of the forthcoming Presidential election the United States would not, or could not, act against Britain in the event that it decided to take military action against Egypt'.[108] As Makins said there was no basis at all for Macmillan's optimism. The fact was, however, that Eden had by this stage lost confidence in his Ambassador and decided to listen to his Chancellor. It was to have disastrous consequences.

At the end of September Makins and Alice began to 'eat their way out of post': a long series of lunches and dinners followed with colleagues, friends and fellow diplomats. On 5 October Makins bid farewell to Eisenhower. It led to yet another despatch to Eden. Makins reported after a conversation with the President that it was 'always a source of great unhappiness to them [Eisenhower and Dulles] when they did not quite see eye to eye with the P.M. and his colleagues. But there was no doubt whatsoever that public opinion in the United States was firmly opposed to the use of force'. On 11 October Makins left Washington for New York where he addressed the executive committee of the Pilgrims Society at lunch. In the morning Makins met Bob Dixon, as Sir Pierson was always known, who reported that he was optimistic about the UN negotiations on the operation of the canal which were taking place between Selwyn Lloyd, Christian Pineau (the French Foreign Minister) and the Egyptian Foreign Minister Fawzi. Makins relayed this optimism in his speech to the Pilgrims Society. Later that afternoon Makins took off from Idlewild for London. As the plane flew over the east coast Makins would have had every reason to believe that the crisis was nearly over, and no doubt would have been thinking more about the daunting prospect of running the Treasury. However, the Suez story was not over yet and the part Makins played in it is taken up in the next chapter.

[107] *Suez Crisis*, p. 33.

[108] Ibid.

Chapter 6
The Treasury Years

The management of the economy in the 1950s was fraught with difficulties as Britain sought to pursue the traditional post-Keynesian objectives of full employment and stable prices while at the same time attempting to protect sterling as a reserve currency. One of the aims of Treasury policy was to maintain of Britain's role in world affairs. This aim was dealt a severe blow in the aftermath of the Suez Crisis. Britain, with inadequate resources, simply could not arrest the haemorrhaging of reserves after the invasion. Her weakness and her reliance on the Anglo-American relationship became clear. What also became evident was that the Anglo-American relationship depended on the officials on both sides of the Atlantic as much as the politicians. Britain desperately needed help from the Americans, and it was the officials who delivered it at a crucial time.

In 1956 Makins moved from the social elite to the intellectual elite.[1] It was the year when he ended a successful Foreign Office career and embarked on a new career as the Joint Permanent Secretary to the Treasury. It was a curious move. It began with Makins being recalled to London by Selwyn Lloyd in April 1956. The reason Lloyd recalled Makins is not known, but it may have been to familiarise himself with events across the Atlantic by talking directly to his Ambassador, or it may have been instigated by Macmillan who had already promised Makins the top job in the Foreign Office but now wanted him for the Treasury. Either way Makins and Macmillan met on 15 April 1956, two days before Macmillan made his first and last budget speech. It was then that Macmillan proposed to Makins that he take the top job at the Treasury.

It is often supposed that it was Macmillan who first suggested Makins for the Treasury. Robert Hall, however, offers a different view. He suggests that Rab Butler, the Chancellor from 1951 to 1955, was not impressed with the top people at the Treasury, and was anxious to bring in someone from outside 'and he mentioned the name of Roger Makins as the man to be brought in'. It seems that Macmillan shared Butler's opinion of the top Treasury officials and he was also an admirer of Makins. The negative view of the senior Treasury civil servants was to continue. When Makins left in 1960 Frank Lee was brought in from the Department of Trade, and when he left in 1962 William Armstrong, a

---

1 Derived from Sampson, Anthony, *Anatomy of Britain*, London: Hodder & Stoughton, 1962, p. 272.

third secretary at the Treasury, was promoted over the head of the more senior officials there. So on three occasions the people at the top of the Treasury were passed over.[2]

The new job of Joint Permanent Secretary at the Treasury was created because of the imminent retirement of Edward Bridges, who had been both Permanent Secretary HM Treasury and Head of Home Civil Service. The dual role, which Bridges had held for 11 years, was very demanding. When Makins once asked Bridges how he managed, he replied 'I don't, I catch about one ball in four'.[3] After Bridges, the job was split into two. Makins became head of the Treasury, and Norman Brook took over as head of the Home Civil Service.

Makins met Macmillan again on 24 April. This time he accepted the position on condition that he could remain in the Foreign Service, and it was agreed that he could return to the Foreign Office after a three years' secondment to the Treasury. Macmillan's suggestion to Makins must have been, as Alice put it, 'something of a bombshell'. It was only a few weeks before that Makins had received a personal letter from Sir Ivone Kirkpatrick, the then Permanent Secretary at the Foreign Office, discussing Makins' succession to Kirkpatrick's position and suggesting that Makins would 'step into his chair in a couple of years'.[4]

The appointment and the organisational changes at the top of the Treasury were announced on 20 July 1956. Macmillan recorded in his memoirs that the appointment of a member of the Foreign Service was a 'startling breach of tradition'.[5] Indeed it was. Sir Leslie Rowan, Second Secretary and Head of Overseas Finance Division, told Macmillan that the appointment of Makins was the biggest blow the civil service had ever received.[6] Rowan, who had eyes on the top job himself, was to leave the Treasury before Makins had served out his term of office. He was a great loss; Robert Hall commenting at the time of his departure wrote 'The Treasury is certainly much weaker with him gone – it is clear now that he was a considerable international figure'.[7]

Rowan's reaction was understandable. Perhaps a more balanced view came from Sir John Herbecq, who held the relatively junior position of Assistant Principal in the Treasury at the time of Makins' appointment. He recalled 'there was a feeling of surprise, resentment was too strong a word but there was a feeling of being slightly miffed that they had to turn to the Foreign Service to find the

2 British Oral Archive of Political and Administrative History (Henceforth British Oral Archive), Lord Roberthall, p. 28.

3 Peter, Hennessy, *Whitehall*, London: Secker and Warburg, 1989, p. 144.

4 Makins Papers, MS Sherfield 527, Letter Kirkpatrick to Makins, 11 February 1956.

5 Macmillan, H. *Riding the Storm, 1956–1959*, London: Macmillan, 1971, p. 2.

6 Cairncross, A. (ed.) *The Robert Hall Diaries 1954–1961*, London: Unwin Hyman, 1991, p. 71.

7 Ibid., p. 180.

head of the Treasury'.[8] Initially, Norman Brook was able to report to Makins, who had clearly been concerned about the possible reaction to his appointment, that 'I have heard nothing to suggest that I was wrong in assuring you that your appointment would be welcomed'.[9] A week later, however, Brook commented 'There is, naturally, a little feeling of regret that there should have been no one available in the Home Civil Service who was fully qualified to fill the job to which you have been appointed'.[10]

The announcement of the Treasury changes caused quite a stir in the press; Norman Brook commented that he 'was quite surprised by the length and the prominence given to this by most of the newspapers'.[11]One paper commented:

> A diplomat seems an odd choice for the economic job, since the Treasury has been for many years a closed priesthood, but Sir Roger is an unusual diplomat. A man of extraordinary intellectual and physical energy, he has made himself the master of many subjects outside conventional diplomacy and, in particular, has had a great deal of first hand experience of international economic questions.[12]

Another article, mindful of Makins' lack of experience in Treasury matters, commented that economic policy and foreign affairs are both professional matters and warned 'That does not mean that the professional is always right, but it is true that the amateur is almost always wrong'.[13] *The News Chronicle*, perhaps more informed of the tension within the Treasury, said 'Sir Roger Makins is one of the most forceful characters in British public life – and not one of the most popular'.[14] In the mixed reaction to Makins' appointment, perhaps the strongest feeling was one of surprise. There was no talk that Makins was not up to the job intellectually, but warning shots were fired with regard to his lack of experience, a criticism which was to be made by one of his Chancellors in due course.

Makins took up his appointment on 15 October 1956. On his desk he found a letter and a bundle of documents from Bridges. The letter and attachments, which Makins would undoubtedly have found useful, only serves to underline how unprepared and ill equipped Makins was to run the Treasury. The papers included a note detailing how the budget committee actually worked including detailed advice on how to put a budget together, a memorandum on Prices Wages and Costs (a 'confusing subject', said Bridges), a bundle on what to do in the event of

---

8 Note of Author's Conversation with Sir John Herbecq (Henceforth Herbecq Notes), 17 January 2012.

9 Makins Papers, MS Sherfield 529, Letter Brook to Makins, 21 July 1956.

10 Makins Papers, MS Sherfield 529, Letter Brook to Makins, 28 July 1956.

11 Makins Papers, MS Sherfield 529, Letter Brook to Makins 21 July 1956.

12 *Observer* Newspaper, Pendennis Column, 22 July 1956.

13 Ibid.

14 *News Chronicle*, 20 July 1956.

a dollar drain and a note from Sir Robert Hall covering the economic outlook.[15] Had the Joint Permanent Secretary been appointed from within the Treasury it is unlikely any of these notes would have been required. Sir David Butler, who had been Makins' press officer in Washington, recalls visiting Makins during his first day at the Treasury. On his desk he saw a book which Bridges had sent. It was the recently published *Treasury Control* by Samuel Beer – a book which deals with the very basics of how the Treasury works.[16]

When Makins joined the Treasury he had access to a considerable array of talented people, many of whom he had known from his time running the Economic Departments within the Foreign Office and from even earlier in his career. These people had the confidence and ability to address the Chancellor directly, a practice developed under Bridges partly because of the pressure he was under carrying out the two functions of running the Treasury and the Civil Service. Makins, while he was still learning on the job, was caught in a 'cross fire of flimsies', the copies of his subordinates' submissions to the Chancellor. He says 'it took me about a year to get some sort of control of what was going on'.[17]

His first few months at the Treasury were dominated by the Suez Crisis. Here it is worth making two points: firstly, Makins' appointment to the Treasury was made in April 1956, long before the Suez Crisis erupted and before Nasser took over the Suez Canal on 26 July 1956 – it is clear that Makins' return to London was not connected with the Suez incident or his handling of it with the Americans; secondly, Makins is unique amongst British officials in that he was involved both in the early stages of the crisis while he was in Washington and in the later stages after he moved to London. This gave him an unusual perspective on the Suez debacle.[18]

During his first few days at the Treasury Makins met with Bridges, Brook and the Second Secretaries. He also met with the junior ministers in the department: Sir Edward Boyle, the Economic Secretary and Reginald Maudling, the Financial Secretary. He very quickly became curious why neither Macmillan, Eden nor Lloyd wanted to see the returning Ambassador from Washington and be briefed on the American view of the Suez situation and other matters. As Makins put it in his memoirs 'there was an unnatural hush in Whitehall and, as an old Whitehall warrior, I made it my business ... to find out what was afoot'.[19] He met with Kirkpatrick on 16 October and it is a testament to Kirkpatrick's trust in Makins that he disclosed that Eden was in the process of being seduced by the so called Challe Plan. The plan, which had been presented to Eden and

15 Makins Papers, MS Sherfield 562, Letter Bridges to Makins, 12 October 1956.

16 Note of Conversation between the author and Sir David Butler, 24 August 2011.

17 British Oral Archive, Makins, p. 66.

18 I am grateful to Saul Kelly for this observation which is contained in Kelly, Saul and Gorst, Anthony. (eds), *Whitehall and the Suez Crisis*, London: Frank Cass, 2000, p. 157.

19 *Suez Crisis*, p. 36.

Anthony Nutting (Minister of State, Foreign Office) at Chequers the previous weekend by Albert Gazier (French Minister for Social Affairs) and Major General Maurice Challe (Deputy to French General Chief of Staff), entailed encouraging Israel to attack Egypt, and then using the ensuing hostilities as an excuse to enter Egypt, in particular the canal zone, on the pretext of being a policing force with the objective of separating the two sides.

Makins points out in his memoirs that both Kirkpatrick and Sir Archibald Ross (Assistant Under Secretary of State), the only two Foreign Office officials to know about it, advised Nutting against the plan on the basis that it would undermine Britain's position in America, the United Nations, the Commonwealth and the Middle East. Kirkpatrick was still in favour of force but not this particular plan. Nutting tried to relay their concerns to Eden, who dismissed them and secured the support of other Ministers. Eden and Lloyd then went to Paris on 17 October to meet with Guy Mollet (French Prime Minister) and Christian Pineau (French Foreign Minister) to convey British acceptance of the plan. Makins was astonished to learn of Eden's support for the French plan and it never occurred to him that the British government would consider taking such action without full American support. Later, he wrote 'I realised immediately that there would be a disaster and I began to prepare myself mentally for it'.[20]

On 23 October Eden informed his cabinet of his 'secret conversations ... in Paris with representatives of the Israeli government'. Lloyd had returned to Paris on 22 October and met with the French and Israelis to discuss further coordinated action against Egypt. On 24 October two British officials, Patrick Dean, Chairman of the Joint Intelligence Committee, and Donald Logan, Selwyn Lloyd's assistant private secretary signed the so called Sevres Protocol, a document which, as Makins put it, saw Britain, France and Israel secretly declare war on Egypt.[21] It was made without any consultation with the Americans, Britain's principal ally, and a country who, through Dulles, was still seeking a peaceful settlement of the Suez Crisis.

The tension in the Middle East had put considerable pressure on sterling and the Treasury was fretting about the reserve position even more than usual. Bridges had warned Macmillan on 8 August that Britain's gold and dollar reserve position was going to be under considerable strain in the coming months. Macmillan was also warned of the need for American support during a period of strain on Britain's reserves.[22] Leslie Rowan wrote a note on the consequences of Britain going to war in Egypt; in it he proposed two hypotheses: Hypothesis A – full US and UN support and Hypothesis B – limited US, Commonwealth and

---

20 *Suez Crisis*, p. 35.

21 *Suez Crisis*, p. 38.

22 TNA, T272/380, Memorandum Bridges to Macmillan, 8 August 1956.

other support.[23] The conclusion was clear. Britain would be in severe difficulties without American support for her plans if she went to war. Both Makins and his Treasury colleagues were agreed then that the lack of consultation with America was disastrous.

On 25 October 1956 Makins chaired his first meeting of the Budget committee, the beginning of the long process towards the presentation of the next budget in the spring of the following year. He also met with Macmillan in the House of Commons; Macmillan did not discuss Sevres, but he did raise the issue of the precarious state of Britain's gold and dollar reserves. The Treasury was predicting that the reserves would fall by $80 million during October alone, and that they would fall below the psychologically important $2,000 million level by the end of the year. The Treasury and the Bank of England disagreed over the timing of any approach to the International Monetary Fund (IMF) in order to seek help with the reserve position. The Treasury favoured an early approach before the situation became too serious; the Bank of England, in the form of Cameron Cobbold (Governor Bank of England 1949–61), argued that any approach would be seen as a sign of weakness. What was universally agreed was that any breakdown in Anglo-American relations would put at risk any assistance from the IMF.

The following weekend Makins entertained Cynthia and Bill Martin at Sherfield. Cynthia was Alice's sister and Bill was the Chairman of the Board of Governors of the Federal Reserve System. This is another example of how well connected Makins was to the American establishment. During the weekend Macmillan summoned Makins to Birch Grove, his country house in Sussex. Here, on 26 October, Macmillan told Makins that 'now the expedition force has sailed I can talk to you'.[24] He said that the invasion force had been given the go ahead and proceeded to tell Makins what he already suspected, that there was to be an imminent attack on Egypt by Israel and a subsequent intervention by the French and British.

Makins was baffled. He could not understand why such action could not wait until after the American Presidential election on 6 November. He was also aware of the catastrophic negative effect this action would have on the Anglo-American relationship. Makins asked Macmillan what 'was being done to liaise with the Americans'. He suggested later that since nothing had been done this question had a 'startling effect' on Macmillan who apparently was like a man coming out of a trance.[25] But it is difficult to believe that Macmillan,

---

23 TNA, T273/380, Note prepared by Rowan *Economic and Financial Measures in Event of War with Egypt*, probably dated 9 September 1956.

24 *Suez Crisis*, p. 40. The expedition force did not leave Malta until 30 October. Makins believed that Macmillan's reference to 'has sailed' must have been a reference to the redeployment of Naval ships from Cyprus.

25 *Suez Crisis*, p. 40.

who visited America frequently, met with Eisenhower only a few weeks before, and had been Foreign Secretary had not thought about the consequence of this action on Anglo-American relations. It is equally unlikely that as Chancellor, he had not sought to do anything about it when he had been warned that the pressure on sterling would only mount as the fact of an invasion became known. Either Makins' account of Macmillan's behaviour is wrong, or Macmillan was continuing to play the game he had been playing all along; deliberately downplaying the effect on Anglo-American relations of Britain using force to solve the Suez problem, and encouraging Eden to believe that the Americans were almost indifferent to such action and that the consequences would, at least from an Anglo-American perspective, be limited.

In accordance with the Sevres plan Israel invaded Sinai on 29 October, and both France and Britain issued ultimatums to Israel and Egypt. Further, they vetoed both the American and Soviet resolutions for a ceasefire at the UN Security Council and ordered the invasion force, which was assembled at Malta, to set sail for Egypt. The American reaction was as Makins had predicted; Eisenhower and Dulles were furious and the Americans felt betrayed.

By 2 November $50 million had been lost from the reserves within 48 hours. The Treasury predicted that if the Suez Canal was shut down Britain's oil imports would fall by 25 per cent and have to be made up from other sources, which would cost over $500 million, and further there would be a fall in industrial production putting a strain on exports and hence the balance of payments. The tension and the conflict escalated. The Egyptians blocked the Canal, the Israelis rejected the ceasefire, and the British Cabinet approved the parachute drops into Port Said and Port Fuad. On 5 November, the day the airborne troops landed, two ministers resigned; Anthony Nutting from the Foreign Office and Edward Boyle from the Treasury. Makins remarked to Boyle 'privately I do not blame you; you realise what has happened'.[26] At this stage Makins suggested that 'he was waiting to see how events unfolded before broaching with Macmillan the subject of emergency measures by the Treasury'.[27]

He did not have to wait long. As Kyle commented 'The sterling area's currency reserves were haemorrhaging as dealers hastened to get out of the currency of a country which was manifestly isolated on the international scene'.[28] There was particularly heavy selling in New York as the Federal Reserve protected its positions. Makins' contacts with the American establishment, like Britain's as a whole, amounted to nothing at this stage. In ordinary circumstances America would have come to Britain's aid by way of a loan or by facilitating drawing rights from the IMF but, as Makins had

26 *Suez Crisis*, p. 42.

27 Ibid.

28 Kyle, *Suez*, p. 464.

predicted, in these circumstances America was in no mood to help. Macmillan had been frantically telephoning New York overnight. It was made clear to him that there would be no help unless a ceasefire was in place by midnight. At this point the Anglo-American relationship was bankrupt and Britain was on a similar trajectory. The Cabinet met on the morning of 6 November. Macmillan informed his colleagues that another $280 million had been lost in the first week of November, and told them the American response to requests for help. He and the Cabinet capitulated and complied with the American demands. Eden announced the ceasefire in the House of Commons at 6.00pm that evening and that it was to be effective from midnight that day.

The historian Diane Kunz has argued that Macmillan deliberately inflated the reserve loss figure when presenting the arguments to his cabinet colleagues.[29] As noted above Macmillan told his colleagues that the loss to the reserves was $280 million. In fact, the Treasury reported on 7 November that the figure was nearer to $85 million. Makins' comment on this is that he did not believe it was deliberate on Macmillan's part, suggesting that 'it was not his style at all'. He further commented that he did not know the reason why he got the figures wrong, but it may simply have been due to a miscalculation by Macmillan himself.[30] This is yet another curious example of Macmillan, to put a generous interpretation on it, being wrong footed during the Suez Crisis.

Makins was now in no doubt that protecting the reserves and thus the pound was the priority and that the only weapon the British had was to re-establish some sort of relationship with the Americans. It was a field in which he was able to excel. The problem Britain faced was that with the run on the pound it would be difficult to maintain the exchange rate at $2.80 while preserving sterling as a major trading currency without drastically depleting the reserves. At a meeting held on 7 November at 11 Downing Street between Makins, other officials and the Chancellor the options were reviewed. They might draw from the IMF, sell Treasury owned dollar securities, obtain a credit from the Export Import Bank of the United State (EXIM bank) and even ration oil. Before any action was taken, they decided to consult with the Bank of England and the British Embassy in Washington.

When Makins met Cobbold on 9 November, Cobbold commented rather predictably that 'sterling is a major casualty of recent events, and that radical treatment was required to save it'.[31] The options suggested by the Bank were similar to those the committee had discussed two days before. It was clear that virtually all the options, or at least the palatable ones, required American

29 Kunz, D., *The Economic Diplomacy of the Suez Crisis*, Chapel Hill, North Carolina Press, 1991, p. 132.

30 *Suez Crisis*, p. 42.

31 *Suez Crisis*, p. 44.

support. The essential conclusion, and the one drawn by Makins, was that it was necessary, indeed vital, to secure an immediate improvement in Anglo-American relations.

Unfortunately Harold Caccia, recently arrived in Washington, was reporting that the chances of the Americans agreeing to an IMF drawing or an EXIM loan were slim. The Americans continued to make demands on the British before offering any support. They now called for a complete withdrawal of troops rather than merely a ceasefire. Meanwhile sterling continued to have a difficult time. Makins knew George Humphrey, the Treasury Secretary, well and, with Dulles in hospital, Humphrey was perhaps the closest advisor to Eisenhower. Makins suggested to Bill Harcourt (the Treasury official attached to the embassy) that he should meet with Humphrey to ease the tension and explore the best timing and method of an approach for assistance. On 21 November he also drafted a message from Macmillan to Humphrey which dealt with the broader picture, the political background and consequences of what was unfolding in Britain. He knew that in spite of all that had happened, the last thing the Americans wanted was a sterling crisis. Bill Harcourt reported from Washington that 'although the Administration was refusing to assist Britain, he thought this would change when things were really desperate'.[32]

The nadir of the financial crisis was probably reached on 23 November. Approximately. $48 million was lost from the reserves in the two days prior to 22 November and a further $20 million on 23 November. There was near panic over sterling in New York and Cobbold reported that for the first time the City began to fret over the situation.[33] The Treasury and the Bank considered implementing crisis measures including reducing overseas commitments and raising taxes. Shortly after this, however, the result of Makins' initiative in Washington began to bear fruit. Caccia and Harcourt were able to report that Humphrey and the Administration were beginning to share Britain's concerns over the position of sterling. Humphrey indicated that a drawing from the IMF of $561 million and an EXIM loan might be forthcoming 'once Her Majesty's Government had shown, in a way which the world could accept, that we were conforming to rather than defying the United Nations'.[34]

Makins persuaded Macmillan to delay releasing the November reserve figures for a day until 4 December so that more time was available for discussions with the Americans. He argued that another 24 hours might make all the difference. If the discussions were successful, any statement made to accompany the figures might be a little more optimistic. The strategy proved successful. Makins informed Macmillan that the loss of reserves for November

32 *Suez Crisis*, p. 47.

33 Ibid.

34 *Suez Crisis*, p. 48.

amounted to $401 million, although this was disguised by selling American securities, bringing the published figure down to $279 million. Then, in early December Britain faced a large dollar deficit due to scheduled loan repayments to America and Canada. This meant that the reserves would stand at $1,965 million at the end of November, and would fall to $1,789 million or lower by the end of the year – way below the psychologically important level of $2,000 million. It was this that persuaded Macmillan and his cabinet colleagues of the need to withdraw forces from Egypt and give in to American demands.

On 3 December Selwyn Lloyd made a statement to the House of Commons informing MPs that troops would be withdrawn by mid December if an effective UN force was in place. This was enough to secure American support, and when Macmillan announced the reserve figures on the following day he was also able to announce that he was, with American backing, seeking support from the IMF and a waiver of American loan repayments. Within three days of Lloyd's statement to the House oil supplies were on their way to Britain. By the end of the year Britain had received over $2,000 million of aid from the IMF and the EXIM bank. Makins' knowledge and experience of dealing with the Americans had been an important ingredient in the negotiations which led to sterling being saved.

However, the Suez Crisis left Makins in a difficult position. Eden, broken both physically and politically, had left Britain on 23 November to recuperate in Jamaica on his doctor's orders. When he returned on 14 December Britain was a different place and Eden's position was untenable. He resigned on 9 January 1957 and Macmillan outmanoeuvred Rab Butler, his only serious rival for the Premiership, and moved into 10 Downing Street. Makins, who had given up his Foreign Office career to work directly for Macmillan at the Treasury, was now to find himself with a new Chancellor, one who had considerably less respect for him than Macmillan had. Nevertheless Makins now had a patron with all the powers of patronage of the Prime Minister's office.

On 13 January Makins was confronted with three new ministers: Peter Thorneycroft, the new Chancellor, Enoch Powell, the Financial Secretary and Nigel Birch, the Economic Secretary. They were three out of a total of 11 ministers under whom Makins would serve during his time at the Treasury. Thorneycroft had been the President of the Board of Trade for five years and was regarded as capable and competent. Makins has said that his relations with Thorneycroft were perfectly amicable. Amicable they may have been, smooth they were not. Powell moved to the Treasury from the Ministry of Housing. Makins regarded Powell as 'strange' and believed that he was the architect of the subsequent difficulties. Birch came to the Treasury by way of demotion, having been Air Secretary. He was both rich and clever, and independent financially and intellectually. Makins regarded him as a 'rather reckless character'. Whatever

Makins thought of these three ministers, one thing is certain: their appointment was the prelude to a difficult period at the Treasury for Makins.

The initial period of Thorneycroft's Chancellorship was not particularly controversial. Given that the economy was operating in the aftermath of Suez the outlook was promising. The first task for the incoming ministers was to agree the budget proposals. As was the usual practice, the budget committee had been meeting since October. On 7 March Makins met with the Chancellor to confirm that the committee was recommending tax reductions of between £50 million and £100 million. The cuts included surtax and purchase tax reductions and allowances to companies operating abroad. The concessions were to be balanced by reductions in the defence budget. It seems that there was little difference of view over the budget between the ministers and the officials. Although it was Makins' first budget and he had no experience of putting budgets together, he did, as Robert Hall pointed out, have one advantage. Since he 'had not grown up in the aura of extreme agitation' which preceded budgets, he was able to help keep the temperature down by remaining calm.[35]

On 9 April 1957 Thorneycroft stood up in the House of Commons to make his first (and last) budget speech. He was able to tell his backbenchers that he saw 'some grounds for cheerfulness'.[36] This was important psychologically so soon after Tory confidence had been shattered by the Suez debacle. He cheered them further by announcing tax reductions amounting to £108 million (£130 million in a full year).[37] The speech was seen as a success and the budget was broadly welcomed by Macmillan and the Conservative Party. The budget speech also contained details of a new committee under Lord Radcliffe, set up to look in detail at the various options for monetary policy which might be available to the government. For Makins, with his limited experience of monetary policy or indeed the workings of the Treasury and the Bank of England, the need to prepare for and give evidence to this committee over the course of the next two years added considerably to his work.

While the conservatives might have been pleased with the budget, the Bank of England had its concerns. In May, the month after the budget, Cobbold wrote to Thorneycroft 'in very gloomy terms ... about growing anxieties over the longer term future of sterling, growing doubts about whether any Government would be able to reverse the inflationary drift that seemed to beset the UK economy and the consequential growing difficulties

35 Hall, *Diaries*, p. 106.

36 Dell, *The Chancellors*, p. 226.

37 TNA, T171/478, Budget Summary.

with Exchequer financing'.[38] At the same time the three Treasury ministers were beginning to focus on what, in their view, was the main problem – inflation, which at that time was running at around 4 per cent. This was not particularly excessive, particularly when viewed against the rates it reached in later years, but there was a feeling that it was becoming endemic within the economy. The government faced constant criticism for allowing inflationary wage settlements. In early 1957 the railway workers secured 5 per cent and the shipbuilding and engineering workers 6.5 per cent. It led the *Financial Times* to comment that the government has 'given up the fight against inflation'.[39]

This was not the case. In July 1957 Thorneycroft sent a paper to his Cabinet colleagues expressing his concerns regarding inflation and suggested that government spending plans needed to be curbed to help combat it. On 7 August he gave his officials instructions to prepare a study to consider 'the possibility of bringing about a measure of deflation in the economy'.[40] He was serious about introducing new measures to limit inflation: he and his ministers felt that the consensual approach, which relied on trade unions not making excessive claims and management not agreeing to them, was not working.

Towards the end of July the exchange rate fell to $2.78, which was closer to the lower level allowed under IMF rules. This was probably a result of speculative pressure, notwithstanding a current account surplus on the balance of payments. The pressure was exacerbated by the partial devaluation of the French Franc. Thorneycroft believed there was a connection between the pressure on sterling and the inflation within the British economy. Many, including most treasury officials, did not agree. But the sterling crisis made the Chancellor even more determined to introduce deflationary measures, using fiscal and monetary instruments to counteract the level of inflation and the supposed threat to sterling.

Thorneycroft thought that, in order to control inflation, government expenditure for the next financial year, 1958–9, should not exceed spending in 1957–8. As a minimum the government must set an example in terms of restraint. His monetary approach was to attempt to hold down the liquidity in the economy by asking the banks to restrict their lending, and at the same time to increase the bank rate significantly. These measures were announced on 19 September and became known as the September measures. They were accompanied by a statement which emphasised that the government was determined to maintain the external and internal value of the pound. It also said 'There can be no remedy for

---

38 Fforde, John, *The Bank of England and Public Policy 1941–1958*, Cambridge: Cambridge University Press, 1992, p. 674.

39 Peden, G.C., *The Treasury and British Public Policy 1906–1959*, Oxford: Oxford University Press, 2000, p. 488.

40 Samuel, Brittan, *The Treasury Under the Tories 1951–1964*, London: Penguin, 1964, p. 191.

inflation ... which does not include ... a control of the money supply. So long as it is generally believed that the government are prepared to see the necessary finance produced to match the upward spiral of costs, inflation will continue to go up.'[41] As Peden points out it would be wrong to regard these measures as an early form of the monetarism practiced by Margaret Thatcher in 1979 but it might be regarded, as Enoch Powell later suggested, as 'a gleam in the eye' of monetarism.[42,43]

It was at this stage that the relationship between the Treasury ministers and Treasury officials began to break down. Thorneycroft, when he was appointed Chancellor, wanted to bring Frank Lee, his Permanent Secretary at the Department of Trade, with him. It might have been better if Macmillan had agreed to this. Samuel Brittan commented that Frank Lee, who replaced Makins in January 1960, albeit under completely different circumstances, was the 'first post war Head of the Treasury to be fully at home in current economic controversies'.[44] Thorneycroft always felt that he knew more about economics than Makins. He complained that while Makins disagreed with what he, Thorneycroft, was doing, he never had any alternative advice to offer other than to ride out the storm. Makins would not be surprised if he were reading this. In his memoirs he noted that Thorneycroft thought, and not without some reason, that he knew more about domestic finance than Makins did.[45]

The extent of the breakdown in the relationship between ministers and officials over that summer might be gauged from an entry in Robert Hall's diary made on 27 August 1957.

> I have had a chat with Makins who has so far come in every day of his leave, and is a bit bewildered by this turn of events. He repeated what he has said to me many times before, and I to him before that, that this government is led by gamblers (he calls them plungers) and he thinks that they are now meditating what he calls an economic Suez.[46]

Hall threatened to resign on two occasions over the summer but was dissuaded from doing so by Makins, who apparently told Hall that he thought the Chancellor was 'a bit of a bull in a china shop' and that there would be a new chancellor before long.[47] Hall did not object so much to the September measures

---

41 Dell, *The Chancellors*, p. 233.

42 Peden, *The Treasury and British Public Policy*, p. 487.

43 Thorneycroft was appointed to the Chairmanship of the Conservative Party in 1979.

44 Brittan, Samuel, *Steering the Economy*, London: Secker and Warburg, 1969, p. 39.

45 Lord Sherfield's Memoirs, section entitled *The Little Local Difficulty The Treasury –January 1958* (Henceforth *Local Difficulty*), p. 1.

46 Hall, *Diaries*, p. 125.

47 Peden, *The Treasury and British Public Policy*, p. 487.

themselves, but the way in which they were presented.[48] As was mentioned above, Thorneycroft for his part 'was disturbed by the thought that he, as a lay minister, knew more about finance than Makins'.[49]

Up until the autumn the Chancellor had the support of his Prime Minister if not his officials. The pressure on sterling eased after the September measures were announced and in October the reserves started to build once more. Thorneycroft, however, remained determined to hold the level of public expenditure for 1958/9 at the same level as the current year, an aspiration which was consistent with a minute circulated by Macmillan to his cabinet colleagues on 10 August 1957.[50] But Macmillan, perhaps under pressure from Roy Harrod (advisor to Macmillan and Fellow in Economics at Christ Church Oxford), was beginning to succumb to his inflationary instincts.[51]

When the annual estimates were presented to the Treasury by the various spending departments in December 1957 the Treasury ministers were horrified. The total of the civil estimates for the year was £275 million greater than the original estimates for the current year.[52] Powell sent a note to Thorneycroft which he copied to Makins; if the demands were met they would constitute 'the biggest increase ever recorded in peacetime'.[53] Powell made the point that the increases were overwhelmingly due to government policies and could, therefore, be reversed. He concluded his note with 'we cannot go blundering on as we are at present'. Sir Thomas Padmore (a Second Secretary at the Treasury) sent a note to Makins indicating that there was little option but to 'blunder on'. Makins' response was to point out that it was not blundering but something which flowed from precise policy decisions. The point was that the Treasury ministers wanted cuts or suggestions for cuts, not clever arguments to avoid them.

A cabinet committee was formed to consider the estimates. Macmillan introduced Macmillanesque arguments to counter his Chancellor: 'public expenditure should be reduced but ... the reductions should not be of a nature which might jeopardise the government's long term objective of establishing wage restraint.'[54] He was moving away from his Chancellor and reverting to expansionism, presumably with an eye to the next election. The Chancellor restated that his aim was to keep the 1958/59 figures in line with the likely out turn for the 1957/58 year. This would entail a reduction of some £153 million in the estimates. Any reductions would require significant policy decisions,

---

48 Hall, *Diaries*, p. 122.

49 Brittan, *Steering the Economy*, p. 128.

50 TNA, PREM 11/2306;Civil Expenditure M405/57, 10 August 1957.

51 In the post-war period Harrod was an advocate of the use of fiscal and monetary expansion to stimulate maximum economic growth.

52 Peden, *The Treasury and British Public Policy*, p. 492.

53 Heffer, S., *Like The Roman*, London: Wiedenfeld & Nicholson, 1998, p. 226.

54 TNA, CAB 130/139, GEN 625, 11 December 1957.

which individual ministers in the spending departments would have resisted. So, 1957 ended with a standoff between Macmillan and the majority of his Cabinet who accepted the need for reductions but not at the expense of wage restraint, and the Treasury ministers who insisted on cuts of £153 million, which they felt were necessary to contain inflation and protect sterling.

The first week of the New Year was occupied with a series of Cabinet meetings; there were three between 3 and 5 January 1958. Tension was high. Ministers debated a number of cuts, and after considerable discussion the Cabinet reached a point where ministers agreed a reduction in the estimates of £100 million, £50 million less than Thorneycroft wanted. On Sunday 5 January Macmillan made a final plea to Thorneycroft to accept the position. The Chancellor said he had not made up his mind. Macmillan, however, believed that 'he had made up his mind to resign, unless he got his full demand'. One might speculate as to how Macmillan knew this and the extent to which he was talking to Makins and other officials at the Treasury. It is highly probable that he was.

During the hectic few days before Macmillan reached his conclusion Makins attended several meetings with the Chancellor, the junior ministers and other officials. He comments that 'he had been rather surprised to find in these meetings that the three Treasury ministers had coalesced, and were united in their determination to reduce the estimates overall by a specific sum'.[55] His surprise is puzzling. It is difficult to find any evidence that the ministers ever wavered from their belief that this was a crucial issue for them and not merely some sort of negotiating position. On Friday 3 January Makins commented to Robert Hall that it would be 'very odd indeed' if by Monday we found ourselves without a Chancellor or either of the two junior ministers. Makins added that tempers were rising over the Chancellor's 'determination to get the estimates down at any cost and that he was being egged on by Birch and Powell who in their different ways are both rather mad'. At this stage Makins did not believe that the Chancellor would be so 'rash' but thought that his resignation was 'on the cards'.

Throughout this Makins must have been passing information on to Macmillan. It seems that Makins, along with Sir Norman Brook, had been deputed by Macmillan to see the ministers and persuade them not to resign. It seems curious that officials were prepared to be used in this way. On the evening of 5 January Makins went to 11 Downing Street to make a 'last ditch attempt' (clearly there had been others) to dissuade Thorneycroft from resigning. Makins describes the atmosphere as tense. The three ministers were standing and talking to each other. Makins was politely received and felt for a moment that he had managed to shake Thorneycroft's resolve. Norman Brook was then announced, causing a flurry of excitement when for a brief moment the occupants of the

---

[55] *Local Difficulty*, p. 6.

room thought he may have come with a message of compromise from the Prime Minister. It transpired that he had come on the same errand as Makins. Both Makins and Brook failed on their political errand for Macmillan.[56]

On the morning of 6 January Makins 'as was my custom at moments of crisis' arrived early at Treasury chambers. On his desk lay Thorneycroft's letter of resignation. Shortly afterwards Macmillan telephoned Makins, 'You are not to worry, Roger. I am leaving for Australia tomorrow morning as arranged. Derick [Heathcoat-Amory] will take over the Treasury and will come over to see you this afternoon'. Macmillan was sure of Makins' loyalty, evidenced when he wrote in his diary on the day of the resignations, 'As far as I can judge the Treasury officials have had no hand in it and have disapproved of it'.[57]

Makins' views of his ministers seem clear. He seems to have been very glad to see the back of Powell and Birch and relieved by the resignation of Thorneycroft.[58] While acknowledging that it was an 'extraordinary episode' he suggests that the 'resignations had caused no more than a ripple on the political scene' and that to 'raise [the issue] to a level of principle was really absurd in the circumstances'.[59] He further asserts in his memoirs that it was he who got it right and Thorneycroft who was wrong.[60] It is difficult to know exactly what Makins is referring to, but it seems a rather sweeping statement and it presents a rather rosy view of his time under Thorneycroft, and indeed, his time at the Treasury.

There is an alternative view. The three ministers were attempting, probably for the first time since the war, to address a malaise that had characterised economic policy since 1945, and to stand up against the post-war consensus which had dominated policy. That consensus usually resulted in giving way to vested interests, almost whatever the consequences. As Edmund Dell points out 'Thorneycroft's instincts told him that there must be something wrong with a country's economic management when it led to one crisis after another'.[61] Thorneycroft and his junior colleagues were making a stand against the way things had been run; it was to take a further 20 years before their approach began to win through.

In the circumstances, perhaps the ministers deserved more support from their officials. It is possible that had the Treasury officials been a little less in awe of Macmillan, less timid at the thought of opposition from vested interests, and stronger in terms of supporting their ministers the outcome may have been different. Powell in a private memorandum written two weeks after his resignation said 'If the Official Treasury had been headed by a strong personality,

56 *Local Difficulty*, p. 5.

57 Bodleian Macmillan Diaries, 6 January 1957.

58 Hall, *Diaries*, p. 143.

59 *Local Difficulty*, p. 6.

60 British Oral Archive, Makins, p. 64.

61 Dell, *The Chancellors*, p. 234.

the Departments – and through the Departments, the departmental Ministers – might have been permeated for months past with a different attitude towards the prospective level of expenditure in 1958/59'. In a rather damning criticism of Makins, Powell refers to 'the general attitude of cynicism or defeatism which characterised senior levels of the official Treasury. Though that attitude in the last year or two may have been strengthened with the weakness of the official head [Makins], it must itself be of longer growth'.[62] Thorneycroft was rather more pungent 'He [Makins] only comes in one day in three and when he does he's against me'.[63]

Criticism of Makins was not confined to Ministers. Bruce Fraser who was a third Secretary in the Treasury at the time and who in 1960 became Powell's Permanent Secretary at the Department of Health wrote:

> Makins was certainly very seriously to blame for what he did (or, rather, didn't do) during those events ... I thought then, and think still, that Peter Thorneycroft ... was wrong both in his political judgement and in his ministerial tactics. But at least he was trying to do his job. Makins wasn't. He had no interest in the management of expenditure and made no attempt either to give leadership to officials or to frame sensible advice for the Chancellor.[64]

Sir Leo Pliatzky, an official with considerable experience of the control of public expenditure from the 1940s to the 1970s, thought that the Chancellor's defeat in 1958 had seriously undermined the authority of the Treasury'.[65] Makins played a part in that defeat.

The new Chancellor was Derick Heathcoat Amory, the former Minister of Agriculture Fisheries and Food. He was a politician who was admired and trusted by MPs on both sides of the House of Commons. He was also liked by officials. Makins described his relationship with Heathcoat Amory over the two years of working with him as extremely agreeable, adding that he was very easy to work with and for.[66] Hall commented that he liked the Chancellor and found him sensible and sympathetic.[67] The new Chancellor had the added benefit for Macmillan of being weak and malleable. Macmillan was able to effectively run the Treasury through Heathcoat Amory, and may have been helped by having a Permanent Secretary who was at least as loyal to the First Lord as to the Second Lord of the Treasury. A number of junior ministers

[62] Churchill Archives, Churchill College Cambridge, Powell Papers (Henceforth Powell Papers) Poll 3/1/15 Memorandum written by Powell shortly after resignation.

[63] British Oral Archive, Powell, p. 13.

[64] Powell Papers, Letter Bruce Fraser to Powell 12/1/89.

[65] Peden, *The Treasury and British Public Policy*, p. 493.

[66] British Oral Archive, Makins, p. 65 and p. 76.

[67] Hall, *Diaries*, p. 145.

served under Heathcoat Amory. Powell was replaced by Jack Simon (Junior Minister in the Home Office and subsequently a Law Lord) who became the Financial Secretary. The position of Economics Minister was not filled until October 1958 when Freddie Erroll (Parliamentary Secretary in the Ministry of Trade) took the position.

The first task of the new regime was to reassure the markets. A statement drafted by Makins was issued: 'The Change in Chancellor means no change in the Government's economic or financial policy.' The statement continued 'The strengthening of sterling and a stable internal price level are the dominating aims of the Government's economic policies, and nothing whatever will take precedence over them.'[68] Nothing, that is, until Macmillan felt the need, some time later, to reflate the economy in order to secure an election victory. By the time Heathcoat Amory got to the Treasury the economy was beginning to respond to the anti inflationary measure that both Macmillan, as Chancellor, and Thorneycroft had put in place. The economy was, in fact, stagnating, if not in recession. When Heathcoat Amory delivered his first budget speech, on 15 April 1958, unemployment was rising and industrial output was falling. There were a number of by-election defeats for the government in early 1958 and Macmillan began to put pressure on his Chancellor. In March 1958 he wrote to Heathcoat Amory: 'I have been thinking about your budget. I hope that ... you will feel able to give back a considerable sum', adding 'the people need some encouragement.'[69] But on this occasion the Treasury was able to resist the Prime Minister. Makins, probably under the influence of Robert Hall, wrote to the Chancellor suggesting that 'circumstances do not permit this year any striking remission of taxation'.[70] In the event the budget was a cautious one with Macmillan probably accepting that it would not be in his interests to provoke another crisis so soon after losing Thorneycroft. The amount 'given away' was £51 million in the current year or £101 million in a full year.[71]

In addition to domestic issues Makins was called upon to consider a number of external financial policy matters. In early 1958 Macmillan wrote to the Treasury asking them to reconsider the question of floating sterling, moving away from fixed exchange rates, and also to consider the issue of the convertibility of sterling. Both the Bank of England and the Treasury came out against floating sterling.[72] Perhaps they believed that to float the pound would remove the discipline of a fixed exchange rate, leading to a depreciating rate, inflation and 'economic irresponsibility of every kind'.[73] In a note to Makins,

68 TNA, T199/633, Statement by the New Chancellor of the Exchequer.

69 TNA, T171/487, Letter from Macmillan to Chancellor, 5 March 1958.

70 TNA, T171/487, Note Headed Budget, 28 February 1958.

71 TNA, T171/487, Budget Summary 1958.

72 TNA, T236/5404, Note by Butler to Macmillan, 31 May 1958.

73 Dell, *The Chancellors*, p. 249.

Rowan commented that Robert Hall, Denis Rickett and himself had held meetings with representatives from the Bank of England and concluded that 'although conditions might arise where a voluntary move to a flexible rate was a necessary or even desirable course, they do not obtain today'.[74]

Convertibility was a different matter. It had been an objective of all governments since the war and as Makins observed, 'it would be no mean achievement to realise this objective'. Makins sent a note to Heathcoat Amory in August 1958 recommending convertibility in the autumn.[75] This note followed conclusions drawn by both the Bank of England's and the Treasury's external finance section.[76] The circumstances were for once favourable for a move towards convertibility. The balance of payments was forecast to show a significant surplus in 1958; the reserves had increased to over $3 billion; inflation was down; and the American economy, which had been in recession, was showing signs of recovery. Because discussions needed to be held with both the IMF and European partners convertibility was delayed until 29 December 1958, when sterling held by non-residents became fully convertible.

Earlier in the summer of 1958 the Conservatives had began to rally in the polls. Macmillan saw his opportunity. The problem was that the outlook was not good. By the autumn of 1958 unemployment was approaching 2 per cent and there was a concern that the figure might reach 3 per cent by the following spring. Over the summer months Heathcoat Amory started to put an end to the credit squeeze; he removed 'the restrictions on the total level of bank lending' and eased 'control over the raising of capital and credit'.[77] Discussion also turned to increasing the level of government expenditure. Heathcoat Amory was under pressure from Macmillan and his Cabinet colleagues to reflate the economy. The Chancellor's concern, however, was to preserve the balance of payments forecast which was projected to be a £450 million surplus for the year. With convertibility imminent the Chancellor was also worried about the international community's reaction to Britain instituting inflationary policies. He also thought it possible that a recovery was already under way.

Macmillan, however, was taking no chances. Prone to hyperbole and now determined to inflate the economy the Prime Minister heaped even more pressure upon his Chancellor:

> There is at stake, more perhaps than in normal times, the whole future of the country. I am not merely concerned with political success; but I really feel that a

[74] TNA, T230/373, Paper on exchange rate Policy Rowan to Chancellor and Makins, 2 April 1958.

[75] TNA, T236/5405, Note by Makins to Heathcoat Amory, 22 August 1958.

[76] TNA, T230/373, Papers on Exchange Rate Policy Rowan to Chancellor and Makins, 2 April 1958.

[77] Macmillan, *Riding the Storm*, p. 722.

> socialist victory at the next election would put back the clock and perhaps be the final blow to the growing influence of Great Britain in the world. The only thing I feel that can beat us now is the unemployment figures coupled with the figures of underproduction. We must get this right at all costs. If we should go a bit too far, we can always pull back again. I feel myself much more fear of the slump coming than I have of another boom.[78]

It is doubtful if there was anything anyone, either at the official or ministerial level, could have done to dissuade Macmillan from his course, and the Chancellor and the Treasury complied. The budget delivered on 7 April 1959 predicted an overall deficit for the year of some £736 million, the largest deficit since the war. The government was to spend its way out of the problem and the population was to be rewarded with considerable tax reductions amounting to some £360 million in a full year.[79] As Edmund Dell put it 'The Chancellor launched not a recovery but a boom'.

Makins must have met with Macmillan to discuss his personal position sometime in April 1959. One can imagine the conversation. Makins was clearly unhappy at the Treasury, an election was looming and there was a possibility of Labour gaining power. Makins would have wanted to secure his next position while Macmillan still had the power of patronage. It was also the case that his initial appointment was for a period of three years, a period which would expire in October 1959. Makins suggests that he was offered the choice of the top job at the Foreign Office or the Chairmanship of the UK Atomic Energy Authority (AEA). To what extent this was a real choice or whether Macmillan pressurised him into the decision he subsequently made is difficult to judge.

It was not entirely surprising that Macmillan turned to Makins to chair the AEA. Makins had a certain amount of experience in the atomic energy arena and he knew some of the principal players at the AEA including Sir William Penney. Perhaps a more important reason, however, was the fact that Macmillan wanted a safe pair of hands at the AEA after the Windscale nuclear accident. On 10 October 1957 there was a serious fire at Windscale, Britain's first nuclear plant. While the government smoothed over the disaster as quickly and quietly as possible and a speedy investigation into the fire's causes and effects was instigated Macmillan, with his highly tuned political instincts, knew that public awareness of the whole nuclear issue was increasing. A safe pair of hands at the AEA would have suited Macmillan very well.

Makins says that 'after a great deal of reflection and some consultation with various people' he elected to take the Atomic Energy Authority. He offers several reasons for this choice. Firstly, he suggests there were 'a number of people

[78] TNA, T171/496, Macmillan to Heathcoat Amory, 2 November 1958.

[79] TNA, T171/496, Budget Summary 1959.

who were perfectly capable of taking the Foreign Office job'. This is hardly a creditable reason. The fact that others can do a job is no reason to refuse it. There were after all others who could have taken the Permanent Secretary's job at the Treasury when Makins took it. It was also the case, as Selwyn Lloyd pointed out, that while there 'is considerable talent at the top of the Foreign Service ... the loss of your services will be a very real one'.[80]

Makins also suggests that for him to take the job would have meant bringing Derick Hoyer Millar's (later Lord Inchyra) term in office to a premature end.[81] However this does not necessarily seem to have been the case. In a letter to Selwyn Lloyd, the Foreign Secretary at the time, Makins wrote:

> I think the Prime Minister has told you that, at his invitation, I have accepted the Chairmanship of the Atomic Energy Authority from January next in succession to Edwin Plowden. I have done this after much heart searching, as it means I must retire from the Foreign Service on taking up the appointment, and thus abandon my chance of going to the Foreign Office when Derick Hoyer Millar retires.[82]

Makins would not have had to wait very long for the Foreign Office job: Hoyer Miller wanted to retire when he was sixty, in 1960, and expected Makins to come back to the Foreign Office at that time. Because Makins went to the Atomic Energy Authority, Hoyer Millar was forced to work an extra year and had to wait to retire until Harold Caccia became available in 1961.[83]

The final reason Makins offers is that 'they simply couldn't find anybody really available to take the Atomic Energy Authority'.[84] This is at least a plausible reason although William Penney, who was the head of research at the authority in 1959 and who became deputy chairman in 1961 and succeeded Makins as chairman in 1964, must have been a possibility. The most likely explanation as to why Makins took the atomic energy job rather than the Foreign Office position is probably because Macmillan wanted him and urged him to do it. Makins himself said when confiding to Robert Hall that 'he was very uncertain but had gone on the rule to go where he was told to go unless there were strong personal reasons against it'. Whatever his reasoning, Makins, while acknowledging that 'it was a difficult choice', accepted the job. His move from the Treasury was announced on 22 July 1959. Of course, Makins

> had not wanted much to come to the Treasury [and] did not mind leaving it.[85]

---

80 Makins Papers MS Sherfield 563, Letter Selwyn Lloyd to Makins, 25 July 1959.

81 British Oral Archive, Makins, p. 58.

82 Makins Papers, MS Sherfield 563, Letter Makins to Selwyn Lloyd, July 1959.

83 British Oral Archive, Lord Inchra, p. 17.

84 British Oral Archive, Makins, p. 58.

85 Hall, *Diaries*, p. 207.

One of the last functions Makins attended as Joint Permanent Secretary was a dinner given in his honour by the Bank of England. The purpose of the dinner which was held on 17 December 1959 was to thank Makins for all the help he had given the Bank including the help with the Radcliffe Report. Cobbold in his speech said 'how much their safe survival owed' to Makins. Virtually the whole of the Court was there as well as all the senior members of the Treasury team. It was 'an unusual if not unique event'.[86] In the week following this dinner Makins wrote to the Secretary of State for Foreign Affairs, the letter brought to an end his life in public service and Makins lost forever the opportunity to lead the Foreign Office.

> I am taking up my appointment as Chairman of the United Kingdom Atomic energy authority on 1st January and this has involved my resignation from public service.
> It has been hard for me to give up my membership of the Foreign Service, in which I have spent so much of my life and to which I owe so much. But you know, and I hope understand, the circumstances in which I was invited to take the Chairmanship of the Authority.[87]

Shortly after it was announced that Makins would be leaving the Treasury at the end of 1959, the *Economist* ran an article entitled 'After Sir Roger'. The article purported to confine itself to general principles rather than personalities. It failed in that the article was seen as not only a criticism of the new structure of a joint permanent secretary responsible solely for economic affairs, but was also a criticism of the first incumbent under this new structure. Two criticisms were offered. Firstly, under Makins there had been an increase in the 'traditional Treasury view of economic policy at the expense of the professional economist view of it'. This was consistent with the way Makins operated, which was to basically accept whatever Robert Hall, who he met nearly every day, told him. There is no evidence that Makins sought to master the issues or even to discuss economic theory with economists outside the Treasury. The second criticism was that 'the experiment had not led to tighter and more efficient control over government spending and over the mechanics of tax raising'. This was almost certainly true. It is also interesting to recount one of the stories Thorneycroft told about his Permanent Secretary. Makins presented Thorneycroft with a note which was advising the Chancellor to authorise expenditure. Makins had minuted on it before it went to the Chancellor 'I agree. Bis dat qui cito dat' (to

---

86 Hall, *Diaries*, p. 223.

87 Makins Papers, MS Sherfield 563, Letter Makins to Selwyn Lloyd, 23 December 1959.

give quickly is to give twice). Thorneycroft's comment was 'what a motto for the Permanent Secretary of the Treasury'.[88]

Criticism of Makins in his role at the Treasury is not restricted to Thorneycroft and Powell. 'The choice of Sir Roger Makins ... as the Treasury's economic chief was a bold gamble that did not quite come off' (Samuel Brittan).[89] 'It was not obvious that it [Makins' appointment] made any ... contribution to economic management' (Edmund Dell).[90] 'It would seem ... that for most of the 1950's neither Bridges nor Makins provided as effective leadership as might have been expected of men of their undoubted intellectual capacity' (G.C. Peden).[91] The question is why Makins was so ineffective. There seem to be two reasons, possibly connected. Firstly, Makins had no experience or knowledge of domestic finance or indeed monetary policy. Secondly, he loathed the work and the assignment. Sir Edward Playfair, who was a third secretary at the Treasury and who had got to know Makins in Washington offered the following comment:

> Roger is a very old friend of mine ... and he is still a marvelously good friend. But it was a very funny appointment. At first I thought it absolutely marvellous until I discovered that he simply loathed it. I took him out to lunch once and tried to get him to confess that there was anything at all in the Treasury which he enjoyed and he wouldn't agree that there was anything he enjoyed whatsoever. He loathed the assignment ... his face dropped when he was in the Treasury. He wasn't smiling anymore ... . The result was that he didn't really interest himself in any part of the Treasury except those bits which were connected with his previous economic work in the Foreign Office. I think you must write that [his time in the Treasury] off as being possibly the only dud period in Roger's life.[92]

88 British Oral Archive, Powell, p. 13

89 Brittan, *The Treasury Under the Tories*, p. 52.

90 Dell, *The Chancellors*, p. 216.

91 Peden, *The Treasury and British Public Policy*, p. 435.

92 British Oral Archive, Playfair, p. 31.

Chapter 7
Atomic Energy Authority and 'Retirement'

In January 1960 Makins succeeded Edwin Plowden as Chairman of the Atomic Energy Authority (AEA). The background to the appointment was discussed in the previous chapter; it seems clear that Macmillan wanted someone of his own at the top of the AEA. Macmillan had taken direct responsibility for the AEA during a period between the resignation of the Lord President, Lord Salisbury, in March 1957 and October 1959 when he formed his new government. It is likely that Macmillan considered the political risk associated with atomic energy to be particularly high. The whole issue of atomic energy had become heavily politicised with the Campaign for Nuclear Disarmament (CND) being launched in 1958 and campaigning against both civil and military uses of atomic energy. Furthermore, the nuclear accident at Windscale in 1957, had shown that nuclear power was not without its downsides. Accordingly Macmillan sought a safe pair of hands. He wrote to Makins and confirmed his appointment as Chairman of the Authority. The job was full-time, and brought a salary of £10,000 a year, a significant increase on the £7,500 he received at the Treasury and the highest salary of his official career. But what did the AEA actually do and in what way was Makins qualified to run it?

The Atomic Energy Authority was set up by Churchill in 1954. Churchill and Lord Cherwell, his scientific advisor during the war and a Cabinet minister in his newly elected government in 1951, had long thought that Britain's nuclear enterprise, hitherto the responsibility of the Ministry of Supply, should be managed by a new non-Departmental organisation along the lines of the American Atomic Energy Commission, but the Labour government disagreed. Immediately after Britain detonated her first atomic bomb at Monte Bello in October 1952 the government launched a review into the management of atomic energy. It set up a committee under Lord Waverley (formerly Sir John Anderson, the wartime minister responsible for Britain's atomic energy project) to plan the transfer and make proposals as to 'the most suitable form for the new organisation, due regard being paid to any constitutional and financial implications'.[1] The committee recommended a new body, 'more akin to the

---

[1] Command Paper 8986, *The Future Organisation of the United Kingdom Atomic Energy Project*, p. 3.

structure of a big organisation than to that of a Government department'.[2] Its conclusions led to the Atomic Energy Act of 1954, which set up the new Atomic Energy Authority to take over all atomic energy responsibilities from the Ministry of Supply, together with a staff of 20,000.

The AEA had the power 'to produce, use and dispose of atomic energy and carry out research into any matters therewith'.[3] Lord Plowden became chairman, and the members included Sir John Cockcroft (responsible for Scientific Research), Sir Christopher Hinton (Engineering and Production), and Sir William Penney (Weapons Research and Development). In addition there were a number of part time members, including Lord Cherwell. These were all people with whom Makins had worked when he dealt with atomic energy at the Washington Embassy and Whitehall during and after the war, and Plowden, Cockcroft and Penney were all good friends, and regular guests, of the Makinses.

The Authority was something of a hybrid organisation, neither a government department nor a nationalised industry. It was set up outside of government partly because it was proving difficult to attract talent on civil service pay scales. But, it was also thought that a 'civil service type of organisation' was not 'suited to carrying on a large pioneering industrial undertaking, and that such an undertaking ought to have the maximum practicable freedom and scope for initiative'.[4] However, because of its political importance and the security aspects associated with atomic energy, it was not thought appropriate to use the standard nationalised industry model. Since it was likely to be a long time before it would become self-financing, its funding was voted by Parliament and paid from the Department of the Lord President.

When Makins took over as chairman, a programme for nuclear power stations was well under way. Britain had always understood that there could be civil applications of nuclear fission and even during the war there had been a limited amount of research into the possibility of generating useable power from uranium. A report on atomic energy produced for the War Cabinet in July 1941 was in two sections: 'Use of Uranium for a Bomb' and 'Use of Uranium as a Source of Power.'[5] Understandably, in wartime, research on weapons was given the top priority, and this carried over into the immediate post-war period when Britain was striving to make her own bomb. In June 1952, however, the government was able to approve the first civil reactor programme. This was followed by a White Paper which stated that 'however crude and primitive

[2] Ibid.

[3] Atomic Energy Act 1954.

[4] Makins Papers, MS Sherfield 563, Report of the Committee on the Future Organisation of the Atomic Energy Project, 23 July 1953.

[5] Pocock, R.F., *Nuclear Power: Its Development in the United Kingdom*, London: Unwin Brothers, 1977, p. 6.

our first nuclear power reactors may appear to future generations, we can look forward with confidence to the time when industrial power from the atom will be a major factor in the world's economy'. Such was the euphoria surrounding the civil applications of nuclear power that the White Paper continued: 'Indeed, it is not too much to say that the exploitation of nuclear energy may come to be regarded as the most important step taken by man in the mastery of nature since the discovery of fire.'[6]

In 1955, shortly after the AEA was set up, the government published a White Paper entitled *A Programme of Nuclear Power*.[7] It outlined the need for Britain to develop new sources of energy in order to meet growing needs. Power stations were predominantly fuelled by coal, although oil was beginning to be used. Britain did not produce enough coal to meet her own needs, and British coal was expensive by international standards, and nuclear power stations could help to bridge the gap. The White Paper outlined a provisional programme which would add capacity of 1,500–2,000 megawatts by 1965 (the capacity of the existing conventional electricity generating stations at the time amounted to some 20,000 megawatts).

Work was already taking place on the development of a reactor capable of generating electricity at the time the White Paper was published, and in October 1956 the Queen opened Calder Hall, a nuclear powered generating station, located in Cumberland. It was the first time in Western Europe that a nuclear powered station had supplied electricity to the National Grid. Buoyed by this success, but also mindful of the pessimistic forecasts for the supply of conventional fuels available to Europe, the government decided to expand capacity further. In another White Paper, issued in 1957, capacity was to be increased to between 5,000 and 6,000 megawatts. By the end of the 1950s the AEA was clearly committed to exploiting nuclear energy for both military and civilian purposes.

Makins, as the Chairman, was responsible to Lord Hailsham who had been appointed the Minister for Science in October 1959. Hailsham had won a Prize Fellowship to All Souls in 1931 and had been a friend of Makins since that time.[8] Makins was fortunate in that Hailsham remained the Minister responsible for AEA affairs throughout his tenure as Chairman, affording an element of stability as well as a friendly ear. By the time Makins arrived Sir John Cockcroft had relinquished his position as the Member for Scientific Research to become a part time member of the authority and his position was taken by Sir William Penney. Penney was responsible for the Research Group, based at Harwell in Berkshire, which was responsible for long-term research

---

6 Cmd. 8986 *The Future Organisation of the United Kingdom Atomic Energy Project*.

7 Cmd. 9389 *A Program of Nuclear Power*.

8 Lord Hailsham, *A Sparrows Flight*, London: Collins, 1990, p. 83.

into non-military problems of atomic energy. The work focused on materials, their basic properties and the effects upon them of radiation. The Research Group also included the Radio Chemical Centre based at Amersham where radio isotopes for industrial and medical uses were manufactured. The group's other sites engaged in the various aspects of research associated with the design of reactors. The Weapons Group was headed by Air Chief Marshall Sir Claude Pelly who took over from Penney in 1959. Based in Aldermaston, this group was responsible for the development of nuclear warheads and associated research.

Before Makins' arrival at the AEA the Industrial Group had been divided into two sections, the Production Group headed by Sir Leonard Owen, and the Development and Engineering Group led by Sir William Cook. Sir Christopher Hinton, who had previously been responsible for the Authority's production activities, had left in 1958 to become head of the Central Electricity Generating Board (CEGB). He was a brilliant design and production engineer who 'towered over his profession both intellectually and physically' and would become something of an adversary for Makins. Both the Production Group and the Development and Engineering Group were located at Risley in Lancashire. They were responsible for running the reactors, the production of radioactive fuel and for the continuing programme of reactor development. The reactors, such as Calder Hall and Chapelcross, were used both for the production of radioactive material and for producing electricity which was supplied to the national grid. At Springfield the radioactive material was converted into useable fuel elements for use in both reactors and weaponry. Risley was also the centre for the development and design of a new range of reactors such as the Advanced Gas Reactor (AGR) and the Fast Breeder Reactors (FBR) which were intended to replace the existing Magnox Reactors.

The scale of AEA's operations, bridging fundamental science and industrial enterprise, were a big change for Makins compared with working for the Foreign Office and Treasury, and he relished the challenge. He himself was based at the Authority's head office in Charles II Street, Mayfair. The head office had a staff of around 200 and included the central finance function of the authority headed by Sir Alan Hitchman. Makins' private Secretary was John Herbecq who was seconded from a relatively junior position at the Treasury. He subsequently worked in the Civil Service Department where he became its second Permanent Secretary from 1975–81. Makins' formal role was 'to co-ordinate the various group's policy decisions and to oversee relations with government departments and other organisations in the UK and overseas'.[9] According to Herbecq he 'was no titular head: he was hands on and worked hard'. Herbecq recalled a time when through a mix up with the diaries there was a clash between a shooting party

9 UK Atomic Energy Authority Annual Reports, Misc 1958–64.

with the Queen Mother and an annual meeting with the AEA's Trade Union representatives. Herbecq said that although it would have been acceptable to have sent a deputy to the meeting since it was a routine matter, Makins declined the shooting and led the meeting himself.[10]

Makins' workload at the Authority can be divided into two parts; the day-to-day routine business of the authority and work on one-off policy issues. The routine issues might include chairing authority meetings, attending international talks (both bilateral talks and international conferences), meetings with government officials and attending and giving evidence to parliamentary committees. The policy issues included subjects such as the choice of reactor designs and the management of relations with the CEGB. The Authority met monthly and the executive fortnightly, with both these meetings chaired by Makins. He was a skilled and experienced chairman, and his lack of scientific knowledge was not necessarily a disadvantage, at least initially. He was, as he himself pointed out, the second layman to be chosen to lead the authority. (He was also the last.)

These regular meetings were a way of keeping in touch with what was going on in the authority. This was no easy task given that by the time Makins joined the AEA it employed over 38,000 people who were widely dispersed throughout the UK in over 20 locations.[11] The agenda for Authority meetings covered items such as the research and development programme, weapons development, international relations, health and safety, capital expenditure and finance. Makins managed to exert his authority at his very first meeting. The executive, apparently concerned by the strain on senior staff caused through the necessity of constant travelling, asked that the case for acquiring a permanent executive aircraft should be examined. The idea was quashed. Makins, who himself was never prone to extravagance particularly with public money, knew that it was he who would have to face the Public Accounts Committee and that purchasing an executive aircraft could become very controversial.[12] Makins also kept in touch with what was going on by travelling to the authority's various establishments to meet members of staff or accompany visitors. The Authority was a relaxed body and relationships between members were good.[13] Makins was no newcomer to the UK atomic energy scene. He knew all the members of the Authority and many others who worked below them. He was sensible enough not to pretend to knowledge that he did not have: he had many other skills, however, and these

10 Herbecq Notes.

11 7th Annual Report UKAEA, p. 68.

12 TNA, AB 16/3441, Monthly Summary of Authority and Executive Proceedings, January 1960.

13 Herbecq notes.

were recognised by those who worked for him. He was highly respected within the authority.[14]

Makins' particular expertise, of course, was in international relations. He spent a considerable amount of time travelling abroad or dealing with overseas visitors to the Authority. The Authority's policy in the field of international relations had three principal aspects: the exchange of scientific information and personnel in unclassified fields (such exchanges often took place at international conferences); special exchanges, usually bilateral, in certain limited areas where commercially sensitive or classified information was involved; and promoting nuclear exports and negotiating commercial contracts for the provision of raw materials.

One of the most significant international organisations in the field at the time was the International Atomic Energy Agency (IAEA). The agency was set up in 1957 in response to President Eisenhower's 'Atoms for Peace' speech to the United Nations in 1953. Its purpose was to promote safe, secure and peaceful nuclear technologies.[15] During his time as Chairman Makins led the UK delegation to the Annual General Conferences of the Agency which were held in Vienna. He often spoke at the conference and in doing so promoted the interests of the authority on the world stage. The AEA also took part in many other international organisations. These included the European Nuclear Energy Agency which operated under the auspices of the OECD, the European Atomic Energy Society and Euratom.

Euratom comprised the six countries of the European Steel and Coal Community and the Common Market. Its original objectives were the pooling of research and resources with a view to a joint atomic energy programme. Britain had not joined Euratom, but a Bilateral Cooperation Agreement between the UK government and the Euratom commission was signed in February 1959. The agreement resulted in some exchange of information and collaboration on certain projects. In early 1960 Macmillan, who was angling for entry into the Common Market, directed that a new review be made into the possibility of Britain joining Euratom. The arguments for joining were that Britain might lose out technically if she did not and even lose nuclear leadership in Europe. Non-membership might lead to exclusion from European markets in the field, and failure to join would prejudice the growth of European cooperation generally.

Makins was yet again very quick to demonstrate his Atlanticist credentials. The authority put together a number of arguments against joining. There was cooperation anyway, and the AEA believed that national organisations could be more efficient than international ones. Euratom did not itself place orders for nuclear technology and there was no reason why corporations within the

[14] Ibid.

[15] Website www.iaea.org.

individual six countries could not place orders with the AEA. But the clinching argument was that joining Euratom would seriously prejudice Anglo-America cooperation in the area.[16] Makins wrote directly to Hoyer Millar, Permanent Secretary at the Foreign Office, and told him that he had discussed the matter with John McCone, Chairman of the US Atomic Energy Commission, who had informed Makins that if the UK endeavoured to join Euratom it would be a 'very grave matter' and furthermore, that it would not be possible for the UK to maintain the existing Bilateral Agreements with the US. Makins informed McCone that 'the AEA realised that membership of Euratom would have a very serious effect on their operations'.[17] He wrote to Harold Caccia, the British Ambassador in Washington, 'The AEA are strongly opposed to the proposal that the UK should join Euratom and I myself consider that membership of Euratom would no longer enable the authority to carry out its present mandate'.[18]

Makins took every opportunity possible to strengthen the Anglo-American relationship. Within a month of joining he had accepted an invitation to visit the US Atomic Energy Commission. During a visit to Washington in May 1960 Makins' discussions with the Americans covered a range of topics including a weapons exchange programme, raw material agreements, and improved cooperation in research and development.[19] It must have felt like old times for Makins who had been discussing these issues with the Americans in various guises since 1945. The visit was one of many to the US during his time as Chairman of the authority; there was, however, no comprehensive agreement negotiated by him during this period, in part, because Anglo-American agreements in this area already existed. The UK/US agreement relating to civil uses of atomic energy had been in place since 1955 and a mutual defence (nuclear) agreement came into effect in 1958.

Much less important than negotiations with the US, but still interesting from a public relations perspective, were the Authority's and Makins' relations with the Soviets. The AEA had maintained contacts with Soviet scientists since its inception. In November 1955 a party of British atomic scientists visited the Soviet Union and there were also a number of reciprocal visits. In April 1956 Igor Kurchatov, the scientist responsible for the Soviet atom bomb project, joined the Khrushchev/Bulganin visit to Britain. The Soviet leaders visited Harwell and Kurchatov discussed fusion research with Cockcroft and the other scientists at the establishment. In October 1961, Makins, in pursuit of further collaboration, undertook a ten day visit to the Soviet Union where he

[16] TNA, AB16/3858, Brief for Chairman's US and Canada Visit UK/Euratom Relations, 19 May 1960.

[17] TNA, AB16/3858, Letter Makins to Hoyer Millar, 2 June 1960.

[18] TNA, AB16/3358, memorandum to the Ambassador, 2 June 1960.

[19] TNA, AB16/3858, Letter Kratzer to Gaunt, 11 May 1960.

had discussions with the Chairman of the State Committee on Atomic Energy. The programme included visits to the I A Kurchatov Institute (Kurchatov had died in February 1960), the Institute of Theoretical and Experimental Physics in Moscow and the Nuclear Power Institute at Obninsk. During the visit Makins formulated a new agreement on future collaboration and arranged a further series of exchange visits.[20]

Makins' international work was not limited to collaboration agreements and flag waving; he also got involved in hard commercial negotiations. For example, he renegotiated a uranium ore contract with Canada. When the AEA was first established in 1954 there were predictions of a shortage of uranium ore for the foreseeable future. Accordingly, a contract was drawn up with the Canadians for the delivery to Britain of large quantities of uranium ore. On the strength of this contract the Canadians had invested heavily in production capacity and opened new mines. By the time the Canadians were ready to start shipping the uranium, however, the situation had changed. Not only was it possible to obtain the ore for a fraction of the price from South Africa, but also the whole nuclear power programme was slowing down. Furthermore, design improvements in the reactors had led to lower initial loadings of uranium, so less was required per unit of energy produced. By the time Makins arrived the AEA's commitments under its long term uranium contracts were greater than its requirements.[21]

Sir John Herbecq recounts the story of how Makins managed to unpick the contract with the Canadians:

> The starting position was that Makins did not have a leg to stand on; the contract was binding and the product had to be taken at a specific price at a specific time and in specific quantities. Makins was negotiating with six Canadians including two Ministers. He opened up by acknowledging the commitment and accepting it, but went on to say that the circumstances had changed and the authority had no need of the ore at all. The Canadians then told their tale of how much money they had spent and the capacity they had built and so on. Makins made no attempt to counter what they said but merely repeated that times had changed and the difficulty the Authority was in. Makins was skilful in not negotiating in too forthright a way which, in turn, may have led the Canadians to just say 'too bad'. He just went on and on repeating his position. After an hour the Canadians began to look a touch uneasy; they were beginning to feel that Makins was leading up to renouncing the contract completely. Without acknowledging the Canadian change in mood Makins went on and on again 'like a record stuck in a groove'. After some time the Canadians suggested that there might be some sort of deal. Makins implied that it might be possible to discuss the price, the

20 TNA, AB16/3141, Monthly summaries November 1962 Chairman's visit to USSR.

21 TNA, AB 22/10, 6th Annual Report UKAEA, p. 37.

> quantity to be taken and time of delivery. At this point Makins adjourned the meeting and handed it over to his staff. In the end the Canadians agreed to store the uranium and the Authority took it over a much extended period of time and at a reduced price.

According to Herbecq 'it was a brilliant piece of negotiating; for Makins, negotiating with another country on behalf of Britain was very much in his blood'.[22]

One of the major tasks for Makins while he was Chairman of the Authority was to manage relations with the CEGB, which was responsible for building nuclear power stations. The AEA was responsible for research and development into nuclear reactors to be used in power stations, the supply of nuclear fuel for the reactors, and the provision of consultancy services. The two bodies did not always share the same views and there was constant friction between them during Makins' term of office. In addition to differences over reactor design there were differences over the pace and scale of the development of nuclear power.

Within months of Makins taking office a meeting between the authority and the CEGB was called by Hinton.

> The principal point emphasised by Sir Christopher Hinton was that, in his opinion, the AEA did not manifest in their relationship with the CEGB a sense of commercial responsibility consonant with the enormous sums which the CEGB were obliged to put at risk in the nuclear power business. The CEGB were obliged to regard the Authority as, in a sense, a contractor; and the CEGB had found that Authority staff acted in their relationship with the Board in a manner which the Board would not have expected or tolerated in the case of a commercial contractor.[23]

Makins, who attended the meeting, welcomed the opportunity for frank discussions with the Generating Board so early after the assumption of the AEA Chairmanship ... adding that 'he took the view that at the present stage of the nuclear power programme all parties would need to work together in unison to ensure the success of the venture'. He suggested in classic understatement that 'He had sensed some defect in the relationship between the two bodies'.[24] It was a defect which was never really resolved during Makins' time as Chairman.

There were two other areas of concern for the CEGB: firstly, the scale and pace of the nuclear power programme and secondly, the design of the reactors

---

[22] Herbecq notes.

[23] TNA, AB 16/3364, Aide Memoire of discussions between Members of the A.E.A. and Members of the CEGB, 4 April 1960.

[24] TNA, AB16/3364, Notes of discussion, 4 April 1960.

to be used in future programmes. Britain's original civil nuclear programme had originally planned for 1,500–2,000 megawatts by 1965. After the Suez Crisis and the perceived threat to oil supplies, this was increased to 5,000–6,000 megawatts by the end of 1965. In June 1960 shortly after the first meeting with Hinton a White Paper was published announcing a new programme which limited capacity to 5,000 megawatts, with that capacity not scheduled to be in place until 1968.[25] Makins described the announcement as a 'change of pace rather than a change of policy'.[26] The reality was a little different. The CEGB was concerned that the cost of electricity generated by nuclear power was too high; the White Paper noted that 'for stations designed today, conventional power costs are about 25% less than nuclear costs in the United Kingdom'.[27] The Generating Board had successfully managed to limit the scale of the nuclear programme.

The Board then began to question the type of reactor design which the AEA was proposing to develop. The reactors being built in the early 1960s for the CEGB were the Magnox type. They were proven in engineering terms and worked well, but the cost of the electricity they produced was uncompetitive compared with conventional coal fired stations. As a result, a number of other reactor designs were being investigated by the AEA (and also by the Atomic Energy Commission in America). The CEGB, who would be expected to buy the new designs, was keen to have a say in their development. The AEA felt that research and design was its concern.

The Authority favoured the Advanced Gas Reactor. It had spent eight years developing it, and it was their reactor of choice for the second phase of the commercial nuclear programme, due to start in the late 1960s. The CEGB was not convinced by the underlying economics and Hinton, who had long experience of industrial production and costing, caused something of a crisis by publishing his arguments in an article in the *Three Banks Review*. He put forward three main arguments: firstly, different countries had adopted different reactor philosophies and at any given time a reactor developed abroad might have benefits over one developed in Britain; secondly, it was not necessary for a country to develop every invention in a field in order to have a sound technical position in that field (here, Hinton was obviously referring to the AEA's all-encompassing approach to nuclear technology); thirdly, 'ultimately everyone connected with the development, design and construction of nuclear power plants must decide his research and development programme on the basis of what his customers find most economical and what he can develop and sell to give him a profit and then power at the lowest possible cost'.[28]

---

25 Cmd, 1083.

26 Williams, R., *The Nuclear Power Decisions*, London: Croom Helm, 1980, p. 87.

27 Cmd, 1083, p. 3.

28 Williams, *Nuclear Power Decisions*, p. 89.

The disagreements between the two bodies began to be taken up in Parliament. Evidence given by the CEGB to the Select Committee on Nationalised Industries in response to earlier evidence given by the AEA summarises the dispute:

> Some of the statements made [by the AEA] do not exactly accord with the picture as we see it but we do not think that this is unnatural. The Atomic Energy Authority is primarily a research and development organisation and is staffed by people who have been trained for these activities; the picture that they paint is naturally of the view as seen by an enthusiastic research staff.

The CEGB's evidence went on to suggest that it had to operate as an organisation carrying heavy financial and commercial responsibilities.[29] When asked by a member of the committee whether the research and development programme undertaken by the AEA was guided by the Generating Board's requirements, Hinton replied 'I think that their activities are guided by what they think our requirements ought to be'.[30]

The Public Accounts Committee, meeting in the same year as the Select Committee, was aware that the AEA had been working on a number of reactor designs, in particular the AGR, and also of the *Three Banks Review* article and what lay behind it. The Chairman, Douglas Houghton, put the position very bluntly to Makins, referring to what he called an 'extraordinary situation'. He said 'you can, therefore, sit there developing your nuclear power with very little prospect of selling it at home and with little prospect in the export trade and you then become a dead loss to the community'.[31] It is hardly surprising that 'Makins, as everyone did, loathed meetings of the Public Accounts Committee'.[32]

The focal point of the differences between the Authority and the Generating Board was whether or not to adopt the AGR for the second nuclear programme. In the end the decision had to be made by ministers. Lord Hailsham, the minister responsible for the AEA, supported the AEA in its promotion of the AGR. However, in an effort to assuage the feelings of Frederick Erroll, the Minister of Power, and the CEGB, the White Paper indicated that the Generating Board would issue an enquiry for tenders for an AGR but, at the same time, would also be prepared to consider tenders from British industry for other types of reactor design. It was typical political fudge although in the end the AGR was chosen.

Makins resigned from the Authority in November 1963, one year earlier than he had originally planned and curiously enough within a month of

29 Williams, *Nuclear Power Decisions*, p. 94.

30 Ibid.

31 Williams, *Nuclear Power Decisions*, p. 56.

32 Herbecq Notes.

Macmillan resigning as Prime Minister and being succeeded by Sir Alec Doulglas-Home.[33] The argument Makins advanced for resigning early was that Penney, his deputy chairman and chosen successor, was 'a prime target for other important posts'.[34] Another possible explanation, given the problems which ministers were faced with over the AGR issue, was that a change at the top of the AEA seemed desirable. It is interesting that a scientist, who would fully understand the issues, was put in charge for the first time. Makins at the time wrote 'I think the time has come for someone with a scientific and technical background to take the Chair'.[35] In any event Makins left the Authority in January 1964 and so ended a long career in public service.

Makins, however, was not yet ready for retirement. He was to have over 30 years of active life left and he spent this time involved in a range of activities which included the House of Lords, working with academic institutions and holding a number of positions connected with the City. Although of less interest to historians, the period of Makins' life after he left public service was almost as long and, in some way as remarkable as his earlier career.

Makins was created a hereditary peer on 15 July 1964 and it was one of the last hereditary peerages to be created. Within two weeks of taking his seat Makins made his maiden speech. He spoke on the John F. Kennedy Memorial Bill. After President Kennedy's assassination in November 1963 the British wanted to establish a permanent memorial to Kennedy and Makins was the Chairman of the committee which was to supervise how the memorial should be put into effect. It was not a long speech and although mainly perfunctory in character it was not without eloquence as the end of the speech shows:

> Perhaps it was the younger generation who were most affected by the death of the late President. Many of them, I think, found it almost intolerable that, in a world which seemed to be largely run by old men, the one representative of their own generation who had broken through to the summit of power was the one to be struck down, I think that this project will serve as a living memory to the President, and that it will appeal particularly to young people.[36]

Shortly after entering the Lords, Makins became a member of the Select Committee on the European Communities and became the Chairman of its energy subcommittee. Makins' main interest, however, was in the area of science and technology and he was a regular speaker in debates which were concerned

---

33 Makins Papers, MS Sherfield 563, Letter Makins to RM Geddes, 5 November 1963. See also MS Sherfield 563 Letter Macmillan to Makins, 21 July 1959.

34 Lord Sherfield's Memoirs section entitled *ICFC*, p. 1.

35 Makins Papers, MS Sherfield 563, Letter Makins to RM Geddes, 5 November 1963.

36 Hansard, 28 July 1964.

with those areas. Such was his interest in this area that when, in 1979, the House of Commons reformed its committee structure and disbanded its Science and Technology Committee Makins, together with Lord Shackleton, submitted a proposal for a House of Lords Select Committee on Science and Technology to be established. The proposal was adopted and thus Parliament had at least one committee monitoring government policy with regard to science and technology. Makins chaired this committee from 1984 until 1987 and it was during this period in 1986 that Makins was elected to the Fellowship of the Royal Society – it was a rare event and a considerable honour for a non-scientist to be elected to the Society's fellowship.

Makins spoke a total of 203 times in Lords' debates and he spoke in every one of his 32 years in the Lords bar three. His final contribution was made on 19 May 1995 and fittingly enough he spoke on the Atomic Energy Authority Bill which was proposing to privatise the Atomic Energy Authority. Pragmatic as ever Makins indicated that while he had never been in favour of privatisation across the board because he believed that the circumstances of each case should prevail, he was in favour of the privatisation of the authority.[37]

Education was an area which interested Makins and this interest manifested itself in many forms during Makins' 'retirement'. Makins was involved with a number of universities: Oxford, of course, was close to his heart and he retained a connection with the university throughout his adult life. Makins was a Fellow of All Souls from 1925 until 1939 and from 1957 until he died in 1996. In 1963 Makins had the pleasure of seeing his son Christopher elected to a Prize Fellowship thus facilitating the rare occurrence of a father and son being Fellows of All Souls at the same time. From 1957 onwards Makins was a Distinguished Fellow and conscientious in attending College Meetings. Although Makins was sorry when All Souls abandoned a scheme for post-graduate students in favour of Visiting Fellowships, Makins, always the realist, understood that in the end it was the resident academic Fellows who should ultimately decide. Makins also retained his connections with Christ Church and became an Honorary Student (Fellow) there in 1973.

Makins' academic interests were not confined to Oxford. He was the Chancellor of the University of Reading from 1970 until 1992 and he was the Chairman of the governing body of Imperial College from 1962 until 1974. Makins brought in first William Penny (1967–73) and then Lord Flowers (1973–85) as Rectors of the College. The 1960s were difficult times to be running a university as 'the students were sometimes uncontrollable ... the heads of departments were bewildered and angry, the rest of the staff including

---

37 www.hansard.millbanksystems.com/people/mr-roger-makins.

the technicians, wanted a say in how everything was run'.[38] Notwithstanding these difficulties a number of reforms were introduced while, at the same time, expanding the College and keeping the finances under control.

Makins was a Fellow of Winchester College from 1962 until 1979. For the last five years of this period he was also the Warden, in effect the Chairman of the Board of Governors. Makins was later to remark that ceasing to be Warden was the only job he ever regretted leaving. There was, of course, a close family connection with Winchester as both his father and uncle had gone there and both of Makins' sons attended Winchester. The Makinses were also generous benefactors; both Roger and his son Christopher made significant gifts to Winchester. There are several reminders of the Makins' family association with Winchester including the Sherfield memorial in Cloisters, the Makins' room in the Moberly Library and a sculpture of Roger Makins' head which now permanently looks out onto Chamber Court.

Reverence for Makins, however, was not universal within the Winchester community. Makins, when he became Warden, took it upon himself, presumably with the support of certain Fellows, to sell one of Winchester College's greatest treasures. The story is taken up in the June 1976 issue of the *Trusty Servant* the school magazine:

> This year is also the quingentenary of the setting up of Caxton's press at Westminster, and we have marked that by a less happy event. The Winchester manuscript of Malory's *Morte d'Arthur* has been sold to the British Library for £150,000. The Warden and Fellows are the trustees of the res Wiccamica, our treasures are in their hands, and the decision was theirs ... The result of the negotiations between Lord Sherfield, our Warden and Lord Eccles, for the British Library, were announced just after the school went down in March, and just over half the purchase price is already here, invested, and producing income to help parents with fees. The rest will come later. The Manuscript is already gone. Those are the facts. There was some surprise when the sum realised was announced. There is some pain felt, as after an amputation, where once there was a limb.[39]

It was a divisive move by Makins to sell Winchester's most treasured possession even if its purpose was to fund fees for those whose parents could not afford them. Makins always argued that the manuscript had not been properly cared for and conserved at the College, and the British Library was the appropriate

---

38 Cathcart, Brian, *Penney, William George, Baron Penney (1909–1991)*, Oxford Dictionary of National Biography, Oxford University Press, 2004; online edition, p. 9.

39 *The Trusty Servant*, 1956–2006, A Fifty Year Pick and Mix.

place for it.[40] Even today, however, the act leaves a bad taste in the mouths of some at Winchester College.

After leaving the AEA Makins accepted a number of appointments in the banking and finance field. The first was as a result of an approach by Bob Brand (the Head of the Treasury Delegation in Washington while Makins was posted there in 1944–7). Brand, who was also a Fellow of All Souls, felt that the *Times* Newspaper Board needed strengthening and so recommended Makins for the appointment as a non-executive Director. Makins served on the *Times* Board from 1964–7. Makins, however, was also looking for a more rewarding position and was approached by Lord Piercy the Chairman of the Industrial and Commercial Finance Cooperation (ICFC) who invited Makins to join the board. The ICFC had been set up in 1945 with funding from the Bank of England and the major clearing banks to provide capital for companies that were too small to access the stock market. It was ideal for Makins; it was not a full-time job and hence Makins was able to accept other directorships. It did, however, offer him a full-time secretary, an office, a car and a chauffeur and an emolument of £10,000 per annum. Makins was the Chairman of ICFC from 1964–74 and he took a great interest in the companies ICFC supported and enjoyed visiting them. Makins held other positions including chairing Hill Samuel, the merchant bank, for four years until 1970: chairing Raytheon Europe International Co., an offshoot of the American defence technology firm and he also chaired the International Advisory Council of the American bank Wells Fargo for 12 years until 1984.

Makins remained active until the end of his life and even though he suffered a stroke in his ninetieth year he still managed to attend the House of Lords and speak on the Atomic Energy Bill in the following year. On 9 November 1996 Makins died of cancer and heart failure; he was 92. Makins' funeral was held on 14 November 1996; there were two memorial services, one at All Souls College, the other at St Margaret's Church, Westminster Abbey; both were well attended. Makins is buried next to his wife Alice in the churchyard of St Leonard's Church at Sherfield on Loddon. As if to echo a life lived off-stage the graves are difficult to find. They lay behind the church, away from view, in the shadow of Sherfield Court, the house they lived in for over 30 years. Inscribed on Makins' headstone is a quotation from Ecclesiastes: 'He was a leader by his counsel, wise and eloquent both honoured in his generation and a glory of his time.'

[40] Correspondence with Virginia Makins.

Conclusion

In order to fully comprehend British foreign policy in the post-war world, we need to have an understanding of the personalities involved. This understanding should not be limited to Prime Ministers, Foreign Secretaries and other politicians, but should also embrace the diplomats and other civil servants they work with and rely on. The politicians and the officials are under different pressures and they bring different perspectives to policy making. The story of the post-war world only makes sense if one talks about officials as well as politicians and, indeed, the way they interact with one another. Relationships between officials and ministers are often built up over many years of working together. Diplomats and other civil servants are often portrayed as faceless bureaucrats who simply respond to requests in a level, measured way. This is not always the case and they do, of course, have personalities of their own and they do interact with others, including politicians.

Roger Makins was undoubtedly one of the most prominent civil servants in the immediate post-war period. He ranks alongside men such as Edward Bridges, Oliver Franks and Robert Hall. There is no doubt that these men had considerable influence on ministers and thus on policy. However, given that policy making is a collaborative process, it is often difficult to dissect out the exact contribution one individual, whether that be a politician or an official, makes to the process. One can, however, often discern a guiding light, a principle or an approach which steers an individual's contribution. The light in Makins' case was his belief that Britain's best interests lay in a close association with America, or perhaps, to put it more precisely, in a belief that America should continue her involvement in European affairs with Britain being the preferred partner. This belief, however, was not based on some theoretical notion of international relations; Makins was no George Kennan; there was no theory of containment or any other theory for that matter. Rather Makins' view was based on the fact that Britain needed American dollars, and she needed American cooperation across a number of fields including foreign relations, atomic energy and defence. Makins was a pragmatist who was interested in solving the problem in front of him. At times, however, his eagerness to appease the Americans, to make concessions to them, appeared overly generous and led to criticism from those who were less inclined to the Atlantacist point of view.

The most prominent position Makins held in the field of Anglo-American relations was as the British Ambassador in Washington. The task of an ambassador, according to Makins himself, is to 'get on well with the Government to which he is accredited [and] to do this while retaining the confidence of his own Government'.[1] Makins, although he had many successes in his Washington posting, failed in this objective. This loss of confidence in Makins and his recall from Washington had significant repercussions. The failure, however, does not entirely rest upon Makins' shoulders. Certainly Makins' telegrams could be strident in tone, and he often sided with the American point of view. His pitch did alienate colleagues in the Foreign Office, but perhaps the clash was also caused by the fact that Eden, while recognising Britain's decline relative to America, could never quite reconcile himself to it.[2] Makins, on the other hand, had been a part of Bevin's inner circle which had struggled with the realities of Britain's decline in the immediate post-war years; they were secure in their understanding of Britain's position in the post-war world and of Britain's position relative to America. Eden, however, out of office for six years, was out of touch and failed to understand the new realities of Britain's situation. The declining relationship between the Ambassador and his Foreign Secretary is a clear example of how the interaction between an official and a politician can affect policy.

Aside from being identified with the pursuit of close Anglo-American relations, Makins' career has also been associated with his work in the economic policy and atomic energy fields. It has been suggested that he roamed 'freely through the jungle of economic and atomic policy making'.[3] While it is right to identify Makins with these areas, the part he played in them and the success he had in them, has been exaggerated. It was noted in Chapter 3 that while Makins was given the title of Economic Minister when he served at the Washington Embassy there was very little economics involved. When Makins moved back to the Foreign Office, even though his role was to head up the economic departments, there was not a great deal of policy work taking place within these departments; they were responsible for mainly gathering and disseminating information. It is true that Makins sat on a number of interdepartmental committees which considered economic policy and made recommendations to ministers, but these committees were dominated by Treasury officials. Makins' role was more about liaison with the Treasury, keeping them informed of Bevin's thinking and keeping Bevin abreast of Treasury thinking, rather than about making economic policy. Makins' role when he served under Bevin was much broader than this; he offered counsel and advice across a wide range of issues. Indeed Makins' strength was that he was not a specialist and he could focus on a range of problems and quickly get to grips with them and make recommendations to ministers.

---

1 *Mission to Washington*, p. 22.

2 *Shuckburgh Diaries*, p. 21.

3 Alex Danchev, 'Makins, Roger Mellor, first Baron Sherfield (1902–1996)', *Oxford Dictionary of National Biography*. Oxford University Press, 2004; Online edition.

Makins' period as Permanent Secretary of the Treasury could, of course, be described as being concerned with economic policy, but it is difficult to describe the appointment as a success. Makins did, however, play a vital role in securing Britain's financial position during his time at the Treasury, particularly during the Suez Crisis, but his part was founded upon his close connections with the American administration rather than because of his economic prowess. Relationships between politicians and officials can shape careers and they can shape policy. Makins' appointment to the Treasury would not have come about if he had not developed a relationship with Macmillan during the war. It was a curious, almost inexplicable, move and one which had significant consequences for policy. It is very doubtful that Thorneycroft and his ministers would have resigned in 1958 had Thorneycroft been allowed to take Frank Lee, his Permanent Secretary, from the Board of Trade with him to the Treasury.

Makins' traditional association with atomic energy policy is even greater than that with economic policy; he even earned the sobriquet 'Mr Atom'. While he was a civil servant Makins, however, was but one part of an elaborate policy making process with respect to atomic energy and the part he was most heavily involved in, that is, continued Anglo-American cooperation, was not a great success. The period 1945–55, the time when Makins was most involved in seeking Anglo-American cooperation, stands out as the period when least cooperation was forthcoming. This is not to say that Makins was necessarily responsible for failing to secure cooperation, or that anyone else could have done better. America was very determined not to share her atomic secrets, but simply to point out that Makins was not the success in this field that many have suggested he was. Indeed Makins can be, and has been, criticised for conceding more than he gained when he was negotiating with the Americans. His failure to analyse the American weaknesses closely enough arose, in part, because he was too trusting of, and possibly too close to, the people he was negotiating with. Makins' association with the atomic energy field was strengthened with his appointment, again by Macmillan, to head the Atomic Energy Authority. He was an able Chairman, and a good international ambassador for the Authority, and the experience he gained with the Authority would have served him well for his subsequent commercial career. The above is not to suggest that Makins was not a diligent and able civil servant, but simply to point out that to associate Makins with these policy areas on the basis that the association had necessarily been a great success is a misnomer. Makins' achievements resided not so much in his domination of policy areas, but in his outstanding abilities as an individual.

It is difficult to draw general conclusions from the study of the career of one man, and one must not claim too much in this regard, but several points can be made. Firstly, the positive influence an official can have over policy seems to be directly related to the extent of trust that exists between an official and his minister, and that in turn, is closely related to whether or not there is an identity of view between them. Makins developed a very close working relationship with Bevin, in part, because they were both committed to the notion that Britain's best interests lay in a strong Anglo-American relationship. Bevin respected Makins' ability to find his way around the American establishment and used Makins to find ways around potential obstacles to influencing American policy. One such obstacle, for example, was the concern some Americans had regarding the left wing elements within the Labour Party. Makins, with his clear understanding of Washington politics, was able to advise Bevin on the approach to take with the Americans and Bevin was receptive to that advice. A similar situation existed in the Second World War when both Macmillan and Makins were committed to winning the war and they, at the same time, had mutual respect for each other's talents. The political work in Algiers where Macmillan and Makins built strong relationships with both American and French officials was an important element in the success of the Mediterranean campaign. Secondly, informal networks are important; private contacts between officials, within and between departments, are extensive and can have an impact on policy. One clear example of this is the correspondence between Makins and David Eccles during the war. Eccles was concerned that Hugh Dalton, Head of the Ministry of Economic Warfare, would institute tough sanctions on both Spain and Portugal and thus drive them into alliance with Germany. Eccles communicated his concerns to the Foreign Office through private and extensive correspondence with Makins. Together they were able to subvert the wishes of Dalton and thus avoid a potentially disastrous policy. Thirdly, closeness to a foreign power is both a blessing and a curse. This is an old problem and one identified by Harold Nicholson in his seminal work *Diplomacy*. Makins was very close to certain members of the American administration and used that to great effect on Britain's behalf. However, as noted above, in the end this led to certain elements of his advice being discounted.

The fact is that more work needs to be done on the part officials played in British post-war history; all too often the officials have tended to tell their own story, often escaping the scrutiny that the politicians have been subjected to by historians and others.

Bibliography

Acheson, D. *Present at Creation.* New York: Norton, 1969.

Aldrich, R. *The Hidden Hand Britain and America and Cold War Secret Intelligence.* London: John Murray, 2001.

Aldrich, R. and Hopkins, M. *Intelligence Defence and Diplomacy British Policy in the Post War World.* London: Cass, 1994.

Ambrose, S. *Eisenhower the President 1952–1960.* London: Allen and Unwin, 1984.

Barclay, R. *Ernest Bevin and the Foreign Office 1932–1969.* Published by the author, 1975.

Bartlett, C.J. *A History of Post War Britain 1945–1974.* London: Longman Group, 1977.

____. *The Special Relationship A Political history of Anglo-American Relations Since 1945.* London: Longman, 1992.

Baylis, J. *Anglo American Defence Relations 1939–1984.* London: Macmillan, 1984.

Beer, S. *Treasury Control.* Oxford: Oxford University Press, 1956.

Berridge, G.R. *Diplomacy Theory and Practice.* Basingstoke: Palgrave, 2002.

Berridge, G.R. and James, A. *A Dictionary of Diplomacy.* Basingstoke: Palgrave, 2001.

Boyle, P. (ed.) *The Churchill-Eisenhower Correspondence, 1953–1955.* Chapel Hill: The University of North Carolina Press, 1990.

____. *The Eden Eisenhower Correspondence, 1955–1957.* Chapel Hill: The University of North Carolina Press, 2005.

Brittan, S. *The Treasury Under the Tories 1951–1964.* London: Penguin, 1964.

____. *Steering the Economy.* London: Secker and Warburg, 1969.

Bullock, A. *Ernest Bevin Foreign Secretary.* London: Norton, 1983.

Butler, D. and Butier G. *Twentieth Century British Political Facts 1900–2000.* London: Macmillan Press, 2000.

Cairncross, A. (ed.) *The Robert Hall Diaries 1947–1953.* London: Unwin Hyman, 1989.

____. *The Robert Hall Diaries 1954–1961.* London: Unwin Hayman, 1991.

Colville, J. *Foot-Prints in Time Memories.* London: Collins, 1976.

____. *The Fringes of Power Downing Street Diaries 1939–1955.* London: Weidenfeld & Nicolson, 2004.

Craig, G. and Gilbert, F. (eds) *The Diplomats 1919–1939.* Princeton, NJ: Princeton University Press, 1994.

Crooks, S. *Peter Thorneycroft.* Winchester: George Mann, 2007.

Dalton, H. *The Fateful Years 1931–1945*. London: Frederick Muller, 1957.
____. *High Tide and After Memoirs 1945–1960*. London: Frederick Muller, 1962.
Danchev, A. *Oliver Franks Founding Father*. Oxford: Clarendon Press, 1993.
Dell, E. *The Chancellors A History of the Chancellors of the Exchequer, 1945–90*. London: Harper Collins, 1996.
Dickie, J. *Inside the Foreign Office*. London: Chapmans, 1992.
Dilks, D. *The Diaries of Sir Alexander Cadogan 1938–1945*. London: Cassell, 1971.
Dimbleby, D. and Reynolds, D. *An Ocean Apart*. London: Hodder & Stoughton, 1988.
Dockrill, M. and McKercher, B. *Diplomacy and World Power Studies in British Foreign Policy, 1890–1950*. Cambridge: Cambridge University Press, 1996.
Dow, J.C.R. *The Management of the British Economy*. Cambridge: Cambridge University Press, 1965.
Eden, A. *Memoirs: Full Circle*. London: Cassell, 1960.
Eccles, D. *By Safe Hand Letters of Sybil and David Eccles 1939–1942*. London: The Bodley Head, 1983.
Fforde, J. *The Bank of England and Public Policy 1941–1958*. Cambridge: Cambridge University Press, 1992.
Frankel, J. *British Foreign Policy 1945–1973*. Oxford: Oxford University Press, 1975.
Gladwyn, Lord. *The Memoirs of Lord Gladwyn*. London: Weidenfeld and Nicholson, 1972.
Gore-Booth, P. *With Great Truth and Respect*. London: Constable, 1974
Gowing, M. *Independence and Deterrence Britain and Atomic Energy 1945–52 Volume 1 Policy Making*. London: Macmillan, 1974.
____. *Independence and Deterrence Britain and Atomic Energy 1945–52 Volume II Policy Execution*. London: Macmillan, 1974.
Hailsham, Lord. *Lord Hailsham: A Sparrow's Flight*. London: Collins, 1990.
Hahn, P. *Caught in the Middle East U.S. Policy Toward the Arab-Israeli Conflict, 1945–1961*. Chapel Hill: The University of North Carolina Press, 2004.
Harvey, J. *The Diplomatic Diaries of Oliver Harvey 1937–1940*. London: Collins, 1970.
Heffer, S. *Like the Roman: The Life of Enoch Powell*. London: Weidenfeld and Nicholson, 1998.
Hennessy, P. *Whitehall*. London: Secker and Warburg, 1989.
____. *Having it so Good: Britain in the Fifties*. London: Penguin, 2006.
Hewlett, R. and Anderson, O. *The New World 1939–1946 Volume I of A History of the United States Atomic Energy Commission*. Pennsylvania: The Pennsylvania State University Press, 1962.
Hoopes, T. *The Devil and John Foster Dulles*. London: Andre Deutsch, 1974.

Hopkins, M., Kelly, S. and Young, J. *The Washington Embassy: British Ambassadors to the United States, 1939–77*. London: Palgrave Macmillan, 2009.

Howard, M. and Roger Louis, W.M. (eds) *The Oxford History of the Twentieth Century*. Oxford: Oxford University Press, 1998.

Howard, N. *The Basic Papers of George M Humphrey 1953–1957*. Cleveland: The Western Reserve Historical Society, 1965.

Ismay, Lord. *The Memoirs of Lord Ismay*. London: William Heinemann, 1960.

Jay, D. *Change and Fortune A Political Record*. London: Hutchinson, 1980.

Johnson, G. (ed.) *The Foreign Office and British Diplomacy in the Twentieth Century*. Abingdon: Routledge, 2005.

Joyce, J.A.*Broken Star the Story of the League of Nations 1919–1939*. Swansea: Christopher Davies, 1978.

Kelly, S. and Gorst, A. (eds) *Whitehall and the Suez Crisis*. London: Frank Cass, 2000.

Kirkpatrick, I. *The Inner Circle*. London: Macmillan, 1959.

Kunz, D. *The Economic Diplomacy of the Suez Crisis*. Chapel Hill: The University of North Carolina Press, 1991.

Kyle, K. *Suez*. New York: St Martin's Press, 1991.

____. *Suez Britain's End of Empire in the Middle East*. London: I.B. Tauris, 2011.

Leffler, M. *A Preponderance of Power*. Stanford: Stanford University Press, 1992.

Leventhal, F. and Quinault, R. (eds) *Anglo-American Attitudes From Revolution to Partnership*. Aldershot: Ashgate, 2000.

Lloyd, S. *Suez A Personal Account*. Published by Lord Selwyn Lloyd and others, 1978.

Louis, Roger W.M. (ed.) *Penultimate Adventures With Britannia*. London: Tauris, 2008.

Louis, Roger W.M. and Bull, H. *The Special Relationship Anglo American Relations Since 1945*. Oxford: Clarendon Press, 1986.

Macmillan, H. *Winds of Change, 1914–1939*. London: Macmillan, 1966.

____. *The Blast of War, 1939–1945*. London: Macmillan, 1967.

____. *Tides of Fortune, 1945–1955*. London: Macmillan, 1969.

____. *Riding the Storm, 1956–1959*. London: Macmillan, 1971.

____. *Pointing the Way, 1959–1961*. London: Macmillan, 1972.

____. *At the End of the Day, 1961–1963*. London: Macmillan, 1973.

____. *War Diaries: The Mediterranean, 1943–1945*. London: Macmillan, 1984.

Mallalieu, W. *British Reconstruction and American Policy 1945–1955*. New York: Scarecrow Press, 1956.

Manderson-Jones, R.B. *The Special Relationship Anglo American Relations and Western European Security 1947–1956*. London: Weidenfeld and Nicholson, 1972.

Moran, Lord. *Churchill: The Struggle for Survival 1940/65*. London: Constable, 1966.
Murphy, R. *Diplomat Among Warriors*. London: Collins, 1964.
Nicolson, N. (ed.) *Diaries and Letters 1939–1945*. London: Collins, 1967.
____. *Diaries and Letters 1945–1962*. London: Collins, 1968.
Northedge, F.S. *The League of Nations its Life and Times 1920–1946*. Leicester: Leicester University Press, 1986.
Norwich, J.J. *The Duff Cooper Diaries*. London: Wiedenfeld and Nicholson, 2005.
Ovendale, R. *The Foreign Policy of the British Labour Government 1945–1951*. Leicester: Leicester University Press, 1984.
Paul, S. *Nuclear Rivals Anglo American Relations 1941–1952*. Columbus: Ohio State University, 2000.
Peden, G.C. *The Treasury and British Public Policy*. Oxford: Oxford University Press, 2000.
Peele, G. and Cook, C. (eds) *The Politics of Reappraisal 1918–1939*. London: Macmillan, 1975.
Plowden, E. *An Industrialist in the Treasury the Post War Years*. London: Andre Deutsch, 1989.
Pocock, R.F. *Nuclear Power Its Development in the United Kingdom*. London: Unwin Brothers, 1977.
Pressnell, L.S. *External Economic Policy Since the War Volume I*. London: HMSO, 1986.
Raffo, P. *The League of Nations*. London: The Historical Association, 1974.
Ramsden, J. *The Oxford Companion to Twentieth Century British Politics*. Oxford: Oxford University Press, 2005.
Reynolds, D. *Britannia Overruled British Policy & Power in the Twentieth Century*. London: Longman, 1991.
Roberts, A. *The Holy Fox: The Life of Lord Halifax*. London: Phoenix, 1997.
Robertson, T. *Crisis The Inside Story of the Suez Conspiracy*. London: Hutchinson, 1965.
Rowse, A.L. *A Cornishman at Oxford*. London: Jonathan Cape, 1965.
Salter, Lord. *Memoirs of a Public Servant*. London: Faber and Faber, 1961.
____. *Slave of the Lamp A Public Servants Notebook*. London: Weidenfeld Nicholson, 1967.
Sherman, A. *Island Refuge Britain and Refugees from the Third Reich 1933–1939*. Berkeley, CA: University of California Press, 1973.
Shuckburgh, E. *Descent to Suez Foreign Office Diaries 1951–1956*. London: Norton, 1987.
Smith, M., Smith, S., and White, B. (eds) *British Foreign Policy: Tradition, Change and Transformation*. London: Unwin Hayman, 1988.
Thorpe, D.R. *Selwyn Lloyd*. London: Jonathan Cape, 1989.
____. *Alec Douglas-Home*. London: Sinclair-Stevenson, 1997.

____. *Eden: The Life and Times of Anthony Eden First Earl of Avon, 1897–1977.* London: Chatto and Windus, 2003.
____. *Supermac: The Life of Harold Macmillan*. Chatto and Windus, 2010.
Vital, D. *A People Apart: The Jews in Europe 1789–1939*. Oxford: Oxford University Press, 1999.
Watt, D.C. *Succeeding John Bull*, Cambridge: Cambridge University Press, 1984.
____. *Personalities and Politics*. London: Longmans, 1965.
Waller, P. and Rowett, J. *Chronology of the Twentieth Century*. Oxford: Helicon, 1995.
Wevill, R. *Britain and America after World War II Bilateral Relations and the Beginnings of the Cold War.* London: Tauris, 2012.
Williams, R. *The Nuclear Power Decisions.* London: Croom Helm, 1980.
Young, J. (ed.) *The Foreign Policy of Churchill's Peacetime Administration 1951–1955.* Leicester: Leicester University Press, 1988.
____. *Britain and the World in the Twentieth Century*. London: Hodder Headline, 1997.
Young, K. *The Diaries of Sir Robert Bruce Lockhart*. London: Macmillan, 1973.
Zametica, J. (ed.). *British Officials and British Foreign Policy, 1945–50*. Leicester: Leicester University Press, 1990.

Index

#0009 - 250915 - C0 - 234/156/14 [16] - CB - 9781472446497